TRAVELS
FROM
INDIA TO ENGLAND

TRAVELS
FROM
INDIA TO ENGLAND

COMPREHENDING A

VISIT TO THE BURMAN EMPIRE,

AND

A JOURNEY

THROUGH

PERSIA, ASIA MINOR, EUROPEAN TURKEY, &c.
IN THE YEARS 1825-26

by

JAMES EDWARD ALEXANDER, ESQ.

GYAN

Published by

Gyan Publishing House
5, Ansari Road
Daryaganj, New Delhi-110002
Phone: 011-47034999, 9811692060
E-mail: books@gyanbooks.com

Distribution Network
gyanbooks.com
India, USA, Canada, UK, Australia, France

ISBN : 978-81-212-2492-5 (PB)
First Published, 1827

2nd Impression 2021

Printed at: Gyan Press, Delhi.

Travels from India to England
Author: James Edward Alexander

TRAVELS

FROM

INDIA TO ENGLAND;

COMPREHENDING A

VISIT TO THE BURMAN EMPIRE,

AND

A JOURNEY

THROUGH

PERSIA, ASIA MINOR, EUROPEAN TURKEY, &c.

IN THE YEARS 1825-26.

CONTAINING A

Chronological Epitome of the late Military Operations in Ava; an Account of the Proceedings of the present Mission from the Supreme Government of India to the Court of Tehran, and a Summary of the Causes and Events of the existing War between Russia and Persia;

WITH SKETCHES OF NATURAL HISTORY, MANNERS, AND CUSTOMS,

AND

ILLUSTRATED WITH MAPS AND PLATES.

BY JAMES EDWARD ALEXANDER, ESQ.

LIEUT., LATE H.M.'S 13th LIGHT DRAGOONS,

AND ATTACHED TO THE SUITE OF COLONEL MACDONALD KINNEIR, K.L.S., ENVOY EXTRAORDINARY TO THE COURT OF TEHRAN.

LONDON:

PRINTED FOR PARBURY, ALLEN, AND CO., LEADENHALL STREET.

1827.

JAS. EDW. ALEXANDER.

R J Lane litho del.

C Hullmandel impr.

TO

MAJOR-GENERAL

SIR ALEXANDER BRYCE,

KNIGHT OF THE ROYAL HANOVERIAN GUELPHIC ORDER,

OF THE ORDER OF ST. FERDINAND AND MERIT,

AND OF THE MOST HONOURABLE MILITARY ORDER OF THE BATH,

DEPUTY INSPECTOR-GENERAL OF FORTIFICATIONS,

&c. &c. &c.

THIS WORK

IS RESPECTFULLY INSCRIBED,

BY

HIS AFFECTIONATE NEPHEW,

THE AUTHOR.

PREFACE.

A young writer, who ventures for the first time before the world, with a diffidence of his own powers and a distrust of his pretensions, whilst he entertains a latent hope that his labours may not prove altogether unworthy of public regard, is under some embarrassment with respect to what he shall say of his work.

The author of this volume finds himself precisely in such a dilemma. This is his first literary effort upon a large scale; and although he is conscious that he labours under many disadvantages, in comparison with those who have been favoured with leisure and opportunity to cultivate letters, owing to his having left England at an early age, when the benefits of study and application just begin to be perceived, and owing to the profession in which he engaged, a profession generally hostile to literary pursuits, yet he is equally sensible that he enjoyed facilities for observation, especially in Persia, which do not fall to the lot of many travellers.

The

The advantages he possessed in having the good fortune to be attached to the suite of the British Envoy, and to journey in the company of persons familiar with the country, were not inconsiderable; in addition to which, his acquaintance with the Persian language exempted him from the inconveniences and impediments encountered by such as are entirely ignorant of the medium of intercourse with the people they visit.

It would have been easy for the author to have extended his work, and rendered it, in the estimation probably of some readers, more interesting, by incorporating with his own narrative facts borrowed from preceding travellers; but he has carefully abstained from so doing. Acting not merely upon his own judgment, but upon that of others, he has confined himself to a simple statement of the occurrences and remarks which he daily committed to his journal on his route. If, therefore, the reader regrets the absence of copious and elaborate disquisitions upon history, antiquities, and manners, he may console himself with the assurance that the author has recorded what he knows to be true from actual observation, and the evidence of his senses. He might have infused more apparent learning into his work without augmenting its value, and increased its bulk without adding to its interest.

The chronological epitome of the late military operations in Ava, which he has subjoined in the Appendix, is an attempt

attempt to supply an omission of his friend Colonel Snodgrass, in his concise and ably written "Narrative," *viz.* to furnish at a glance the events of the Burman War, and the loss sustained in that arduous and prolonged conflict. The summary also of the causes and events of the existing war between Russia and Persia, he conceives, will be particularly acceptable at the present period, when so few authentic details on this subject are before the public. The particulars he has given were collected chiefly upon the spot from the most unexceptionable sources; and the itinerary of his route will be serviceable to future travellers.

Although the second part of the volume may be deemed the most important portion of the work, the author presumes to think that the sketch he has furnished of the country and people of the Burman Empire will prove of use, even for the sake of collation, with the reports of previous travellers, since it is the result of actual examination, without reference to books. The details he has also been enabled to supply respecting the Andaman islanders, may not be devoid of interest.

The illustrations from sketches by the author were executed under the direction of that eminent artist Mr. R. J. Lane; and Mr. Hullmandel has done them ample justice, from the careful manner in which he has printed them.

In conclusion, the author submits his book to the candour of the public, and trusts that his youth and comparative inexperience will plead in extenuation of its defects, and secure it an indulgent reception.

Powis-House,
Near Stirling, N.B.

CONTENTS.

PART I.

BURMAN EMPIRE.

CHAPTER IV.

CHAPTER V.

CHAPTER VI.

CHAPTER VII.

CHAPTER VIII.

PART II.

PERSIA, ASIA MINOR, &c.

CHAPTER XII.

CHAPTER XIII.

CHAPTER XIV.

APPENDIX, No. I.

APPENDIX, No. II.

APPENDIX, No. III.

ILLUSTRATIONS.

PART I.

PART II.

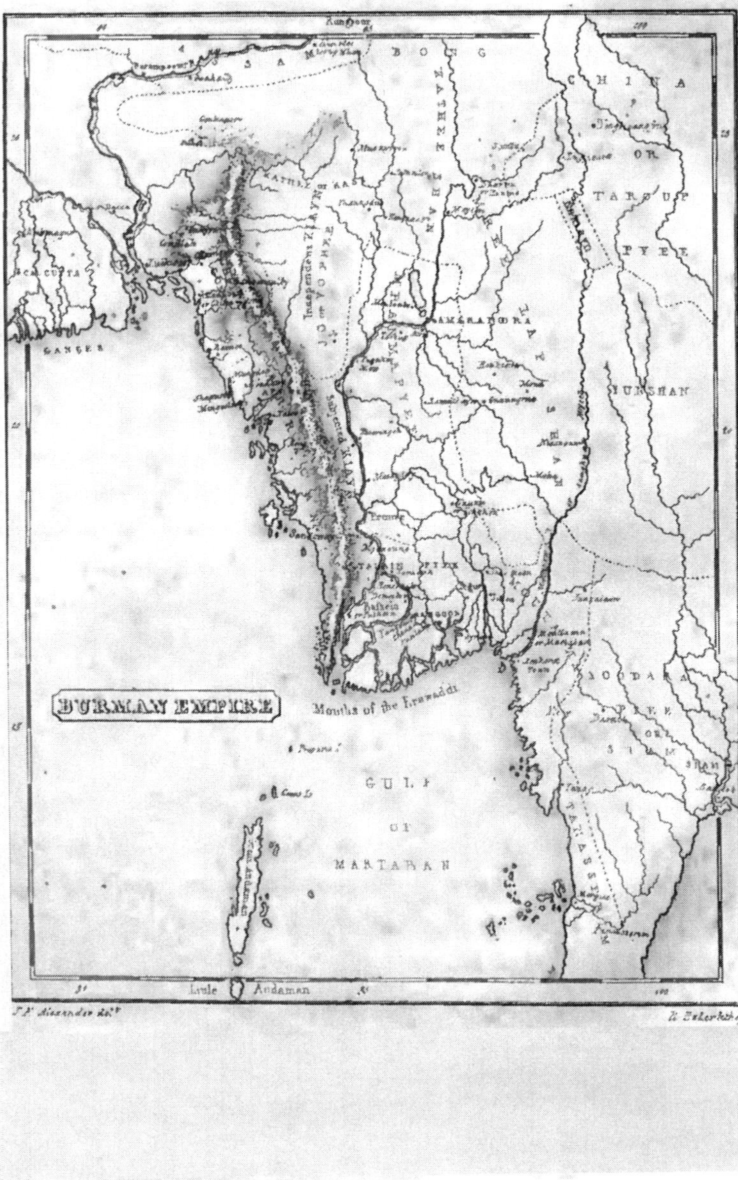

J. F. Alexander del.

R. Baker sc.

TRAVELS

FROM

INDIA TO ENGLAND.

PART I.

BURMAN EMPIRE.

CHAPTER I.

Sailed from Madras to Rangoon......Obliged to put into the Little Andaman Island for a supply of Water......Attacked by the Inhabitants......Skirmish with them...... Description of the Island......Arrival at Rangoon.

On the 16th October 1825, having taken leave of my much-esteemed friends at Madras, I embarked on board the Honourable Company's transport, *Earl Kellie*, 500 tons burthen, Captain Edwards commander, with four companies of that highly distinguished corps, his Majesty's 45th Foot, and one hundred Madras Pioneers; the whole under the command of Major Hilton, and destined for foreign service in Ava. The troops came off through a heavy surf, in high spirits, in the large and elastic Masoolah boats, the drums and fifes playing inspiring tunes. We weighed anchor, and stood out of the roads with a favouring breeze, passing under the stern of

the

the *Golcondah* transport, containing the head-quarters and remaining companies of the 45th. At night-fall we lost sight of the arid plains of the Carnatic.

The vessel, which was manned by natives, was a very heavy sailer, and excessively crowded, there being a soul on board for every ton. The officers (with the exception of the three seniors, who had cabins) roughed it in the steerage, which was so close and hot, that it was utterly impossible to sleep till towards morning. Swarms of cock-roaches and centipedes infested this as well as every other part of the ship: some of the latter were a foot in length, and of the thickness of a finger. I slept, during the whole of the voyage, on deck, which presented a curious spectacle at night; most of the European soldiers doing the same. As some recompense for the miseries experienced during the night, we were extremely comfortable during the day; a better or more abundant table I have scarcely ever seen. In the intervals between meals, we either read or sauntered beneath the thick awnings. In the evening, the men sat in circles on the deck, amusing themselves with songs or stories. Mirth and hilarity reigned on board, diversified by a few occasional curses vented at the slow progress of the ship.

In about two or three days it fell calm, and we saw, as usual, turtles, dolphins, and sharks. The *Golcondah* was observed astern of us hull down. Whilst we were in smooth water, the men were exercised by being marched in quick time, and made to run round the decks to the sound of lively music: a practice which cannot be too much recommended on board transports, since it is attended with the most beneficial effects; our men were thereby kept in high health; they enjoyed the amusement almost as much as quizzing the

the pioneers, whom the Europeans perpetually made objects of their sport and ridicule. These unfortunate fellows, never having been to sea before, suffered dreadfully; they tumbled about in a state of complete helplessness, and fancied it was all over with them.

It continued a dead calm until the 24th. During the evening we amused ourselves with dancing, fencing, or other recreations, to pass away the time; or we rowed round the vessel in the jolly-boat. On the 25th and 26th we had very heavy squalls, attended with torrents of rain: one of which took us so unexpectedly that the vessel was on her beam-ends; we shipped several seas at the quarter-deck ports, and the masts were expected to go every instant, until we were under double-reefed topsails and foresail. Until the 1st of November we had hard squalls with variable winds; which precede the setting in of the north-east monsoon. As we had provisions and water only for thirty days on board, with the prospect of a tedious passage, the troops were put on half rations.

On the 4th, it being calm, an immense *balæna physalus*, or fin-whale, approached us; near it floated a large tree covered with barnacles, on which white fish preyed. We killed the following birds: *columba migratoria* (passage-pigeon), *falco subulco* (hobby hawk), and a black bird of the genus *procellaria*, or petrel. The *phaëton æthereus*, or tropic bird, appearing like a white cross in the heavens (called by seamen the boatswain, from the resemblance its tail bears to a marling spike), and gannets, were seen winging their weary way over the fathomless deep. They soared too high to be touched by the detonators. In the afternoon there was an alarm of fire. The men had heaped on too much fuel in the caboose; the

 forecastle

forecastle was in a blaze, and the flames had nearly reached the foresail, which was beginning to blacken, when they were fortunately extinguished.

On the 10th we had only reached half way across the Bay of Bengal. The monsoon was steadily against us, and we could only tack up and down the Bay, so as to endeavour to make a slanting course towards the shores of Ava. The breeze, though adverse to our progress, proved highly favourable to our health: those who had become enervated and debilitated by a residence in India, were now completely restored to vigour.

Our water was now very putrid and nearly exhausted. There was some talk of putting back, which would have been to me a most severe disappointment. Before and after the commencement of hostilities, I had twice volunteered for Ava, and had met with the mortifying reply, that a cavalry officer could not be spared from his duty. However, on the 11th at noon, the North Centinel, an island of the Andaman Archipelago (the *Insulæ Bonæ Fortunæ* of Ptolemy, a designation which includes the Nicobars), was seen, bearing N.E. by E., low and covered with jungle. Carrying all sail, we passed immense branches of sea-weed.

On the 12th, we saw from the mast-head the South Centinel, bearing E.N.E., distant five leagues. Next day, steering a south-east course, hove in sight of the Little Andaman Island. At day-break the land was four leagues distant. Saw a brig, hull down, bearing north-west, steering to the south-east; bore up and stood in for the land to get a supply of water, and sounded on a coral reef eight, nine, ten, and sixteen fathoms, patches, the bottom very plainly seen under the ship. Numerous sharks followed the vessel,

one

one of which we succeeded in killing. On the surface of the water was seen swimming a *murœna ophis*, or sea-serpent, in length about four feet; the colour of the back black, the belly white, and a row of dark spots along the sides, the tail rounded: it was unprovided with the caudal fin. A monstrous fish also made its appearance near us apparently of the genus *raia;* its length about twenty or twenty-five feet, and its breadth nearly the same; the colour of the back reddish.

There was a very heavy swell on the bank. Steering from N.N.E. to N.W. to haul off it, ran a distance of four knots, when the water deepened to twenty fathoms. Whilst on the coral shoal, in eight fathoms water, the extremes of the island were from 8½ N. to N.N.E., with a small bay in the centre. This island, unlike the Great Andaman, is upon a level with the water's edge: it is covered with a very lofty jungle, and is of coral formation. The length is twenty-five miles, the breadth fifteen. We saw a light on shore, brought up off the north-west point, and anchored in eight fathoms and a-half, at two miles and a-half distance from the land.

The next morning, at day-light, the chief mate and myself left the vessel in one of the cutters, intending to search for water. We had six Bengal Lascars on board, armed with muskets, besides the tyndal or coxswain, who was a Malay. In pulling towards the shore we observed on the beach a woman and child, who appeared to be collecting shell-fish: on perceiving the boat approaching they ran into the jungle. We discovered a little sandy bay (which I took the liberty of christening after the name of our ship), with coral reefs running out from both extremes, over which a tremendous surf was breaking: the water inside was perfectly smooth. Anchoring the cutter a few fathoms' length from shore, and leaving a couple of hands

hands in her, we landed with the remainder of the crew, and proceeded along the beach towards the north-west point, in search of two runs of water mentioned by Horsburgh, in his *Directory*. We had not gone far, when, at an angle of the jungle which covers the island to within a few yards of the water's edge, we came suddenly upon a party of natives, lying on their bellies behind the bushes, armed with spears, arrows, and long bows, which they bent at us in a threatening manner. The Lascars, as soon as they saw them, fell back in great consternation, levelling their muskets, and running into the sea towards the boat. It was with great difficulty we could prevent the cowardly rascals from firing: the tyndal was the only one who stood by the chief mate and myself. We advanced within a few paces of the natives, and made signs of drinking, to intimate the purpose of our visit. The tyndal salaamed to them, according to the different oriental modes of salutation; he spoke to them in Malay, and other languages: they returned no answer, but continued crouching in their menacing attitude, pointing their weapons at us wherever we turned. I held out my handkerchief towards them, but they would not come from behind the bushes to take it. I placed it upon the ground, and we retired in order to allow them to pick it up: still they did not move.

I counted sixteen strong and able-bodied men opposite to us, many of them very lusty; and farther on six more. They were very different in appearance from what the natives of the Great Andaman are described to be, namely, a puny race. The whole party was completely naked, with the exception of a stout man, nearly six feet in height, who was standing up along with two or three women in the rear: he wore on his head a red cloth with white spots. They

were

were the most ferocious and wild-looking beings I ever saw. Their hair was frizzled or woolly; they had flat noses, with small red eyes. Those parts of their skin which were not besmeared with mud (to defend them probably from the attacks of insects) were of a sooty black colour; their hideous faces seemed to be painted with a red ochre. I may here remark, that the natives of the Andamans, who are decidedly a negro race, differing widely from the inhabitants of the neighbouring continent, are supposed to be the descendants of the survivors of an Arab slave-ship wrecked on one of the islands some centuries ago. The Chinese, who occasionally resort to these islands to collect the edible swallows'-nests and *beche de mer*, affirm that they are anthropophagi. It is certain that part of the crews of several junks, who have lately fallen into their hands, were never heard of.

At this juncture the other cutter, with two or three of the officers on board, neared the beach; and observing what was going forward, they called to us to retire a short distance, and allow the tyndal to go up and speak to the savages, as they might be afraid of Europeans. We accordingly fell back to the water's edge, and having desired the tyndal (who evinced no signs of fear) to strip, in order to convince them he was unarmed, he approached the natives within a few paces, and offered them handkerchiefs, making at the same time signs of drinking; but upon his attempting to advance closer they drew their bows in a menacing manner. Seeing this, we called him off; and not knowing how to act in this emergency without advice from the ship (as we had been directed not to molest the natives), both cutters returned. Upon reporting what had occurred, a subaltern's party was ordered to accompany us. We left the ship again

in

in the four boats, with the water-casks, and a party of pioneers to fill them, and landed at the same place as before. Not seeing any thing of the natives, we proceeded along the beach towards the southward. Upon turning a point we discovered a hut on the edge of the jungle; approaching it, we found it to be about fifteen feet in height, of a conical shape, and thatched with rattan leaves to within a foot and a half of the ground, leaving just room to crawl in underneath. The floor inside was strewed with leaves, and there were several cots, or raised sleeping-places, consisting of four stakes driven into the ground, on which was fixed a bamboo grating.

Ranged round the walls were the smoked skulls of a diminutive species of pig. From the roof was suspended a piece of red and white chequered cloth, which seemed to be of Madras manufacture. In conical baskets there were pieces of jack fruit, with a nut resembling a chestnut, and several roots. In a corner I found several large mangroves. At a fire the following shells were roasting: the green *murex tribulus, trochus telescopium, cypræa caurica,* and several varieties of muscle. The drinking cups were *nautili.*

The weapons were a bow, from six to seven feet in length, which is bent with the feet, the archer sitting on the ground; and a hand-bow, of four feet. The strings were made of the dark red fibres of a tree; the arrows were three and four feet in length, the upper part of a very hard white wood, inserted in a stock of cane, so as to quiver in the wound. The soldiers shot several of them at a tree: they penetrated a couple of inches into the solid timber, and it required the joint strength of two men to pull them out, and even then the points were not injured. Several arrows were found with two, three, and four prongs. The hand-nets were formed of black

filaments

filaments of bark. In one of the baskets, carefully wrapped up in a cloth, were the head of a harpoon with two barbs, a Malay chopping-knife, and several spike-nails and ring-bolts. These last were probably from the American ship *Dove*, which was wrecked here several years ago. We saw no idols of any description, nor canoes or rafts.

Naturally concluding that there was water near the hut, we penetrated into the entangled jungle in the rear of it, consisting of dammer trees, red-wood, the Alexandrian laurel, aloes, ground rattans, many *convolvuli*, and a very lofty and straight tree, about twelve feet in girth, the wood of which, if not too heavy, would answer admirably for masts. Having advanced about thirty or forty yards from the beach, we came to a pool of good water; but its position being inconvenient, we were looking for another, when we observed our people left in charge of the boats in considerable alarm, and making signs to us that there was danger in the jungle. Advancing towards the spot at which they were pointing, we discovered a party of sixty or seventy of the natives waiting in ambush our approach. We went towards them in order to induce them to shew us another pool. So little intention had we of molesting or injuring them, that we had brought with us several looking-glasses, cloth, and baubles to give them. However, we had no sooner got within fifteen yards of them than we were assailed with a shower of arrows, which struck several of us. I received a scratch in the leg which lamed me for several days after. We immediately extended the files to skirmishing order, and returned with a round of musketry, which killed and wounded several of them. Fixing bayonets, we then charged them; but they, well knowing the intricacies of the jungle, and being extremely nimble, succeeded in not only effecting their escape, but also in carrying off the disabled of their party. We were brought up by a deep pool, and saw them making off on the other side, shouting *Yahun! yahun!*

After this encounter we continued our march along the beach, and discovered another pool of very good and sweet water immediately opposite the vessel, and just within the skirts of the jungle. Having sent for the water-casks, and hoisted a jack at the pool (being a preconcerted signal to those on board), we left half the party there, and proceeded with the remainder along a path into the jungle, expecting that it would lead to a village where we might get live stock. We advanced about a couple of miles without seeing any more huts, or natives, and no quadrupeds of any sort. The wood into which we penetrated, and in which the bugle alone kept us together, was one of the most gloomy and dismal that can possibly be conceived: it was, indeed,

"Nemus atrum horrenti umbrâ."

The trees were of great height, in many places thickly interwoven with rattans and bushrope. The sunbeams being unable to penetrate the entangled foliage, the atmosphere, in consequence, bore the semblance of twilight. The broad boughs hung rich with heavy dew-drops, and the air was loaded with a damp and pestilential vapour, occasioned by the rotting twigs, leaves and fruit, with which the swampy ground was thickly strewed.. The death-like stillness was occasionally interrupted by a solitary parrot winging its noisy flight overhead; but owing to the luxuriance of our vegetable canopy, it was almost impossible to gain even an imperfect view of him. Numerous snakes were observed stealing along amongst the bushes.

From

From several we had narrow escapes: those we succeeded in killing were all furnished with poisonous fangs, and many bore a striking resemblance to the *coluber prester*, or viper, but generally they were spotted.

Tired with our excursion, we returned to the watering pool; and having rolled the casks up to it, we sat down to a slight refection previous to commencing the filling. Whilst busily engaged with our repast, a strong party of the natives stole down upon us, and threw in a shower of arrows, which killed one and severely wounded three of the soldiers. We quickly formed, charged them, killed and wounded several, and continued skirmishing with them till sunset; for they made several desperate attempts to cut off the pioneers engaged in filling, and it required the greatest alertness to keep them off. At last, the pioneers having completed their task, we gave them a parting volley, and pulled off from Kellie Bay for the ship. But a strong current at that time setting to the N.E., at the rate of four knots an hour, we found that, instead of being able to gain the vessel, we were drifting fast out to sea; we therefore anchored the water-boats, and the two others having gone alongside, the ship's anchor was weighed, and dropping down to the long-boat and cutter, she was brought up in thirteen fathoms, and by midnight we got on board, after a hard day's work, and laden with bows, arrows, shells, &c. During the night the savages collected from all parts of the island, and kept shouting and yelling in defiance on the beach; but having got what we wanted, we did not humour them by a second visit.

Our present connexion with the Burman empire, which will lead to frequent intercourse with that country by sea, renders it highly desirable that some attempts should be made to conciliate the natives

 of

of the Andamans. The Little Andaman would be a convenient watering-place, besides affording abundant materials for refitting or building ships. Under existing circumstances, a visit to this island is extremely hazardous, as the foregoing details will prove.

Next morning we weighed and stood through Duncan's Great Passage. At 10 A. M. we got on a coral reef not laid down in any chart, least water five fathoms, with the following bearings: North end of the Little Andaman S.S.E.; the north-west point, S.W. by S. The centre of the South Brother, S.E. by E.½E., distant four miles; and the centre of the North Brother, E.½N. Both these islands, like the Little Andaman, are flat, and covered with high trees, without a rising ground of any sort on them. We kept away to the northward, and got twelve fathoms all the way between the South Brother and Sisters:—an eight-knot breeze during the day, which put us in high spirits.

On the 16th, the favourable breeze still continuing, at 7 A.M. we saw Barren Island, distant ten leagues. On this there is a volcano which has frequent irruptions. All hands quite alive at the prospect of a speedy termination to a most tiresome voyage. A considerable portion of a wreck passed us, on which was the stump of a mast; likewise several barnacle-covered trees followed by shoals of fish. On the 18th we were in soundings, forty fathoms with a muddy bottom. In the afternoon one of the pioneers fell overboard from the shank of the little bower anchor: a form was quickly thrown him from the poop, the jolly-boat lowered, and he was picked up a mile from

* The account of our visit to the Little Andaman Island appeared in The Edinburgh Philosophical Journal.

from the vessel. Never did I see a man in such a fright; even after he was safe it was a long time before he recovered his composure. We had previously lost two natives from sickness.

On the 19th our longing sight was gratified by a distant view of the seat of the war, being Bargue Point, a part of the Burman empire. The appearance of the land was low, and covered with trees. In the evening we anchored. Next morning we weighed, and saw three vessels bearing down upon us, and another steering the same course as ourselves, the last being a transport with a native regiment on board: two of the first bound for Calcutta, and the remaining one the bark *Nimrod*, which had been sent out in search of us, with supplies of provisions and water. I boarded three of the vessels, and found there was no likelihood of peace.

At daylight, on the 21st, we saw the Elephant, a grove of trees at the mouth of the Rangoon river, one of the mouths of the mighty Irawaddy, and what the Hooghly is to the Ganges. The pilot came on board from the pilot-brig lying at anchor outside the bar, on which it was nearly all over with us, for we got into a-quarter less three fathoms, were touching, when down anchor, and swung into five. After getting within the mouth of the river (three miles in breadth), we were caught in a severe squall, and obliged to beat up the whole way to Rangoon, twenty-four miles. The land on each side was low and covered with jungle, out of which rose at intervals the black spires of the trumpet-shaped praws or temples: the appearance of the richly gilded praw of Shoé Dagoon, behind the town, was splendid in the extreme. In the evening we anchored off the King's wharf.

CHAPTER II.

Description of Rangoon......Persons, Dress, and Manners of the Natives......The Military......War-Boats......Money......The Priests......Description of the Great Shoé Dagoon Pagoda.

The appearance of Rangoon,* the principal seaport of the Burmese empire, is not at all imposing. The wooden buildings extending along the bank of the river resemble ancient barns, behind which is the stockade, composed of massive pieces of timber about fifteen feet high. In the back ground towers the great Shoé Dagoon, in the midst of its subordinate spires, which formed a splendid object, glittering in the evening sun. The river was full of transports, with about half a dozen British men of war. The small canoes of the natives glided about with the rapidity of the wind, so that the river presented a lively sight, strongly contrasting with the sombre dusky town. The Rangoon river is about half a mile broad. The Dalla, or west side, is a level plain, interspersed with clumps of trees and a few ruined pagodas.

Having shaken hands with a few old acquaintances, I took up my abode with my friend Major Home, in a gilded temple surrounded with lofty pagodas. Their tinkling bells soothed and composed the mind, after the tumult of a crowded transport. The temple was surrounded

* The exact mode of pronouncing this word by the Burmese is *Yanghoon;* they are unable to articulate the initial *R.*

surrounded by a breast-work, and defended by two long twelve-pounders. As it was situated on an eminence in the rear of the city, it commanded an extensive view of the country, which consisted of jungle, with plains and patches of water interspersed.

The principal part of the city is situated within the stockade, which extends a mile along the river; the streets are wide and at right angles. One or two houses only are built of brick and chunam, the chief of which is the custom-house. The dwellings of the common people are constructed of posts driven into the ground, at the distance of two or three feet from which is a bamboo grating, forming the floor. The roof consists of the leaves of the palmyra, or long grass twisted round and sewed to slips of bamboo. The houses of the *yahāns* or *rhahāns* (priests) are large buildings of teak, with substantial tiled roofs (sometimes two or three to each house, one above another), and the floors commonly eight or twelve feet from the ground: many of the houses are carved. In these they reside with the images of Gaudma, which are composed of marble or wood highly gilt, and seated on an ark, in which their sacred books are contained. The suburb of Tackally, inhabited by the lower orders and cyprians, is more populous than the town itself.

The inhabitants are stout and athletic: the men are about five feet eight inches in height, seldom taller, with straight muscular limbs; the women are rather diminutive, but well-formed in every respect except the nose, which is commonly flat. Both sexes are of a copper colour: they are lively and inquisitive; they smoke segars constantly: almost all of them read and write; and having no prejudices, they are readily susceptible of improvement and civilization. The women are not immured at home, like those of Hindoostan; they superintend

superintend the domestic economy, and weave their own and their husbands' clothes: the latter are checks, of different patterns, resembling tartans. The men wear a single cloth tucked round the loins, and hanging down to the knee; the loose part is thrown across the shoulders, strongly resembling the ancient mode of dress amongst the Scottish Highlanders. Both the men and the women wear the hair of the head long, but eradicate with pincers the hair from the other parts of the body: the men have neither whiskers nor mustachios. The head-dress of the men is a handkerchief twisted round, entwined in the hair in front, and tied in a knot. Sandals are worn on the feet, consisting of a sole of leather fixed on the foot by two straps, which unite at the great toe. The dress of the women barely serves the purposes of decency: it consists of a narrow piece of cloth, worn over the breasts and tucked in at either side; in walking one leg is always exposed. Over the lower robe is worn a loose vest with sleeves (commonly white), which reaches to the upper part of the thigh. The hair of the women is divided in front, and tied in a knot behind, in which flowers are entwined. Men and women attain the age of puberty before they marry. Those who can afford it burn their dead; but the poorer classes make a narrow hole in the ground, about three feet deep, and having tied up the corpse in a mat, thrust it in sideways, first carrying it three times round the hole or grave; they then throw the earth over it, trampling it down hard. I observed massive tombstones in several parts of the outskirts of the town, which had been placed over the ashes of *poonghees*, or inferior priests.

Males and females have holes in the lobes of both ears, in which they stick their segars: they dye their teeth and the edges of their eye-lashes eye-lashes with antimony. The greatest compliment that can be paid a Burman, is to take the lighted cheroot from your mouth and present it to him; he, immediately after placing it in his cheek, performs the *shiko*, or salaam, with both hands. They are very fond of drinking tea and brandy with Europeans, and eat and drink with them without the least scruple. When the men and women quarrel they fight it out; the men with their fists, and the ladies with their slippers: they despise the Hindoos for confining their contests to abuse, without coming to blows.

They account it to be very injurious to the growth of animals to be deprived of the maternal milk; wherefore they never milk their kine, which consequently excel in size those of Hindoostan. The children are suckled for a couple of years; and I have seen a child, after taking its fill from the nipple, smoke a segar with great relish.

The men are tattooed very closely, from the waist to below the knee, with different figures of animals, charms, &c.: I saw a woman with *the white of one of her eyes tattooed.* The process is performed with a long steel needle, loaded at one end, and divided at the other to contain the liquor, which is either red or blue: it draws blood at every stroke.

The sitting attitude is the most respectful: when an attendant presents any thing to his superior, he falls on his knees and hands it to him.

Pickled tea-leaves, the areca nut, and betel-leaf, are chewed; and the grades of rank are denoted by the betel-box being either of gold, silver, or wood, as well as by the articles of furniture and dress. The Burmans are extremely curious in examining the texture of the clothes worn by Europeans: they approach in a respectful manner,

and

and feel the dress all over. For an old red jacket, or a piece of broad-cloth, a Burman would part with any thing, even his wife for a season. Of their complaisant disposition in this respect the European officers availed themselves; most of them having one, and some two Burman wives, who proved very faithful, and made excellent servants. They were purchased for fifty or sixty rupees: some of the ladies bore Anglo-Burman children.

The disproportion of females to males in the population of the Burman empire, owing probably to the wars which have occurred there, has been the occasion of a custom amongst the Burmans of selling their wives and daughters, particularly the latter.

Dr. Buchanan mentions a curious custom of the physicians in this country, which did not occur to my observation. He says that the parents of a young woman attacked by a dangerous illness enter into a compact with a doctor, who undertakes to cure her under the following conditions; namely, if she lives, she becomes the property of the doctor; if she dies, he pays her value to the parents. He adds, that the number of fine young women he saw in the house of a doctor at Meaday made him think that the practice was very common.

The Burmans are not of the penurious disposition of the Bengalees, but live as well as their means afford; they foolishly expend considerable sums upon their spiral or trumpet-shaped temples, where they bury images of silver. All the smaller temples about Rangoon (of which there are several thousand) have been picked by the Europeans for the sake of the small silver Gaudmas. Few steps were taken to check this very culpable practice.

The Burmans are exceedingly fond of music and poetry. They have

have bands of music, consisting of circles of gongs, drums, and pieces of bamboo of different lengths fixed on strings, which being struck with a short stick, produce a sound resembling that of a piano; the effect on the water, on a moonlight night, is very fine. Their dancing consists of turning round slowly on one spot, and gracefully moving the arms and hands in circles.

The food of the Burmans is principally rice, to which they add animal food when they can get it, though they are prohibited from slaughtering domesticated animals. Napee, prepared from putrid sprats and other fish, is a favourite sauce with their rice. They also use a soup made from the stem of the young plantain tree.

The lower orders are extremely abusive: the common terms are "*na lee,*" "*supak loo,*" "*ni maggé loolah,*" &c., which are too indelicate to admit of translation. When they challenge one another to fight, they strike their left arm at the elbow with the right hand, exclaiming, "*youk ya!*" or "here's a proper man for you!". In their boat-races, they exclaim, "*youk ya lahy!*" and *yeyla wallahy!*" which are all terms of defiance.

During my sojourn in Ava I did not observe a single individual pitted with small-pox, and very few deformed: blindness is prevalent.

The arms of the soldiery are muskets (without bayonets), swords and spears; they carry their powder in a horn, and sometimes in a dried pumpkin, or a long cloth bag. The weapon they use best is the ginjal, or swivel, which they fire with great precision. The *dar*, or sword, is used for building their houses, fighting, or preparing their food. The handle is of the same length as the blade; so that they can hold it with one or both hands, and strike a powerful blow with it. Those of the chiefs are cased in gold or silver, and covered

 with

with gems. Their spears are ornamented with horse-hair; they have also a kind of javelin, which is thrown from the back of an elephant, by means of a small crooked stick, in a manner similar to that practised by the natives of New South Wales. The Cassay horsemen are armed with matchlocks, swords, spears, and shields. They ride galloways, about thirteen hands high, that move in a rapid amble; the legs of the riders are defended by a circular piece of leather, which is commonly highly .gilt. When the body-guard of the Governor-General first encountered them, the Cassays were startled and terrified at the sight of Arab horses, fourteen and fifteen hands high.

The main arm of his Majesty of the Golden Feet is his marine establishment, consisting of war-boats: every *rua*, or village, on the banks of the river, is compelled to furnish a certain number. The common length of these boats (which in the native language are called *tee-lee)* is fifty or sixty feet. They are rowed or paddled by thirty or forty men, their weapons placed at their side; they carry also a few soldiers, with a piece of ordnance mounted on the prow, which is made sharp, for the purpose of running down and staving smaller craft. Our man-of-war boats could never get near them: the steam-boat alone tired out the rowers, and when she came up with them they jumped overboard.

The following instance of British intrepidity has never been publicly noticed; it may therefore not be improper to mention it here. At the period when the whole Burman army, headed by the celebrated Maha Bundoolah, surrounded our orce at Rangoon, towards the end of the year 1824, the captain of a transport lying near the mouth of the river left his vessel in his cutter, manned

manned with half a dozen Malay Lascars, in order to communicate with the agent for transports at Rangoon. He had not proceeded far up the river, when six war-boats, filled with men, pushed off to attack him. He ordered his men to pull for the nearest boat, and on coming alongside he jumped on board, followed by his Lascars. The Burmans were so confounded at his boldness, that they abandoned the boat and took to the water, leaving the glittering prize in the quiet possession of the gallant sailor. The other boats, on perceiving the fate of their companion, judged it prudent to retire.

Chiefs of a certain rank are entitled to gild their boats, and to bear a golden *tee* or umbrella.

The boats for passage and those for the conveyance of merchandize are roofed in, with out-riggers, on which the crews sit, and pull or force them along with poles: they occasionally track them with a rope. When the wind is right aft, they hoist a sail of cloth between two poles: having no keel, they cannot beat to windward. The *ledeegee*, or steersman, sits or stands upon the elevated stern, which commands a view of the river. All the smaller canoes are made of single trees; first shaped, then hollowed out, and finally the sides extended by means of stretchers. In rowing, the crew keep time by calling out or singing, "*ye-ee, ee-ee!*"

The Burmans have no coined money: the circulating medium is bullion. A silver *tickal*, or *dinga*, is nearly the weight of a Madras rupee; and before the war broke out, one hundred seers, or about two hundred pounds of rice could be purchased for a *tickal:* the price, however, at Rangoon, during my visit, was thirty. Every shopkeeper has a small box, containing scales to weigh the bullion given in payment for commodities: the weights are modelled after the

the figure of griffins, cows, &c. The inferior currency is lead, with which fish, vegetables, tobacco, &c. are purchased.

Whenever a Burman accumulates a considerable sum, he lays it out in building a brick and chunam pagoda, in which he places several figures of Gaudma, coated with silver, or smaller figures of gold, enclosed in a square box.

The priests are shaven on the head, and wear a long loose yellow robe reaching to the knees: they never cook their own victuals, but subsist upon alms. They issue every morning from their *kiooms*, or monasteries, and perambulate the streets with a black or blue wooden box in their hands, which is filled by the charitable with rice and vegetables. Their employment consists chiefly in attending upon their god, keeping the idols clean, and reciting prayers and discourses on moral duties: they also teach the children to read and write. The vernacular character is circular in shape, and written with a style upon palmyra leaves. The most valued of the sacred books are composed of slips of ivory, and written in the square, or Pali character. The priests, as well as the other inhabitants, keep a sort of scrap-book, or album, which consists of a piece of cloth, smeared with lamp-black (folded up into a small compass), in which they write with a pencil of *steatites*, songs, memoranda, or any thing curious; they also keep their accounts, and preserve sketches of remarkable objects in it. The name of the book, in the vernacular tongue, is *parucek*. Besides the *rhahāns*, *poonghees*, or priests, there are a few antiquated virgins, who shave their heads, and are employed in carrying water to the temples, and in other menial offices in the sacred buildings.

A very considerable part of the population of Rangoon is composed

of

of Chinese, or *Fokis* (as they term themselves), who are merchants, shopkeepers, artizans, and constitute the most industrious portion of the inhabitants of this town.

The great *praw*, or pagoda, is the Shoé Dagoon, or golden temple: it is situated two miles and a half in the rear of Rangoon. Leaving the town by one of the northern gates, a broad fosse is crossed by a causeway; the road then gradually ascends between rows of smaller pagodas, till the eminence is reached, on which stands the Shoé Dagoon, occupying the highest of three platforms. The building is octagonal at the base, and spiral at the top, and is said to be three hundred and thirty feet in height. It is highly gilt. On the top is a *tee*, or umbrella, of open iron-work, surmounted by a vane, and a small globe of glass: bells are hung round the lower part of the *tee*. There are no apertures in the building, which is solid throughout. It has small niches around, which contained images of marble and wood; but these have been removed to England, India, or elsewhere. It was truly melancholy to observe the ravages which had been committed on the smaller pagodas surrounding the Shoé Dagoon: one alone, amongst thousands, was preserved from pillage by the exertions of Dr. Campbell, of the Madras Artillery.

On the southern side of the pagoda is a beautiful pavilion, gilt and picked out with crimson, containing an image of Gaudma of such gigantic dimensions, that an English officer placed his couch, where he reposed, in its left hand! The pagoda and environs were at this time occupied as a military post, having guns and mortars mounted upon the upper platforms. To the north of it was a picquet. From the village of Kemmendine, four miles up the river, to that of Pooja-down, two miles below Rangoon, are the remains of the Burmese trenches

trenches when they invested our army in December 1824. The sallies made by our troops from the great pagoda occasioned much slaughter amongst the enemy. The skeletons of men are constantly met with in the neighbouring jungles.

These jungles consist of the *mangifera Indica*, the *ficus Indica*, different varieties of palm, plants of the *euphorbium* genus, the *laurus cassia*, with plantains, the jack-fruit, the custard apple, a species of cedar, and high reeds in abundance, the abode of swarms of musquitoes.

The animals which inhabit the jungles are the wild elephant and tigers of a large size, some of which I have seen prowling near the stockade which surrounds Rangoon, in search of the pariah dogs; also wild hogs, antelopes, and other deer. The fowls are the common jungle-fowl, with snipes, woodcocks, partridges, and quails.

CHAPTER III.

The Author joins a Detachment under orders for Prome......Kemmendine......Panlang ......Musquitoes......Yan-Yan-Chinia......First Sight of the Irawaddy......Donabew ......Henzada......Shocks of an Earthquake......Shoégeen......Napeezeik......Mioung ......Plunderers......Yangeen......Mnouzeay......Shoédoun......Putdoun...... Arrival at Prome.

A DETACHMENT of infantry and artillery having received orders to proceed up the river from Rangoon to Prome, in consequence of the rupture of the armistice and the recommencement of hostilities, I volunteered to accompany the party. Having stowed my baggage in a large boat, rowed by six men, with a *ledeegee* or steersman, we pushed off from the King's wharf, where there is a battery commanding the river.* Besides the boats which conveyed the troops, there were many others laden with provisions and ammunition: our flotilla consisted in the whole of a hundred and seventy. We passed a thirty-six-gun frigate on the stocks, building for the Imaum of Muscat, and named *the Bundoolah*, after the celebrated generalissimo of the Burmese: she was nearly ready for launching.

The flotilla brought up at the village of Kemmendine, four miles, the

* Owing to the loss of my memoranda of dates, which were blown out of the boat in which I returned to Rangoon, I am unable to be exact in this respect. In the subsequent part of this chapter I have therefore thought it better to omit the dates altogether.

the boats being made fast with wooden anchors having a single fluke, or with poles stuck in the mud. It was in the stockade of Kemmendine that the twenty-sixth regiment of Madras Native Infantry, under Major Yates, withstood for seven days forty successive attacks of a large portion of the Burmese army, and repulsed them; for which they now bear "Kemmendine" on their colours.

Being anxious to push on, and not knowing it to be the commandant's intention to halt at Kemmendine, I proceeded up the Lyne branch of the river, and after being fired at by the gun-brig, I discovered that we had made a wrong turn, instead of holding to the left or entrance of the Panlang creek, and dropped down. Next day we ran up in one tide to Panlang, forty miles. This was formerly an extensive town; it is now a straggling village of bamboo huts. Indigo, cotton, tobacco, and rice, are cultivated in the vicinity.

The narrow and despicable policy of the government, by permitting the highest classes only to construct durable habitations, opposes itself to the improvement and civilization of the country, which would be greatly forwarded if the common people were allowed to imbibe local attachments, which are destroyed by the present system, whereby they are continually moving from place to place.

The musquitoes here occasioned me the greatest torment I ever experienced: whole squadrons of these insects issuing from the high reeds which line the banks of the creek, bit us in a few seconds through sheets and long drawers, and we could get no sleep. A cavalry officer affirmed that he found no protection against them in a pair of leather-breeches; an infantry soldier declared they had bit

him

him through his breast-plate; and an artilleryman, to crown the joke, asserted that he could not secure his head by thrusting it into a mortar! I have since noticed that Colonel Symes sustained equal misery from the same cause, in his passage up the river. He describes this part of it as remarkable for being infested by musquitoes of unusual size, and venomous beyond what he had ever experienced in any other country. The colony of insects, bred and harboured in the reeds upon the bank, extends some miles, so that a heavy vessel must continue for one tide within their action.

Here (at Panlang) I had an opportunity of observing the Burmese mode of weaving, which is exactly similar to the European, except that the treddles are pieces of lead held between the toes: also the manner of husking rice, which is performed by means of a hand-mill, and that of pounding the rice by a wooden hammer. I was freely admitted into the houses of the villagers, who brought their children to perform the *shikothee* or salaam. Many of the children had Spanish dollars suspended round their necks; and their mothers were highly gratified when I gave them some rupee-pieces for the same purpose.

After leaving Panlang, in proceeding up the creek, several huge alligators were observed under the bank. The country, as far as the eye could reach, was a thick lofty forest.

Upon reaching Yan-Yan-Chinia, we were first gratified by a sight of the mighty Irawaddy, here a mile in width. The country is a champaigne tract, and is inundated by the river during the rains. The bed of the Irawaddy is composed of an alluvial deposit, indurated through the petrifying quality of the water. Hitherto I had not met with a single stone, either in the bed of the river or on its

 banks.

banks. From the mud of the river, in any part of its course, from ten to twelve per cent. of gold-dust may be washed.

After proceeding five or six miles up the Myeet, or great stream, we came in sight of Donabew, the scene of the Bundoolah's death, and where, in March 1825, Brigadier-General Cotton, with a force inadequate to the assault of the exceedingly strong stockades and defences erected here, was repulsed with considerable slaughter. The stockade was now prostrate in several places: but the remains of the tree which was scaffolded, with three tiers of guns erected on it, still existed, as well as the abbatis.

I observed here some Carians. This race is derived from Pegu, and they are employed as cultivators. They differ in person from the Burmans in general; they are taller and more athletic; their disposition is however equally good. They inhabit villages in the interior, and are exempt from the Burman law of conscription, by which every male is compelled to serve in the army when called upon. Their dress is a sort of shirt, with holes to admit the head and arms.

Whilst quietly discussing a plate of rice and salt fish, I saw descending the river a crow sitting and feasting upon a dark-looking substance, which proved to be the corpse of a European soldier dressed in a checked shirt. The head had been chopped off.

Flocks of birds appeared of the curlew species, with red bills and white plumage; they skimmed the surface of the water, keeping the bill beneath it. Numerous alligators were likewise seen.

We arrived at Henzada, a large town, in which were many temples and wooden bridges. The inhabitants had returned, and were pursuing their usual avocations. The chief wore a naval uniform, which had been presented to him by Captain Alexander of the *Alligator*.

Alligator. He shewed us his commission, which ran as follows: "Shoé Ma Praw, chief magistrate of Henzada, having drank the "waters of fidelity to the British flag, wears the knife in his girdle "from this date, September 4th 1825." Rice was here abundant and cheap, thirty-six seers for a *dinga*: a bullock cost six rupees. A tremendous current was running past Henzada.

I visited the *poonghee* houses here, and was courteously received by the priests, who examined me attentively, and seemed particularly pleased with the tartan dress I wore. They would not part, however, with any of their sacred books.

Whilst we remained at Henzada, I observed that a group of our boatmen had got an old pack of cards, and were amusing themselves at a game resembling loo. In the arms of some of them pieces of gold and silver had been inserted under the skin, which were intended as charms. Our soldiers, aware of this custom, became very dexterous in making incisions in the arms of the dead Burmans, and in ridding them of their then superfluous talismans.

One evening we experienced ten severe shocks of an earthquake; they proceeded across the river from east to west, and caused a great swell and rise in the water. The boats rolled about and dashed against each other. The shocks were accompanied by a long rolling noise, as if the banks were tumbling in. The thermometer stood at 70°; the air was very still. The Anoupectoumiew, or Arracan hills, were now seen in the distance.

About Sarrawah, on the banks of the Irawaddy, opposite to Henzada, the teak-tree flourishes. In the pools and back-waters, after we had passed Henzada, we daily witnessed the horrible and disgusting sight of dead bodies, in every stage of decay, to the number

number of sixty or seventy together. Some of the individuals were Europeans, who had been either killed by the Burmese, or whose bodies had been disinterred by them. Others were natives, who had either fallen in action, or were victims to the cholera morbus. The stench was extremely offensive.

We passed Shoégeen, an extensive town, filled chiefly with women and children. The policy of the government compels the men to fight by holding their women and children in pledge, whom they massacre, if the men desert the *henza*, or standard of the empire.

We arrived at Napeezeik,* opposite to which was Yeageen, where there was a subaltern's party. After passing this place we were fired upon from a stockade in the jungle. Next day, whilst towing and tracking the boats up some dangerous rapids, the rear of the column was attacked. The enemy kept blazing away from the jungle; but when a fire was opened upon them they were quickly silenced. We arrived at Mioung next day; it had just been burned. At the spot where we anchored (a very dangerous part of the river), two or three miles above Mioung, the skeletons of murdered men were seen whitening on the beach. Look-out houses were erected at the edge of the jungle, where the aged and feeble were placed to observe when boats passed up or down the river. Upon single boats being discovered, or canoes weakly manned, the spies spring a wooden rattle with four clappers, sounding exactly like those which are tied round

---

* *Napee* is the name of a sort of sprat, which is eaten by the Burmese as a sauce to their rice; *zeik* means a landing place, and is a not unfrequent termination of names of places.

round the necks of bullocks to prevent their straying in the jungle; by this contrivance they convey a signal to their own people, who lie in wait in the creeks, without causing alarm to the persons on the river. The plunderers rush out in their boats, and not only rob, but murder or mutilate those who fall into their hands.

After passing Yangeen, where that fearful scourge, the cholera morbus, was raging, on turning a point of land, we found a party of sick sepoys, of the twenty-sixth or Kemmendine corps, engaged with plunderers, who had issued forth armed in two boats, at the usual signal from the look-out bank. They had attacked the boats of the twenty-sixth just as the head of our column came in sight. A volley being fired into the leading boat of the enemy, all hands jumped overboard and the boat was taken: the other pulled into a creek and got beyond the reach of our fire. We observed a strong body of the enemy, with war-boats, on the opposite shore.

The next day we had a skirmish with a body of marauders at the village of Mnouzcay. We drove them out of the village into the jungle, taking a few prisoners, who informed us that their main body was fifteen hundred or two thousand strong, with one hundred horse and five pieces of artillery. Near this village, and only a few days before, Dr. Sandford and Lieutenant Bennet, of the Royals, were taken prisoners by the enemy. They were coming from Prome sick, and having imprudently landed to breakfast on the sand, several men approached them, one at a time, presenting fowls, vegetables, &c., till about a dozen had collected, who suddenly threw a nooze round their necks, and dragged them into the jungle. A China man, who saw what passed, by concealing himself behind a bush, stated that the Burmese stripped the two officers, and tormented them by

thrusting

thrusting sticks into their bodies. Their own boats pushed off the moment they were taken. Many dead bodies passed down the river this day; and whilst walking along the bank I observed the recent corpse of a European, with a spear-wound in the chest, and a stake driven through his neck; also another impaled.

At Mnouzeay were numerous *kioums* or monasteries, some handsome bridges, and enormous figures of griffins, thirty feet high, placed at the entrance of the enclosure surrounding the pagodas, as usual. The appearance of the country had improved; being less flat than it had hitherto been. I noticed a few pebbles of water-worn quartz.

The following day we passed Shoédoun, and brought up at Putdoun, where we had a brush with a strong body of the enemy. The scenery up the river, until we reached Prome, was now enchanting; the country on the banks consisted of hills covered with wood to their summits, and broken into beautiful undulations; the noble Irawaddy, a mile wide, winding between, its margin fringed with foliage, and its bosom resembling an extensive lake studded with islands, forming altogether a scene of the most picturesque description. Gun-brigs were stationed at intervals of twenty miles, all the way up the river, to keep open the communication; the last was a little below Prome.

The city of Prome, situated in latitude about 19° N. longitude 95° E., was the ancient frontier town between Ava and Pegu. On both sides of the river are wooded hills, many of them covered with pagodas, which were all stockaded upon the advance of the English army. The pagodas here have all been preserved entire, as well as the bells, of which there are eleven at the great gilt pagoda. These

bells

bells are struck by devotees (with the horns of antelopes and deer) to awaken the attention of the god. The place was filled with inhabitants, to whom every protection was afforded. The bazaars in the stockade were well supplied. The houses presented a curious appearance; it being the dry season, they were all unroofed: that is, the covering of cadjan leaves and grass was stripped off, and a few mats substituted to keep off the sun: no other covering being permitted through fear of fire.

The luxuries of Prome were of a very limited kind. The English troops were in small danger of incurring the same ill consequences as attended the residence of Hannibal's army at Capua. Beef was the only meat that could be procured; and that highly effective and well-regulated department of the Madras army, the commissariat, deserves great praise for its conduct in procuring and supplying this article. The natives evinced no unwillingness to show the commissariat-officers the stray bullocks and wild buffaloes in the neighbourhood, or to partake of the flesh when killed. The vegetables were yams and sweet potatoes. The price of spirits was eighty rupees per dozen.

The recreations of the British officers were not of a very varied or exalted character. The evening after my arrival at Prome, whilst sitting at the door of the house where I resided, I observed an English officer stealing towards me, armed with a formidable spear, making his approaches cautiously, and partly concealing himself behind a paling. He seemed bent on some bloody deed, and I began to look about for some weapon to meet his attack, if possible, *paribus armis*; when suddenly he dashed from his hiding-place, and hurled his spear at a pariah dog, reposing in fancied security upon a dunghill. The weapon grazed the animal's back, and it ran howling to the jungle. This was one of the most active recreations of the subalterns at Prome. In the monsoon, when the water flowed beneath the elevated houses in which they lived, they amused themselves by fishing with a line let down between the planks of the floor, as they lazily reclined on their cots (whilst a Burman was *tattooing* their skin), or rowed about from house to house in small canoes.

At this place several of the horses of the body guard, and many head of cattle, were destroyed by leeches in the viscera, which they received into the stomach along with the jungle-grass, in which these leeches exist in great numbers.

The soil about Prome is a debris of ferruginous sand-stone. Coal is found higher up, about sixty feet below the surface, containing sulphur and iron pyrites: iron is also met with in considerable quantities. Much of this metal is used at Prome in fabricating various implements, particularly entrenching tools, and *dars* or swords. The blacksmiths have a strange and disgusting custom of eating horse-flesh, under a belief that it makes them strong.

I formerly noticed the petrifying qualities of the water of the river: I now saw a strong proof of the rapidity with which it converts foreign bodies into stone. The pioneers were ordered to remove a house, which would have interfered with the defence of the stockade if the enemy had assailed it. Upon endeavouring to cut down the massive teak pillars on which it was raised, they found that the edges of their hatchets were all turned. On examining into the cause of this, they found that the pillars were petrified throughout, though the house had only been built ten years, and the pillars were under water three months in the year during the monsoon.

It

It will here be convenient to give the reader a brief narrative of the occurrences of the war, between the period of my arrival in Ava and my return from Prome to Rangoon. At the time of my visit to Prome, an attack having been daily expected from the whole Burmese army, breastworks and entrenchments had been constructed round the city.

CHAPTER IV.

Offers of Peace by the British Commander......Armistice......Treaty......Violation of the Armistice by the Burmese Troops......Rupture of the Armistice by express Orders from the King......Enemy advances upon Prome......British Troops retreat from Wuttygaon......Attack on the Burmese positions at Simbike......At Napadee ......and on the West Bank of the Irawaddy......Burmese Witches......Advance from Prome......Flag of Truce......Treaty of Peace......Disaster in Pegu.

Before the commander of the forces advanced from Prome, at the commencement of the cold season of 1825, a communication was made by him to the Burmese commanders, who, at the beginning of October, had established their head-quarters at Meeaday, about forty miles above Prome. The letter of Sir Archibald Campbell urged upon the enemy the policy of putting a stop to the horrors of war, by accepting the offers of peace which he was authorized to make. The Burmese chiefs despatched in return a mission to the British head-quarters, charged to express the wishes of their king and his ministers to establish a lasting peace.

Lieut. Colonel Tidy, the Deputy Adjutant General, and Lieutenant Smith, of the Royal Navy, were thereupon commissioned by the British general to proceed to Meeaday and propose an armistice, to allow time for a meeting between commissioners on either side, duly authorized to arrange a treaty of peace. They were courteously received by the Kee Woonghee, or Burman prime minister; the proposal for an armistice was accepted, and it was agreed upon that the British and Burmese commanders should meet at Nen-ben-zeik,

zeik, attended by an escort equal in number on either side, and there conduct the negociations. The armistice was signed on the 17th September, and the two commanders, attended by their respective guards, met in a temporary building, near the village of Nen-ben-zeik, on the 2d October.

After long discussions, the Burmese chiefs desired that the armistice, which was to continue for a month, might be prolonged for an additional period of twenty days, in order to allow them time to forward the terms of the treaty proposed by the British commander to the court of Amerapoorah.

By the conditions of the armistice, the line of demarcation between the two armies, during the suspension of hostilities, was drawn from Comma, on the western bank of the Irawaddy, and passed through Nen-ben-zeik, and along the road from that village to Tongho.

Sir Archibald Campbell had scarcely returned to Prome, after the conclusion of his interview with the Burmese chiefs, before the enemy's troops violated the armistice by crossing the line of demarcation, plundering the villages on the British side of the line, and committing various excesses, which the Kee Woonghee pretended were without his sanction or knowledge.

At length the commander of the forces announced to his army, in a general order dated October 29th, that he had received information, too circumstantial to be doubted, that the Burmese army was in full march to attack the British position, under express orders from the King of Ava, in open and shameful violation of the armistice concluded on the basis of the plighted faith of the two governments.

The

The Burmese forces advanced upon Prome, with a view of surrounding the British army, and cutting off its communication with Rangoon. The neighbouring districts were overrun with irregular bands, causing General Campbell much anxiety respecting the safety of the valuable convoys on the river. The enemy's army consisted of three principal divisions. The right, under the Suddoowoon, amounting to about fifteen thousand men, crossed the river, and occupied its west bank, stockading themselves strongly, and being defended by artillery, detaching a corps to its front to intercept the communication of the British with the rear; the left corps, amounting also to fifteen thousand men, Burmans, Shans (Siamese tributary to Ava), and Cassayers (chiefly horsemen), was commanded by Maha Nemiow, an old and experienced general, sent down express from Ava to introduce a new system of conducting the war. This corps moved by a route about ten miles distant from the river (an extensive forest intervening), and stockaded themselves in the jungles at Simbike and Kyalay. The centre, from twenty-five to thirty thousand strong, was under the immediate orders of the Kee Woonghee, and moved along the east bank of the river, accompanied by a considerable fleet of war-boats, to a position upon the heights of Napadee, which were a series of hills, stockaded to the summit, and only accessible on one side by a narrow pathway, commanded by artillery: on the river side the navigation was also commanded by batteries of heavy ordnance.

Before the grand conflict took place, Lieut. Colonel McDowall was directed to advance with two brigades of Madras Native Infantry (without Europeans, guns, or scaling ladders) to dislodge a part of Maha Nemiow's corps from the village of Wuttygaon, where they

they had posted themselves, apparently either to harass the right flank, or to fall into the rear of the British army on its advance from Prome, or to annoy the garrison and intercept the communication. Major Evans was directed to move with a native regiment on the enemy's front, and to act in concert with Lieut. Colonel McDowall. The number of the enemy's troops and the strength of his position appear to have been miscalculated. The British troops encountered formidable stockades twenty feet in height, from whence a galling fire was opened, Colonel McDowall, the commandant, being unfortunately killed by the first discharge, and after a considerable time spent in a vain endeavour to carry the defences, the brigades were reluctantly obliged to retreat, with the loss of ten other officers, and two hundred and fifty men killed and wounded. The Colonel's body was put in a dooley and conveyed seven miles from where he fell; but the bearers getting frightened, being closely followed by the enemy, threw it into a nullah, and it was never recovered.

The Burmese army amounted to between fifty and sixty thousand men; the British effective force opposed to this number was but five thousand (after garrisoning Prome), of which three thousand were European.

The prudence of the veteran Maha Nemiow kept the Burmese troops within their formidable stockades and entrenchments, which they were constantly employed in strengthening and augmenting; the British commander, therefore, resolved to become the assailant, notwithstanding the numbers of the enemy, and the extensive and difficult works which surrounded his positions.

On the 1st December, Sir Archibald Campbell advanced upon Simbike to dislodge the corps of Maha Nemiow from its position on the

the Nawine river; the flotilla, acting in concert, commenced a cannonade upon the enemy's centre, to draw his attention to that point. At the village of Ze-ouk, a short distance in front of Prome, the British force was divided into two columns. The right, under Brigadier General Cotton, continued its march along the left bank of the Nawine river; the other, under the direction of the commander of the forces, crossed the river, and advanced upon Simbike and Lombek, in a direction nearly parallel with the other.

Brigadier General Cotton's column first reached the enemy's position at Simbike. The Burmese were taken by surprise. Lieut. Colonel Godwin, who commanded the storming party, at the first stockade, cried out to his men, "never mind ladders, my boys; rush at it and pull it down." The men went in like bull-dogs, and in less than five minutes tore up the bamboo stockade, bayoneting three hundred of the enemy. The whole of the position was immediately carried, the enemy quitting their succession of stockades as if panic-struck. Their old general, Maha Nemiow, who was seventy-five years of age, fell whilst endeavouring to rally his troops; all the enemy's commissariat and stores were abandoned, and a great quantity of gold and silver ornaments, some beautiful swords, and one hundred Cassay horses, were taken.

Sir Archibald Campbell, after joining in the pursuit of the fugitives, at length turned back, and marched to attack the enemy's centre, before the Kee Woonghee could have intelligence of the defeat of his left wing. His Excellency, at daybreak on the 2d, moved from Ze-ouk, where his troops had bivouacked for the night, after a march of twenty miles, and commenced a cannonade of the heights of Napadee, the *Diana* steam-vessel and the gun-boats bombarding;

barding; the sight was grand and impressive. After driving the enemy from all his defences on the plain, the British troops resolutely assailed him in his entrenchments on the heights, his Majesty's 38th regiment in particular driving him from hill to hill, over precipices which could only be ascended by a narrow path, seldom firing a shot in return to continued vollies, till, in about an hour, the whole position, formidable by nature, and nearly three miles in extent, was in their possession. The enemy defended the position for some time bravely; the hills were one sheet of fire. Our loss was severe; Captain Dawson fell whilst leading on his gallant seamen, than whom none are better adapted for scaling stockades. Much plunder was taken.

The right corps of the enemy, under the Suddawoon, was easily dislodged from its position on the 5th. The British troops (the Royals, the 47th, and 89th) drove them from their first line of stockades, in capital style, and came unexpectedly upon a second line, of which they were not previously aware. But the panic-struck troops of the enemy, crowding into these confined works, which became obstacles to their retreat, rather than the means of protection, were broken with ease by the pursuers, and escaped only through the difficult nature of the country.

At the attack of one of the stockades, one of three Burmese witches, who accompanied the enemy's troops to second their efforts against the British by spells and enchantments, was killed by a musket-shot in the breast. She was a beautiful Shan girl, said to be (as well as the other two) of high rank, and possessed of supernatural endowments, particularly the power of turning aside the balls of the English. Besides these three deluded creatures, several other

Shan

Shan women were seen, dressed in male attire, and taking a part in the action.

Taking advantage of the enemy's consternation, the road to the capital being now open to the advance of the British troops, Sir Archibald moved from Prome with his whole army, in two divisions; one under his personal command, the other under Brigadier-General Cotton. They advanced to Meaday without firing a shot, meeting on the route with striking proofs of the enemy's total rout, disorganization, and dismay. At Meaday, owing to the inefficient state of the Bengal Commissariat, the whole of the Bengal division was left behind, and Sir Archibald advanced with the Madras division to Patanagaon, where he arrived on the 27th December.

Before the commander of the forces reached this place, a flag of truce was despatched to the flotilla from the Burmese chiefs at Malloon, where their forces had concentrated. The officer who bore the flag (a Woondock) announced the arrival of a commissioner at Malloon, sent from the capital to conclude a treaty of peace. Commodore Sir James Brisbane sent the Burmese officer to Sir Archibald Campbell, who, on his arrival at Patanagaon, opposite to the stockade of Malloon (which was filled with the enemy's troops), despatched the two officers who had been deputed upon a former occasion (Lieutenant-Colonel Tidy and Lieutenant Smith) to Malloon, to arrange a conference to be held in a boat moored in the centre of the river, between Malloon and Patanagaon. The conference accordingly took place on the 30th December, between the commander of the forces and Mr. Commissioner Robertson, on the one part, and Kolien Menghee (the royal deputy) and the Kee Woonghee, on the other, attended by their respective officers. After considerable

considerable discussion as to the terms of the treaty, it was at length signed on the 3d January 1826; and it stipulated that the four provinces of Arracan should be ceded to the Company, as well as the provinces of Mergui, Tavai, and Yé or Zea: that Assam, Cachar, Zeatung, and Munnipore, should be restored to the former rajahs, or placed under princes to be named by the British Government; that one crore of rupees (about a million sterling) should be paid by the Burmese Court to the East-India Company, at stated periods, by instalments of twenty-five lacs; that a resident should be admitted at Amerapoora, with an escort of fifty men, and a consul at Rangoon, &c.

Previous to the conclusion of peace, Colonel Pepper, who commanded at Pegu, marched with the troops under his command towards Tongho, by direction of Sir Archibald Campbell, in order to co-operate with the main army in its advance upon the capital. He took Shoégeen, without opposition from the enemy, on the 3d January; but upon detaching Colonel Conroy, with the third Madras Light Infantry, unaccompanied with a party of Europeans, to occupy Zittoun, that officer found the place was in possession of the Burmans; and after a fruitless attempt to storm the strongly stockaded height, in which Colonel Conroy fell, and several officers and men, the detachment was obliged to fall back upon Shoégeen. Colonel Pepper, on hearing of this defeat, retrograded and marched to the attack of Zittoun. On coming to the banks of the river which flows under the town, the naked bodies of Colonel Conroy and the others were found suspended by the heels from a gibbet. The intention of this piece of wanton barbarity was very evident; but, far from intimidating our troops, it only served to exasperate

 them,

them, particularly the European part of the force: they rushed up the height in gallant style in three columns, planted the ladders, and succeeded, in spite of the determined bravery of the enemy, in carrying the stockade, but with a loss of several officers and men, whilst five hundred of the enemy were bayoneted.

The Siamese made a shew of aiding us, and despatched several bodies of troops to assist the British commandant at Martaban; but their friendship towards us was all pretence. They were too apprehensive of the resentment of their Burmese neighbours, when we should evacuate the country, to enter heartily into our cause.

CHAPTER V.

Return to Rangoon......Prisoners at Mnouzeay......Executions amongst the Burmese ......Sensation at Rangoon......Murder there......Embark for Calcutta in a Man-of-War......The Voyage......Nautical Anecdotes......Reach the Sandheads......Arrive off Champaul Ghaut.

THERE being no prospect of farther hostilities, I departed for Rangoon in a commodious canoe. Nothing material occurred on the way down; except that, on passing the village of Mnouzeay, I observed the bodies of the prisoners we had taken at this place, as mentioned in Chapter III.; they had been crucified, *in terrorem*, by order of the chief of the district.

It may here be proper to give a description of the different modes in which criminals are executed in this country. The culprit is led to the place of execution (which is commonly an open spot on the banks of the river), where a bamboo grating is set up, to which his extended arms and legs are tied; sometimes he is made to kneel in front of the grating, and the hands alone are pinioned to it. The eyes of the culprit are not bound, so that he witnesses all the appalling preparations for his death. The executioner, who is distinguished by a red cloth crossing the body over one shoulder, and armed with a *dar* or sword, which he holds in both hands, retires about twenty yards from the criminal, and making a rush at him, inflicts a frightful wound in a diagonal direction, from the upper part of the thorax to the bottom of the abdomen, which exposes the viscera: a piercing shriek follows the blow, which is not immediately

immediately fatal, the culprit lingering sometimes for several hours after. This is the punishment for heinous offences. The most common punishment for more trivial crimes is decapitation by a single stroke of the *dar;* or a target is painted on the naked body of the culprit, who is fixed to a tree and fired at. In the latter case, if the executioners miss their object, after a certain number of shots (which they are very ready to do if well bribed), he is permitted to escape. It is extraordinary to observe the apparent unconcern which the Burmese exhibit when led to execution; they smoke a segar on their way, and continue to do so, with perfect *sang froid,* till the fatal moment.

Upon my arrival at Rangoon, I had the satisfaction of being the first to convey the intelligence of the conclusion of peace to Brigadier Smelt, the commandant. The news quickly spread throughout the place, and all the Europeans were dancing for joy in consequence. The Burmese were in ecstacy on another account, namely, the raising of the bell of the great pagoda out of the bed of the river, into which it had fallen several months previous, whilst the prize-agents were endeavouring to ship it for Bengal as a trophy. It was raised in a very simple manner, by attaching two cables to it, which at low water were made fast to a brig moored over it: when the tide rose so did the bell, and it was hauled on shore by thousands of enraptured natives, who testified their delight by many acts of extravagance: they crowned it with flowers; they performed sacrifices to it; they danced before it, and stationed bands of music constantly near it. At the time I left Rangoon they were busily employed in removing it to its former position at the Shoé Dagoon.

The

The satisfaction of the Burmese at the raising of the bell was considerably damped by an apprehension that, in consequence of the peace, Rangoon would be re-delivered to their own government; and they were so little pleased at the prospect, that a large portion of the population was making preparations to quit the place, and proceed to the British possessions in the south.

Whilst I resided here with Captains Todd and Rooke (the Paymaster and the Assistant Commissary-General), we were one morning shocked by the appearance of a ghastly figure—a Burman with his face cut in two. There was one wide wound from the upper part of his forehead to the chin; the bone was little injured, but the flesh of the face might easily have been separated on each side of the nose. He gave the following account of the cause:—He was the servant of the Burman employed by the commissariat to procure canoes for transporting stores, &c. to the army; considerable sums of money passed consequently through his hands, and it was currently believed that he was opulent. A party of armed ruffians, expecting a rich booty, had broken the evening before into his dwelling, which was situated on the outskirts of the town, murdered him and his wife whilst they were asleep, ransacked his house, and inflicted this dreadful wound on his servant, who was endeavouring to make his escape. No traces of the murderers could be discovered.

Brigadier Smelt, who had given me the command of a detachment of Europeans, was kind enough to introduce me to Captain Stoddart, of his Majesty's ship *Champion*, who politely offered me a passage to Calcutta in his vessel, which carried Captain Snodgrass with the peace despatches. The *Champion* is reckoned the fastest sailing vessel in the British navy; she carries the gauntlet, which

no

no other ship has as yet been able to touch. She was built by Captain Hayes, on fixed principles of his own invention; she is very weatherly, sails on an even keel, and is exceedingly roomy: she carries eighteen thirty-two-pound carronades, the carriages of which are on the new construction; the lower platform not recoiling, only traversing; the upper slide recoiling. Two other experimental vessels, the *Pylades* and the *Orestes*, were built at the same time as the *Champion*, under the direction of Sir Robert Seppings and Professor Inman, but they have proved unable to compete with her.

Nearly half our crew (which was a hundred strong) were in hospital. Almost all the men who had gone up the river suffered severely from the bites of musquitoes, which caused obstinate ulcers; some of them had actually lost their limbs, owing to a mortification having commenced. These insects swarmed in the vessel fore and aft, so that I had not an over-comfortable birth, although I swung in the captain's cabin.

We got on board about 4 P.M. on the 9th of January, and expected to have passed the Elephant in the night; but the first thing I heard at wash-deck-time next morning was, "On deck there!" from the captain: "are we below the Larne Tree yet?" (half way down the river).—"No, Sir, right abreast of it." Then, from the officer of the watch: "Below, there! tumble up all the skulkers. Boatswain's "mate, cut down that lazy rascal driving his pigs to market "(snoring) in his hammock there?"—"Aye, aye, Sir," growled the boatswain's mate.

On the 11th, the pilot left us, and we stood out to sea with a fair breeze.

When in the Gulf of Martaban a suspicious sail hove in sight, which

which refusing to shew colours, was consequently chased by the *Champion;* and after thirty shots had been fired at her, without her bringing to, it fell dark and she escaped. She was afterwards captured by a man-of-war, and proved to be an American, laden with arms and warlike stores for the Burmese.

I may here relate an amusing anecdote of the crew of the ship whilst they were crossing the equator. They planted the carpenter's-mate (a green-horn) on the jib-boom-end, with a great hatchet in his fist, in order that he might cut the line, and let the vessel pass. The lieutenant of the watch was let into the joke, and every now and then he sung out from the quarter-deck: "Jib-boom "there!"—"Sir?" from Chips. "Are you all ready to cut away?" —"All ready, Sir."—"See you do it cleverly, then, boy."— "Aye, aye, Sir." After some time: "Can you see it yet?"— "In half a minute, Sir."—"Keep a good look-out!"—"Aye, aye, "Sir." And thus was the unfortunate carpenter's-mate kept astride the boom for half the day. On the same solemn occasion, Neptune and his crew being a long time in coming aft, the captain inquired what they were about. "Shaving the figure-head, Sir, and making "the ship free:" and so the fact was; they lathered and shaved the old Champion's chin in due form, as the vessel had not before crossed the equator.

We got on very well until the 16th, when it fell calm, with light airs morning and evening: the weather during the day was excessively hot. On the 20th a nice little breeze carried us on at the rate of ten knots. We got soundings with forty fathoms line, and changed our course from north-west to west. On the following day we saw the pilot brig off the Sand-Heads; and at ten A.M. got the old fellow on board, with his leadsman. What was our astonishment when he told us that the *Enterprize* steam-vessel had been at Rangoon and back again to Calcutta, with duplicate despatches of the peace, and all since our leaving the Elephant! The captain was excessively annoyed at having been so completely beaten.

In the afternoon, Captains Stoddart and Snodgrass left the ship in the gig for Calcutta, distant a hundred and thirty miles. At 8 P.M. we came to an anchor in Saugor Roads. During the night it blew a gale of wind; the vessel rode it out very well. The pilot offered to take the other passengers and myself in his brig to Kedgeree. We got on board by means of a fishing boat, which was nearly swamped by the heavy sea then running. This pilot vessel, the *Asseerghur*, was kept in capital order; every thing exceedingly clean, the accommodations below splendid, very lofty between decks, and well lighted. Pilots live sumptuously here: gram-fed sheep, fat poultry, and every luxury of the table, are found on board their vessels.

After beating up to within three miles of Kedgeree, the tide failed us, and we were obliged to drop anchor. I got into the brig's boat, and attempted to pull for Kedgeree; but the tide was running so strong, that after three hours' exposure to the meridian sun, I could only get opposite the Light-house. I jumped ashore, and walked to Kedgeree, to endeavour to procure a conveyance to the City of Palaces, distant a hundred miles. By great good fortune, I was kindly accommodated with a lugger for the trifling sum of two hundred rupees!

On

On the following day, by twelve at noon, we reached Fultah, half way up, where we landed, and enjoyed ourselves upon Bengal fare. In the evening we passed Garden Reach, the beautiful approach to Calcutta, and on awaking on the morning of the 24th, we found ourselves lying off Champaul Ghaut.

CHAPTER VI.

Appearance of Calcutta......The Course......The Strand......Manner of living at Calcutta......Renewal of Hostilities, and Fall of Bhurtpore......Nautch......Barrackpore......Take a Passage for Bombay in a Country Ship.

THE first appearance of Calcutta to a stranger is very grand and imposing: the public buildings, mostly of the Grecian order, are extremely handsome; porticoes, colonnades, and piazzas abound every where. The river was crowded with shipping, chiefly European, with budgerows, bolios, and other Indian craft; the whole indicating the commercial prosperity of this flourishing capital of our Eastern empire.

We landed, on the 24th January, at the Ghaut, where we were assailed, as usual, by a crowd of native servants wanting employment, and affecting to be extremely officious. I proceeded to my agents, Messrs. Cruttenden, Mackillop, and Co., and was very kindly received by them. In passing along, I observed that turbans were not so generally worn by coolies and the lower orders as they are on the coast. The vehicles for transporting the natives from one part of the city to the other, called *Karaun-Chees*, are the most paltry conveyances I ever saw, and would be a disgrace to any city: they have large clumsy bodies, painted in a tawdry manner, without glazed windows, exceedingly dirty, and are drawn by two miserable tatoes, or ponies, urged into a jog-trot by the voice and chabook of a naked coachman. Men with huge umbrellas were running about,

about, offering their friendly shade to pedestrians who chose to hire them.

During the period I remained here, I divided my time between the city and Garden Reach. In the evening I mixed with the fashionables on the Course, which was crowded with gay equipages till sunset. The Course is a broad road round a grass quadrangle adjoining the splendid palace of Government, and bounded on two sides by the lofty and handsome buildings of Chowringhee. It commands a view of the river and of Fort William.

The appearance of Lord Amherst on this scene did not exactly correspond with what might have been expected from the Governor-General of India, though it accorded with his unassuming character. He rode in plain clothes on a white horse, not remarkable for its beauty, attended by a single Aide-de-camp, and a couple of troopers of the body guard, who were dressed in red hussar jackets with silver lace, leather breeches and long boots, caps and feathers. His Lordship is a short and spare-made man, his complexion sallow, his hair grey. Lady Amherst appeared in better style, accompanied by her daughter and an Aide-de-camp, in a smart carriage and four: an escort of the body guard attended in front and rear. The vehicles on the Course were of every build, from the dashing landau to the humble buggy. Some of the ladies sported bare arms, and were unbonneted: a few of the gentlemen promenaded in white jackets without hats. Rich natives, baboos and others, were lounging in their coaches; amongst them I observed the Representatives of the Pacha of Egypt, the Imaum of Muscat, &c. Leaving the Course, I took a turn on the Strand, the street which leads along the river, and which is resorted to by the more sober and unostentatious portion

portion of the inhabitants. Here I observed several beautiful Armenian ladies with their golden diadems, the lower part of their faces muffled in white veils, who were enjoying in their carriages the cool breeze from the river.

Close to the Strand is a steam-engine, for raising water from the Hooghly and distributing it over the city. This is a recent improvement, and attended with great benefit and comfort to the inhabitants of Calcutta. There are now runs of water along the streets, which are daily watered.

In proceeding towards Garden Reach, I passed an iron suspension bridge, the design of which is light and elegant, although it is a great deal too narrow to admit of carriages passing each other without considerable risk.

The house in which I resided at Garden Reach was beautifully seated on the river bank, opposite to the Botanic Garden, which I frequently visited: it is kept in high order, under the superintendance of Doctor Wallich. The inhabitants of this capital live in excellent style, and I had just arrived at the proper time for enjoying their luxuries, besides its being the coolest and finest season of the year. Our fare at table consisted of the finest meat, capital fish, European vegetables in perfection and abundance, wines of the first quality, including champaigne, which flew in every direction. The dinners invariably concluded with the care-dispelling hookah.

Among other friends here, I visited the late Surveyor-General of India, Colonel Blacker, whose recent death has been so severe a loss to science in India. His health was then far from being good; but he continued indefatigably employed in his literary labours.

One morning, whilst at Garden Reach, I observed the steam-vessel

Enterprize

Enterprize coming up the river from Rangoon. I quickly pushed off and boarded her, and was greatly astonished to find that hostilities had recommenced. In passing Fort William a royal salute was fired, to our infinite surprise, the cause of which was a supposition that the vessel had brought the ratified treaty from the Burman Court. So certain was Lord Amherst of peace, that he had given orders to fire a salute the moment the *Enterprize* appeared in sight, and preparations had been made at Government House for a splendid fête, at which a couple of transparencies were to be exhibited: the one representing the steam-vessel passing the fort, with the word "peace" at the main; the other, Bhurtpore in ruins, the news of the fall of which had just arrived, and afforded some consolation to his Lordship for his disappointment. When the mistake was discovered, the salute was alleged to have been in consequence of the splendid victory of Malloun.

During this month (February) plays were occasionally performed by amateurs; balls and parties were frequent among the Europeans, and nautches among the natives. I attended one of the latter, given by Baboo Russum Doss Moolk (reputed to be worth one hundred lakhs), on the occasion of the marriage of his son. The salloon in which we assembled was brilliantly lighted up with wax-lights in expensive cut-glass chandeliers. The natives sat on chairs and couches: many of them wore English stockings, shoes, and kid gloves, which made a ridiculous addition to their oriental costumes. The son of one of the baboos, a boy of eight years of age, was dressed in the full uniform of a general officer, with cocked hat, aiguillette, &c. The master of the house having handed round the uttur, and sprinkled the company with rose-water, was succeeded by domestics

domestics offering cool sherbets, fruit, and *patisserie*. The entertainments eonsisted of daneing-girls, sueeeeded by Persian boys, who performed various feats of agility with swords. The seene was interesting, as it differed materially from others of the kind whieh I had seen elsewhere. On the way home I witnessed an imposing speetaele, being a large Indiaman, the *Commodore Hayes*, on fire.

I made an exeursion to Barraekpore, crossed the seene where the much-talked-of affair of the 5th November 1824 took place, and drove through the beautiful park surrounding the eountry residenee of the Governor-General, pleasantly seated on the banks of the river. From thence I proeeeded to Isianpore, where I visited the extensive powder-mills, and returned through the Bùrra bazar and native part of Calcutta, which is exceedingly erowded, and where I was choaked and covered with dust. Satiated, at length, with the festivities of the City of Palaees, I resolved to return to England, and took a passage in the *Glorioso*, a country ship of five hundred tons, eommanded by Captain King, and bound for Bombay, whenee I intended to proeeed by the overland route.

Having proeured letters of introduction (written on emblazoned paper and enelosed in silken bags) to the Pacha of Egypt, the Imaum of Museat, the chiefs at Judda, &e., I embarked on board a schooner at Champaul Ghaut, and on the 20th of February stood down the Hooghly to join the *Glorioso* at Diamond Harbour. On arriving at this plaee, however, we learned that the vessel had dropped down farther. The next day, at four P.M., we observed the ship tacking across the river; we stood towards her, and when eoming alongside our sehooner sprung a leak. The water poured in at the larboard bow, and in a short time the floor of the cabin

was

was an inch deep in water: the exertions of two or three hands at the pumps could not keep it under, and she would have gone down in a few minutes, if we had not made all sail and run her on shore. The *Glorioso's* carpenter, a China-man, repaired the damaged plank and stopped the leak. At six P. M. I got safely on board, with all my baggage. We had three passengers besides myself in the cuddy; the treasurer of the mission to Persia, and several Parsees, Banyans, Armenians, and Moguls, were also passengers.

CHAPTER VII.

Sail from Calcutta.......Pilots.......Turtle......Water-spouts......Ceylon......Lightning ......Medusæ.......Storm.......Calicut.......Mangalore......Goa......Severndroog...... Angria......Arrival at Bombay.

ON the 22d of February we reached Kedgeree, when it came on to blow, and the appearance of the weather was very threatening. Opposite Saugor, where we dropped anchor, we rode out a severe gale of wind from the south-west, which continued all night, a tremendous sea running. We pitched frequently bowsprit under: struck all the upper masts, braced the yards round to the wind, and succeeded beyond our expectation in riding out the gale till daylight. In the morning we weighed, and endeavoured to reach the floating light, as the wind had moderated considerably; but after several ineffectual attempts to get out, the wind having again freshened, we were obliged, as well as other vessels, to put back, and brought up near Kedgeree. Three of the vessels in company sustained considerable damage in their canvass.

On the 25th we again weighed, and fortunately succeeded in getting out to sea. The pilot now quitted us, previous to which the supercargo presented him with two hundred rupees, and twenty-five to his leadsman. This is a great abuse; for which, however, there is no remedy. The pilots are handsomely paid by Government, branch pilots getting seven hundred rupees per mensem and a brig, and masters two hundred and sixty; yet, if a handsome present be not

not made them, upon taking out or bringing in a vessel, the next trip they are sure to lose anchors, cables, &c., and to play the very deuce with the ship. The pilotage paid to Government is, according to the vessel's draft of water, twenty rupees a foot: besides this, the harbour-dues, mooring-charges, &c. are most exorbitant; and as to the custom-house, it is the worst conducted public office, perhaps, in the world. It is impossible to get a ship cleared for several days without the payment of a large fee.

For the next week we had some good runs. On the 5th of March, in latitude 15° N., numerous turtles floated past the vessel, in a calm with light airs; a boat was lowered, the oars muffled, and we pulled for the nearest. We got within five or six yards of him, when the tyndal, or coxswain, slipped overboard, and swimming towards the dosing *testudo*, laid hold of his hind flipper, and capsizing him in the water, held on. The turtle made some desperate efforts to dive and recover himself, but a hand in the boat got hold of one of his fore flippers, and we secured him. In this way we caught three, a hand standing ready with the grains to plunge into their breasts, in case we had failed in mastering them as above. They were the Ascension turtle (*testudo mydas*), with two nails on the fore feet and one on the hind: the largest weighed three hundred pounds, and was in capital case. They seemed to be steering for Edmonstone's Island, at the Sand-Heads, where they repair to lay their eggs; I observed, also, a hunch-backed turtle, which is considered unwholesome eating.

After the 5th of March we had dead calms. The horizon was exceedingly hazy, and at night the sea was so smooth and glassy that every little star was accurately reflected in its bosom. It was ludicrous to observe the mates at one moment whistling for, and

I 2 endeavouring

endeavouring to coax the wind, and then cursing and damning the weather. The heat was most intense, and our situation was far from comfortable; but we endeavoured to console ourselves as well as possible, with the *spes melioris ævi,* and trusting that the change of the moon would bring us relief. At length, on the 10th, the Lascars discovered the new moon; and, as usual, came aft, in high spirits, to make their salaams to the Captain, who presented them with a sheep on the occasion. However, there was no change for the better: the mates still whistled and cursed, and the Lascars were harassed to death, hauling about the yards from the variable cat's-paws. The *Qui-hy* passengers took it easy enough, enjoying themselves with their soda water and hookahs.

On the 13th we had a breeze, which was of short duration, and listlessness and despondency resumed their sway. The evenings were however delightful, for

> The cloudless moon, whose trembling light appears
> Like the faint image of departed years,
> Mournful but lovely now in distance spread
> O'er dim uncertain forms, now nearer shed,
> In gems of sparkling beauty,

and, resembling a canoe of mother-o'-pearl sailing in a cerulean sea, cheered us at the close of the day.

On the 23d, whilst at dinner, the Second Officer announced to us that a boat was pulling towards the ship. With our glasses we perceived a black speck in the horizon, occasionally hidden from our anxious gaze by the swell. I pronounced it to be a wreck, and my fancy converted two white specks upon it into two survivors. The jolly-boat was lowered, into which I jumped with eagerness, and pulled

pulled off to rescue them. We neared it, still thinking it a wreck; and it was not till we approached close to it, that we discovered it to be two large roots of the Aloes tree, the leaves of which sticking up, presented at a distance the appearance of spars and timbers: the white specks were occasioned by the dung of birds. To console us for our disappointment, there were shoals of fish round it, preying on the barnacles which adhered to it, and we were not long in handling the grains. There were sharks of all sizes, from twelve feet to one foot in length; a most extraordinary fish resembling a bat, which I imagine to be a species of *pleuronectes;* it swam on its side, and was called by the Lascars the *putha muchee*, or leaf-fish: we speared one. There were also two fish with long spines proceeding from the back, and with very small mouths: they are probably two species of *balistes.* We drove the grains into a ten-feet shark, which had amused itself for some time by swimming round the boat, with his back-fin above water. We hauled him up under the tree, and had almost got him on board, when, by a tremendous plunge, he bent the grains, and scoured away, followed by the others to suck his blood.

The ship having got a breeze, we were signalled on board. On the 25th some rain fell in the evening, and we observed a water-spout a mile from us. The next day, when in latitude 5° 30′, considerable interest and no small alarm were excited by another water-spout crossing our bows, at a few yards' distance: it swept away to leeward, causing the water to boil up like a mighty cauldron. Rain followed in great quantities, and the appearance of the weather was breezy. On the 27th we had a rattling breeze, and on the following morning we came in sight of the high land about Dondra Head, the southern extremity of Ceylon. At night the whole of the horizon

horizon was illuminated by lightning, which is prevalent here, and renders the coast of this island exceedingly dangerous to navigation. Every year vessels are struck, and one was entirely burned a short time ago.

Whilst standing across the gulf of Manar, in the afternoon of the 29th, the clouds collected in thick masses of *cumuli*. The sea began to swell in a heavy and portentous manner, being at the same time of a leaden hue: presently vivid lightning scintillated from cloud to cloud; the thunder growled in the distance; the clouds congregated overhead, and the atmosphere became of the colour of pitch. A stream of fire darted over our heads, followed by an ear-splitting peal of thunder; large drops of rain descended, and it came on to blow most furiously. The ship reeled and staggered through the troubled sea: a strong gust carried away the topsails of the fore and mizen masts, and we scudded along with the main. Towards midnight the gale moderated, and we were enabled to clear away the streaming remains of our canvas.

On the 30th we saw the high land near Cape Comorin; sounded, and got bottom with fifty fathoms line. In the middle watch, the Captain anxiously looking out with his night-glass, observed breakers on the lee-bow. Ordering the helm to be put hard a-port, it was found that the tiller-rope had broken; a new one was, however, bent in sufficient time to enable us to escape this danger, and next morning we were ten or twelve miles up the coast of Malabar.

Perceiving a strong and offensive odour from the sea, resembling the smell of decayed hay, I looked over the sides and observed a yellowish stripe, a foot in breadth, on the surface of the water, and extending on both sides as far as the eye could reach. I lowered a

bucket,

bucket, and found that the water which I took up was filled with minute brownish particles, oblong in shape, probably a species of *medusa,* if not the spawn of fish: their colour collectively was yellow, individually brown. A delightful breeze set in from the north-west, which carried us on at the rate of five knots.

The following night we had vivid lightning; and at noon on the 2d of April, whilst in latitude 9° 30′, near Cochin, heavy, dense, and threatening clouds collected in the horizon. At 4 P.M. there was a dead calm. In half an hour afterwards the sea began to rise, with a long swell from the north-east; the clouds grew dark and louring, and at length hung in a gloomy canopy overhead. The wind began to blow in gusts, with the lower scud driving rapidly along. On a sudden a rushing and howling sound was heard astern, and on looking towards the east, we saw the water lifted up in white foam, and advancing towards us at a furious rate like a wall. The utmost confusion prevailed on board: the Lascars ran about stupified with fear. All at once, before a single sail could be taken in, a terrific gust took the ship, and laid her on her beam-ends. I expected the masts to go by the board every instant; the upper ones bent like willows. The top-gallant and topsail-haulyards were let go, but the wind was so strong that the yards would not come down on the caps; and we rushed on through a tremendous sea, with the spray washing clean over the bows, and pitching bowsprit under. The sea was coming in at the lee-ports, when suddenly all the sails went streaming in ribbons, with the exception of the fore-topsail, and the ship righted: the main-topsail sheet broke, and the main-yard tilted right up and down. The lightning all this time was darting round the mast-heads, and with the thunder almost deprived

us

us of sight and hearing; the rain fell in torrents. Most of the passengers were paralyzed with fright at our perilous situation.

> ———— Venti, velut agmine facto,
> Incubuere mari, totumque a sedibus imis
> Una Eurusque Notusque ruunt, creberque procellis
> Africus, et vastos volvunt ad littora fluctus.
> ———— Ponto nox incubat atra,
> Intonuere poli, et crebris micat ignibus æther.

The storm continued to rage for several hours; and though we had only one sail to carry us on, we continued to fly through the water. The night was pitchy dark, and the vessel seemed to be driving through a sea of liquid fire, sending out long streams of light from her bows. A hand in the main-top sung out, "A ship "on fire to windward!" Turning our eyes to that quarter, we beheld a great blaze several miles off, which continued to gleam fearfully in the horizon, and all at once disappeared; it was impossible for us to beat toward it. We afterwards learned that it was an Arab ship which had been wrecked on the coast, and the light we saw was a signal of distress.

At ten P.M., the storm having nearly subsided, grog was served out to the Lascars, who were quite exhausted, nodding and falling asleep on the yards whilst unbending the remains of the sails. The Musselmans, though prohibited by their religion, took off the liquor without scruple. The tyndals requested that the light might be previously removed, "for then," said they, "we don't know that we "are drinking forbidden liquor."

On the forenoon of the 3d it fell calm, and we were enabled to repair, in the best way we could, the damage sustained during the preceding

preceding night. We saw Calicut, bearing N.E. by E.½E., and several galliots in the roadstead.

It was truly delightful and heart-cheering to see land again, from which we were distant only two miles; and it was pleasing to reflect, that the spot we now saw was the first land on the continent of India beheld by the enterprizing Portuguese in 1498,

——— Who came
From Lusitanian mountains, dear to fame,
Whence Gama steered, and led the conquering way
To Eastern triumphs, and the realms of day.

Calicut, situated in latitude 11° 18′, lies low, backed by forest-covered ridges. In the distance towered the mighty western Ghauts.

Next day I observed that the sea was covered with sperm in every direction, and multitudes of porpoises were tumbling about. I noticed an extraordinary sea-serpent (*muræna ophis*), four feet in length, chequered yellow and black, with a round tail, shaped like the blade of an American paddle. We passed Mahé, a French settlement, beautifully seated on an eminence near Tellicherry.

It was now determined that we should put into Cananore, as we had exhausted our live stock. We accordingly stood for it, and in the evening came in sight of the commandant's house and barracks: when, to our great chagrin, the wind came to blow strong off shore, and we were obliged to stand out again. In the blue distance we observed Mount Delle, rising majestically out of the water, like a sea-girt isle.

During the night of the 5th it rained, thundered and lightened most fearfully. The forked lightning danced about the poop, attracted by the iron belaying pins on the mizen-mast. Next day, at noon, we got sight of the flag-staff of Mangalore, a flourishing sea-port in South Canara, in latitude 12° 50′. We stood towards it, and brought up in six fathoms water, the flag-staff bearing S.E. by E. We landed in the jolly-boat, through a heavy surf. Owing to bad steering, the curl of a wave took the boat on the starboard quarter, and nearly swamped us. We ran into the mouth of a small river communicating with a lake, on which the town is seated, and passed without accident a tremendous mass of breakers at the bar. Inside were lying numerous patamars and dows, rigged with lateen sails, from Kutch, Arabia, and different parts of the coast, and which repair here for rice, the staple commodity. In sailing up the lake to the Custom-house Quay, the scattered huts of the inhabitants, amidst extensive plantations of areca-nut and palmyra-trees,—the fishermen paddling about in their long narrow canoes,—the Moplas (or Musselmans) with their high blue-and-white caps, together with the general aspect of the place,—presented a scene as completely Indian as I had ever seen in any part of Hindoostan.

Upon landing we proceeded to the house of the commandant, Colonel Waugh, delightfully situated on the crest of the eastern glacis of the fort, overlooking a ditch eighty feet deep. This fort is celebrated in the military annals of the country. In 1783 it belonged to Hyder, and was taken by a force from Bombay. After the destruction of General Mathew's army, it sustained a six months' siege by Tippoo Sultaun, who, although assisted by his French allies, was unable to carry a breach which had long been open, or to force Colonel Campbell and his brave garrison to surrender. At the peace in 1784 it was given up to Tippoo, who in revenge razed the fortifications. It is of small extent; the ditch is a very formidable

formidable one. From the upper part of the citadel there is a beautiful bird's-eye view of the sea, salt lake, and town. Here we were gratified by the intelligence of the final termination of hostilities with the Burmese.

As it threatened to blow a heavy squall, we were reluctantly obliged to leave. We entered the report-boat, a large canoe, as our caterer had not collected his supplies of fowls and fruit, and was to follow in the jolly-boat. We had barely time to get to the nearest patamar, when it came on to blow and rain furiously. The boatmen were afraid to cross the bar, and taking shelter under the lee of the patamar, remained there for a couple of hours till the weather moderated. The patamar was a hundred and fifty candies burden (or fifty tons), loading with rice, and navigated by ten men. We went on board; and one of the crew, having opened a box, took out bundle after bundle, and rag after rag, till at last he produced a small case tied round with string, which he carefully unfastened, and disclosed a compass, which he held up to us to gaze and wonder at; he then displayed to us, as another curiosity, a half-hour sand-glass. These navigators keep a reckoning of time by round pieces of pasteboard strung on twine. We again embarked in the canoe, and got safely on board: an hour after we weighed anchor, and stood out with a fair wind.

Sailing up this coast is very delightful. There is not only a constant change of scene, but the aspect of the country is remarkably pleasing, and often grand. The general features of the coast, with the xebec-rigged boats in the foreground, strongly recalled to my mind many paintings I had seen of the shores of Italy. Very different are the western from the eastern ghauts: the latter present

 to

to the eye sun-burnt and barren peaks; whereas the former are clothed with lofty forests rising out of a rich vegetable mould. The bamboo, as well as the teak, or Indian oak, attains to great size. The former grow in detached clumps, of a height equal to that of the palms: they have open spaces between them, affording a passage to herds of wild elephants. The inhabitants of these jungles construct their habitations by cutting away the inner bamboos of a clump, and thatching the vacant part. They enter from above: thus securing themselves in a natural fortress from the attacks of tigers and other wild beasts.

On the 9th we passed Pigeon Island and Fortified Island; the latter a mile in circumference. It was originally fortified by a Mahratta Rajah, and subsequently by Tippoo, who designed to make it his naval arsenal. It was taken by three British frigates in 1792.

It continued to be delightful sailing, with cool breezes all day, until the 11th. During the previous night we had stood out as usual to gain an offing, in order to be ready for the sea-breeze, which commonly sets in at noon. We sailed along some very high land, the hills rising abruptly from the water's edge, backed by lofty mountains, until four P.M., when it came on to blow a strong north-wester; the ship pitched heavily. We carried the topsails and foresail close reefed, with the royal masts on deck.

On the 12th the breeze was moderate, and we came in sight of Goa, the capital of the Portuguese possessions in India. I observed the Fort of Alguada, and the monastery of Cabo, on two high points of land which form the entrance of the harbour. On the 16th we had another north-wester, which caused the ship to make a great

deal

deal of water. A very large shoal of fish passed us, which appeared to consist of grampuscs, dolphins, &c.; a flock of birds, resembling gulls, hovered over the shoal, picking up the unfortunate flying fish. The sight was altogether lively and curious, from the great commotion in the sea, the screaming of the birds,—and fish of all sizes leaping high out of the water. We struck a large dolphin at the bows, and I found it to be one of the most delicious fish I had ever eaten.

We passed the island of Severndroog, or Goldcn Rock, the strong hold of the famous pirate Angria, who (which is not generally known) was a native of Dundee, in Scotland. He was originally the admiral of the Mahratta fleet, and afterwards cruised on his own account. He and his dcscendants were the terror of this coast for many years, and caused it to bear the appellation of "the Pirate Coast."

On the morning of the 20th of April we saw the Light-house, and entered the harbour of Bombay.

CHAPTER VIII.

Appearance of Bombay......Dock-Yard......Visit to the Governor at Malabar Point ......Fête at Parnell-House......Sail for the Persian Gulf in a Cruiser.

In sailing along the island of Colaba, towards the Apollo Pier, at which we landed, the appearance of Bombay was singular. The high and red-tiled roofs of the houses in the fort, and the windows shaded by wooden verandahs, gave a mean character to the buildings. We presently opened the middle anchorage-grounds, backed by the Ghauts, and the island of Elephanta, Butcher Island, &c., and then the view of the harbour became extremely beautiful. On landing, we could hardly force our way through the cotton bales with which the pier was covered. Large and powerful natives of Kutch, with enormous turbans, were superintending the shipment of the cotton in the patamars and dows waiting to receive it. We entered the fort by the Apollo gate, and crossed a good wet ditch. The streets within were spacious; but from the height of the houses the heat was excessive, it being the commencement of the hot season. I was kindly received by Messrs. Ritchie and Stewart.

In the evening I visited the dock-yards, the master-builders in which, as well as the shipwrights, are all Parsees, the finest and most enterprizing race in India. A large eighty-gun ship was on the stocks building for the Imaum of Muscat, who is possessed at present with the ship-building *mania*. Our Government allow him to build as many vessels as he pleases, as it would be an easy matter

to

to take them from him in the event of a war. Besides this ship there was a smart eighteen-gun sloop of war for the Bombay Marine, almost completed. She possessed the advantage of being sufficiently high out of the water to admit of a tier of scuttles; a most invaluable acquisition in tropical climes, and which is found in none of the King's ships of her size. I saw the keel, sternpost, and stem of a seventy-four, intended for the Royal Navy, which was to be put on the stocks after the launch of the Imaum's ship. The docks do great credit to the engineer who constructed them. The timber used in them comes from the Malabar coast.

From the docks I proceeded to the fashionable resort, which is a road on the esplanade at the foot of the glacis. The equipages were, of course, not so gay as those in the City of Palaces, and there was a great proportion of male and female equestrians. The band of his Majesty's 6th Foot was playing near the tents and temporary bungalows, which are erected on the esplanade during the hot season, for the accommodation of those who have not country-houses, or a residence overlooking the ramparts. The girls of the charity-schools were amusing themselves on the glacis, under the charge of a peon or two: they were dressed in grey frocks, and had a remarkably clean appearance. They are the daughters of European soldiers; and after attaining the years of puberty, are either married or sent to service as ladies'-maids. Some of them, however, are said to disappear in an unaccountable manner.

On the morning of the 22d I drove out to Malabar Point to wait on the Governor, the Honourable Mr. Elphinstone, who had pitched his tents there to pass the hot season. The distance is about six miles, but the roads were excellent. I passed through what is termed

termed the wood, consisting of innumerable cocoa-nut trees (which yield a considerable revenue to Government, one rupee being annually paid for each tree), interspersed with Portuguese chapels and small country-houses. Having gained the summit of Malabar hill, a most beautiful view of Back Bay presented itself. Numerous small vessels were sailing about in it, and beyond them rose a forest of masts of the shipping in the harbour. After breakfast I returned by the Breach-road, so called from a stone dyke (on the top of which is a wide and excellent road), which was constructed to reclaim a large tract of land from the sea; yet although this yields a considerable revenue, the Governor under whose auspices the work was undertaken got no thanks from his honourable Masters, but was censured for his lavish expenditure. I passed through a part of the native town, and was highly pleased with the spacious streets of the Bendy bazar, having footpaths on each side, so different from any thing I had before seen in India. These improvements, as well as many others for the benefit of natives and Europeans, have originated with the present Governor. Mahratta is the language generally spoken in Black Town, and Guzerattee by the Parsees. I saw several Parsee women, who are large and fair, and the young ones very handsome.

On the 24th of April I attended a splendid fête given by the Governor at Parnell House, in honour of his Majesty's birth-day, and to which the whole of the society of Bombay was invited. The road leading to Parnell was crowded with natives in bullock-bandies, on ponies, and on foot, who were hastening to the gay scene. On my arrival, I found a large assemblage. The ball-room was capacious and well-lighted. Two rows of couches extended round it: the front row was occupied by the ladies of the presidency, in white; and along the

walls

walls were rich natives in variegated dresses, appearing like a row of gaudy tulips behind a bed of lilies. The Governor wore the Windsor uniform, with the addition of rich gold embroidery. There was little dancing in consequence of the heat. At twelve o'clock the company repaired to the gardens in rear of the house, passing along an illuminated walk, and under a lofty moslem arch of lamps, to the edge of a large tank, on the opposite side of which fire-works were exhibited. After the representation of the storming of Bhurtpore, our attention was drawn to the tank by several small skiffs stealing along. These were presently enveloped in a thick cloud of smoke, and were then observed paddling with great velocity towards the shore, whilst flames seemed to burst from beneath the hitherto placid waters, in which fire-frogs jumped about, bubbled, and hissed; on the land, cascades of fire and vollies of rockets filled the air. We supped on one side of the tank, under a rustic arcade; and along a terrace on the other side tables were spread for the natives, covered with fruits and sweetmeats. The company began to disperse about two o'clock, and I got home about three, highly pleased with the entertainment, which reflected great credit upon the liberality and taste of the master of the ceremonies.

It had been my original intention to proceed homeward through Egypt; but finding, on my arrival at Bombay, that no vessel would sail for the Red Sea probably for six months, I was obliged to abandon this project, and had now no alternative (besides proceeding round the Cape in the midst of winter) but to travel overland through Persia and Russia. It was proposed to me to attach myself to the mission of Colonel Macdonald, who had just sailed for Persia, which would afford me opportunities for seeing that interesting country, court, and

 people,

people with every facility. It was accordingly arranged that Captain Campbell, second assistant to the mission (who had just arrived at Bombay), and myself should follow the Envoy in company.

The Honourable Company's cruizer *Palinurus* was ordered to prepare for a voyage to the Persian Gulf, to carry the overland despatches announcing the conclusion of peace with the Burmese and the fall of Bhurtpore, and Captain Campbell and myself were kindly offered a passage by the captain. Having only a day's notice to prepare for my journey, it may easily be supposed that I was in a state of considerable confusion; but by great exertions I completed my arrangements, and embarked on the 26th of April.* We weighed at four P.M., stood out of the Bay, and soon lost sight of the shores of India.

'Tis a long and last adieu I bid thee, sunny land,
Farewell for ever to thee, and to thy golden strand;
Along thy bright and sacred streams I never more will stray;
From thy spicy gales and groves of palm I hasten far away.

Land of the sun, I leave thee; but I leave thee not with pain;
Thy luxuries and splendours lost I count exceeding gain.
Though thy dark-eyed maids, with raven locks, I never more shall view,
Again I bid thee, INDIA, a long and last adieu.

I've

* Besides being obliged to submit to the disappointment of not seeing the classic land of Egypt, I was obliged to forego the pleasure of meeting an only brother, Lieut. John Alex. Henderson, 4th Light Dragoons. Having not seen him for five years, I had come round from Calcutta to wait his arrival from England in the May fleet: he arrived a few days after I quitted Bombay.

I've wandered 'midst thy gloomy wilds, thy jungles dark among,
Which the feathered race of every hue enliven with their song:
But the spotted snake lies there concealed, which shuns the face of day,
And tigers fierce are lurking there, and hung'ring for their prey.

I've seen thy fairest palaces, thy richly sculptured fanes,
Where ignorance holds sovereign sway, and superstition reigns:
Which lead the widow to the pile, and drown the aged sire,
And consign the helpless infant to the all-devouring fire.

'Midst thy brightest scenes I long have pined to view my native home,
To my father-land my longing eyes have never ceased to roam:
'Tis with gladness then I leave thee, and thee again I tell,
INDIA farewell—and if it be for ever, fare thee well!

END OF PART I.

PART II.

PERSIA, ASIA MINOR,

&c.

CHAPTER I.

Particulars respecting the Mission of Colonel Macdonald Kinneir, K.L.S., Envoy Extraordinary to the Court of Tehran.

Previous to commencing the narrative of my visit to Persia, it will be convenient to give the reader a short account of the circumstances which led to the mission lately despatched to the Persian court, in the suite of which I travelled.

The importance of maintaining friendly relations with Persia, a country which opposes an obstacle to the encroachments of Russia, and is, in fact, a protection to our Indian territories against invaders from Europe, has induced the British Government, as well as the East-India Company, to send expensive embassies, at various periods, to the court of Tehran. Of late, a British *chargé d'affaires* has constantly resided at the capital; the arsenal has been furnished with the necessary stores from India, and the Persian army has been disciplined by European officers.

During the late war between England and France, Persia received from the former a subsidy of 200,000 tomauns, or £150,000, annually,

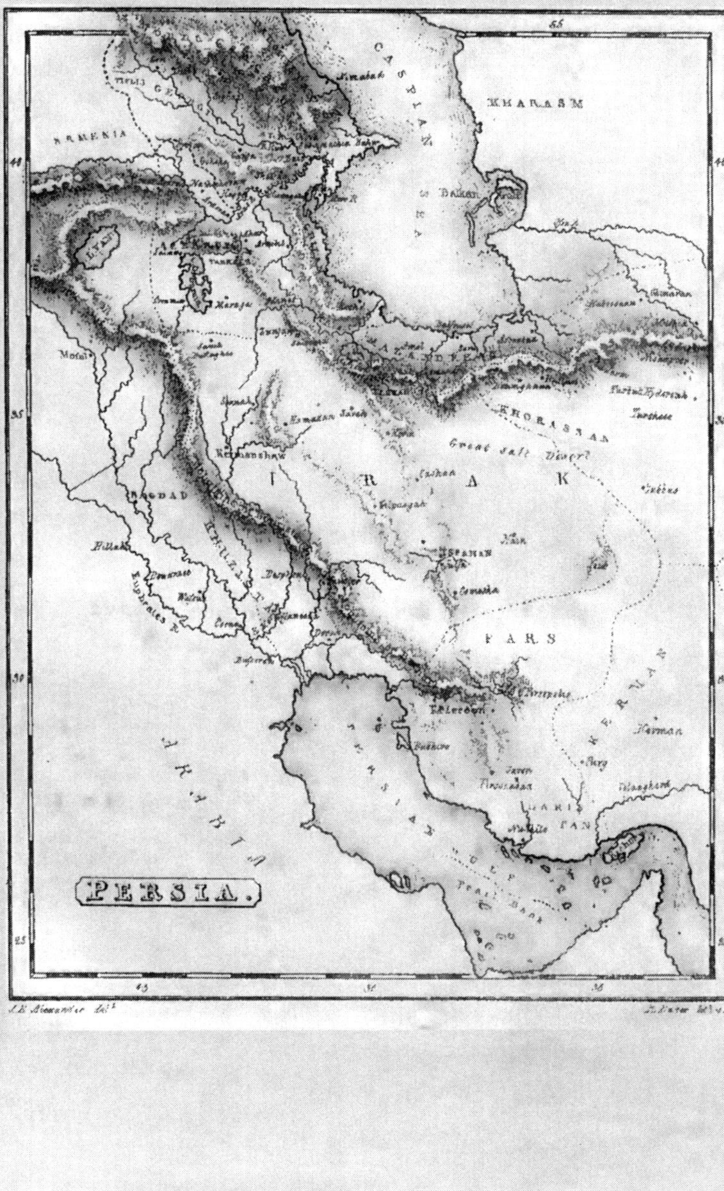

J. E. Alexander Del.[t] ... Sc.

nually, upon the condition that she would prevent the French Emperor from marching through the Persian territories to attack the East-India Company's possessions. When the danger ceased the subsidy was withdrawn; but the British Government was bound by treaty to renew it in the event of a war with Russia, if the latter power was the aggressor.

A considerable balance of the arrears of this subsidy remained unpaid; in consequence of which repeated embassies were sent from Persia to England, and this country was subjected to heavy expenses for the maintenance of the envoys, who were unprovided with funds from their own government. His Majesty's Ministers, consequently, proposed to the East-India Company (from whom the subsidy was due) that the diplomatic intercourse with Persia should be managed by the Company, and that future envoys should be accredited by the Governor-General of India, in order to avoid the delay and expense created by the intervention of the Court of Great Britain.

A mission was accordingly prepared on the part of the East-India Company. The Envoy, Colonel Macdonald Kinneir, was not an accredited ambassador of his Britannic Majesty, like Sir Harford Jones and Sir Gore Ouseley; but, like Sir John Malcolm, was the agent or representative of the Company.

When this change in the political character of the Envoy was communicated to the King of Persia, he refused to receive the mission, alleging that it would be derogatory to his dignity to recognize an envoy from a body of merchants.

There is abundant reason to believe that the Shah was instigated to this course by the Russians, who intimated that if the British envoy was received, they would in future send missions from the Governor-

General

of Georgia, instead of embassies from the Sovereign of Russia, as formerly. It was also insinuated by the courtiers about the person of the heir apparent, and who were in the pay of Russia, that a new and unfavourable treaty was to be proposed.

Notwithstanding the effect which the Russian representations produced at the courts of Tehran and Tabreez, it is a mistaken notion that the Russians were favoured by the Persians: on the contrary, they have always been objects of jealousy. It has been the constant aim of Russia, for several years, to extend her frontier to the river Arras, which would deprive Persia of one of her finest provinces, that of Erivan, the Surdar of which, Hussun Khan, is a brave and enterprizing chief, who repelled the Russians when they attempted to invade the province in the last war. There is no doubt, indeed, that Russia possessed considerable influence over the heir apparent, owing to the stipulation in the treaty of Gulistan, which bound Russia to assist him in securing the throne on the demise of the reigning monarch. This charm is now dissolved.

Colonel Macdonald received his appointment and instructions, as envoy, at Calcutta, in March 1824. Henry Willock, Esq., K.L.S., then his Britannic Majesty's *chargé d'affaires* at the court of Persia, was nominated Secretary and Head Assistant to the Mission;* Captain J. N. R. Campbell, Madras Cavalry, was appointed Second Assistant; Dr. MacNeill, Bombay Establishment, surgeon; and Lieutenant R. Macdonald, Bengal Cavalry, Commandant of Escort.

The

* This gentleman, on his change of character, had the satisfaction to receive the decided approbation of his Sovereign, for the judicious manner in which he had discharged his difficult and delicate functions whilst *chargé d'affaires*.

The members of the mission assembled at Bombay in May, when the obstacles before specified put a stop to their embarkation. Application was made to the Supreme Government for instructions, and the Envoy was directed to remain at Bombay till further orders. The governors of the two subordinate presidencies were, however, of opinion that the mission ought to have proceeded without delay; that its object was of so much importance as to demand expedition; and that had firmness been displayed at first, in disregarding the frivolous objections of the Persian court to the character of the Envoy, the rich presents he carried, and the arrears of the subsidy which he was authorized to pay, would have overcome the scruples of the court, and secured him, eventually, a favourable reception.

In July, Major George Willock, brother to the late *chargé d'affaires* in Persia, arrived at Calcutta on a private mission from the court of Tehran respecting the arrears of subsidy. The subject of the Persian mission had, it appears, undergone much discussion in the council of the Supreme Government of India; and in August the Envoy was informed, by a letter from the Secretary to Government in the Political Department, that the mission was suspended until the receipt of advices from England. The Envoy was directed to remain at Bombay on the salary attached to his rank, with a table allowance of a thousand rupees per mensem.* The other members of the mission were directed to return to their respective duties.

In December, letters from Persia brought advices that a change had

* The full table allowance is five thousand rupees, including servants, carriage, &c. The Court of Directors have restricted the expenses of the mission to £12,000 per annum.

had taken place in the sentiments of the Prince Royal, which was probably brought about by the meritorious exertions of Major Hart, generalissimo of the prince's army, and Dr. Cormick, his physician. Abbas Mirza now urged the Shah to invite the mission to his court, and expressed a decided disapprobation of the sentiments entertained by the ministers of Tehran. The Shah, however, adhered to his former resolutions: he relaxed only so far as to consent to receive the mission with due honour, but refused to allow of the permanent residence of the Envoy, unless he should be accredited by his Britannic Majesty. The mission of Colonel Macdonald still remained in abeyance at Bombay, waiting advices from England.

Meanwhile, Major Willock's mission was proceeding rapidly to completion. It had been publicly recognized by the Governor-General, and his papers were submitted to the consideration of the Council. In the course of two or three months, the Governor-General was pleased to concede all points relative to the subsidy, and to the debt due to an individual named Nubbee Khan; and in January 1825 the Major left Calcutta on his return to Persia, empowered to draw the full amount of the debt, and the sum of 182,000 tomauns (nearly eleven lakhs of sicca rupees), the arrears of the subsidy.

The impolicy of this proceeding is obvious. Whilst the Shah of Persia persisted in refusing to admit an Envoy from the East-India Company, he was taught to believe he could not receive the amount of his pecuniary claims; but by this precipitate measure the Supreme Government relinquished the powerful instrument it possessed of obliging the Persian Court to comply with its views and to receive its Envoy, whilst it strengthened the influence of the British *chargé d'affaires*, *d'affaires*, whom the Envoy was to supersede. The objects of the mission were, by this proceeding, almost entirely frustrated.

Russia availed herself instantly of our errors, under the judicious direction of her resident minister, M. Amburger. The designs of the crafty Alexander, and the process by which the Persian Prince Royal extricated himself from Russian intrigues, will be more properly treated of in a summary of the causes and events of the existing war betwixt Persia and Russia, which will be given in a succeeding chapter. It has been already intimated that the Prince was restored to sounder views of his own interest, and to more friendly feelings towards the English, by the persevering arguments of the British officers in his service.

By the exertions of our *chargé d'affaires*, the Shah was at length induced to abandon his objections to the mission proposed to be sent by the East-India Company, and to receive it in the usual manner. His Majesty was the more easily reconciled to this measure upon hearing that the Envoy was a relation (brother-in-law) of Sir John Malcolm, who is an universal favourite in Persia, owing to his captivating address and liberal disbursement of money—a sure engine in Oriental politics. Since the last embassy of Sir John Malcolm, the English name has stood high in Persia; and when the present mission was first proposed, the Persians urgently solicited that Sir John might be sent, as he had completely won their hearts.

In February 1825 an invitation arrived from the Shah for the mission to proceed to his court. The Supreme Government, however, still deemed it expedient to wait for advices from England: it was, moreover, imagined that an alacrity to accept the invitation might indicate an over-anxiety to court the friendship of Persia; and that a moderate delay would manifest our indifference, and likewise be a proper mark of resentment for the slight which the mission had hitherto experienced. These reasons appear extremely unsatisfactory. With regard to the first, the public good demanded that the mission should proceed whilst the Shah was in a humour to receive it cordially; as to the last, the Shah could scarcely believe we were indifferent to his friendship, after the enormous sums we had disbursed during the last thirty years to secure it. The concessions made through the medium of Major Willock, must effectually have banished all idea of our resentment from the mind of the Shah.

The character of the reigning monarch of Persia is fickle and capricious. Although the dread of Russia, and a strong impression that the English are more to be depended upon than any other ally, may have induced his Majesty to sacrifice his scruples in point of etiquette upon this occasion, still he was not to be depended upon (as, indeed, his change of resolution in this particular proves), and great mischief might have arisen from delay.

In April 1825, the Supreme Government determined not to despatch the mission until another kind of invitation came from the court of Persia. In October a more pressing invitation arrived, when the members of the mission were ordered to be in readiness. In March 1826, a nobleman of the blood royal (Curreem Khan) came to Bombay, in the Hon. Company's cruizer *Ternate,* to attend the Envoy to the Persian court; Colonel Macdonald accordingly embarked in the *Tamar* frigate with his lady, and after a prosperous voyage arrived at Bushire.

CHAPTER II.

Sail from Bombay......Oceurrenee at Barbora......First view of the Arabian Coast ......Cape Muksa......Cape Fillam......Cape Musseldom and the Quoins......Ormus ......Gamberoon......Kishm......Bassadore......Pearl Fishery......Arrival at Bushire.

On the 26th April 1826, Captain Campbell (Second Assistant to the Envoy) and myself embarked at Bombay, as before stated, on board the *Palinurus*, a brig of two hundred tons burthen, carrying eight guns, and commanded by Lieutenant William Rose of the Bombay Marine. We stood out into the Arabian sea, and steered a W.S.W. course. We were very comfortably situated, both in regard to accommodation and messing; and I was extremely fortunate in having Captain Campbell as a travelling companion, since he had resided in Persia for a couple of years, and was well acquainted with the country, the language, and manners of the people. I had not, therefore, the prospect of experiencing what the poet describes:

> Thou dost not know how sad it is to stray
> Amid a foreign land, thyself unknown;
> And when, o'erwearied with the toilsome day,
> To rest at eve, and feel thyself alone.

For some days we had heavy seas and blowing weather. On board there was a detachment of the Bombay Marine battalion, consisting of a naique and eight men. Every cruiser has a detachment of this corps, according to her size, who act as marines, and have frequently distinguished themselves. The men we had being re-

 cruits,

cruits, endeavoured to skulk, feigning sickness; the first officer, however, quickly brought them round, by administering a copious draught of bark and bilge-water.

The second officer had been part-owner and chief officer of the brig *Mary Ann*, which was taken by pirates, a short time ago, on the coast of Africa. As the occurrence made some noise at Bombay, I shall briefly state the particulars of the capture.

The *Mary Ann* had arrived at Barbora, a port near the Straits of Bab-el-mandel (or the Gate of Death), which is not frequented by Europeans, though resorted to by Arabs and Banyans. At this port there is an annual fair, which lasts from February till May. The natives come from the interior to Barbora, bringing gold-dust, coffee, gums, &c., which they barter for iron, cloth, and other articles. There is no town here, the natives living in tents upon the beach, on which also are a few temporary houses. The Arabs and Banyans being jealous of Europeans, and this being the first ship which had entered Barbora, they incited the Caffres to plunder the vessel, which was effected in the following manner. The captain (Lingard) and the first officer being on shore, several boats put off for the ship with cargo, which the second officer prepared to take in, and removed the hatches, when a large body of Caffres jumped on board, killing and wounding several of the crew. The Portuguese Sookannees ran up the rigging. The second officer was desperately wounded and thrown overboard; and it evidently appeared that the Arabs were concerned in this infamous transaction, from the circumstance of the crews of several dows having refused to take him in when he managed to swim alongside, and hauling in their ropes. The vessel was run ashore, plundered of every thing, and broken

up

up for the sake of the iron. The captain and first officer escaped by a miracle. They found themselves prisoners in a house which they had entered, and were desired to prepare for death. Another party, however, that wished their lives to be spared, prevailed, after a good deal of altercation, and they were suffered to escape. They returned to Mocha, and from thence got a passage to Bombay, where they submitted their case to Government, and obtained a promise that, at the next fair, a man of war or cruizer should be sent to blockade the port of Barbora, until the amount of the vessel and cargo was recovered from the native traders.

For several days, during the early part of our voyage, shoals of pilot fish attended us, which daily supplied our table. These fish were unaccompanied by sharks. The weather was remarkably cool and pleasant: the thermometer stood in the morning at 80°, and at noon at 82°: never higher, until we came in sight of the Arabian coast. The prevailing wind was north-west. Sea birds constantly attended us; among which were the fulmar *(procellaria glacialis)*, the tropic bird *(phaëton æthereus)*, and a black species of pintado, called "the carpenter," from the tail resembling a pair of compasses, which frequently alighted on the decks. There was a peculiarity in this species I never before observed: the roof of the mouth was of a deep purple, and the fœces were exactly of the same colour.

Till the 13th of May nothing particular occurred. On the evening of that day we observed the sun set over the high land behind Ras-el-had, a cape in Arabia Felix in 22° 22′ N. lat. and 60° 40′ E. long., which bore N.W. distant twenty-five miles. The cape is low, and backed by lofty mountains. This first sight of Arabia was not prepossessing, for a more parched and barren-looking region I never

never saw; the only appearance of vegetation was a few scattered date trees along the beach. Next day we had a distinct view of the land. Although we were not sufficiently near to distinguish the stratification of the hills, their outline seemed to indicate primitive limestone or indurated sandstone.

Whilst we remained in sight of the land the heat was excessive, in the morning 86° and at noon 95°, the atmosphere close and damp; the night cloudy, with a very heavy dew. On rising from my dormitory on deck I wrung the wet from my cloak, but sustained no bad effects from this exposure to the night damps.

On the 15th we saw Cape Muksa, in Persia: it is low, with a conical hill to the eastward, and behind it high and irregular mountains. On the 19th we were becalmed under very high and bluff rocks, towards which the current was rapidly drifting us: the boats were got out, and succeeded in hauling us off; a breeze sprung up at noon, and carried us out of danger: we were then in lat. 26° 2′ N. and long. 58° 49′ E. We found these rocks to be Cape Fillam, in Arabia, which few navigators have seen. The height of the most elevated point we ascertained, by trigonometrical observation, to be two thousand six hundred feet. The rocks from this height were precipitous to the sea, and presented the appearance of a grey, rugged, and furrowed wall; they seemed to consist of primitive limestone, dipping to the westward, the angle of inclination apparently only six or eight degrees.

On the 21st, in the morning, we saw Cape Musseldom, bearing N.W. and by W., distant five miles; at noon we passed the cape, and Quoins (so called from resembling the quoin of a gun), behind which, piratical boats used to lie in wait. The rock of which the

cape

cape and islands seemed composed was limestone. The dip was westerly: the angle of inclination varied exceedingly; in some places I observed a columnar stratification, indicating basalt. There is no vegetation, either on the islands or main land, except in the clefts of the rock, where wild sorrel is found. Innumerable shoals of fish frequent the Quoins, which are at the true entrance of the Persian Gulf. It is usual here for the native traders to make an offering of flowers, money, and fruit. Sometimes they equip a small vessel, and put in it samples of the different articles of which their cargo is composed: this vessel they set adrift, and if it makes towards the land they infer a favourable termination of their voyage. Some of these miniature barks are occasionally met with many leagues out at sea.

This evening there was a total eclipse of the moon. When she shone forth again, the scene reminded me of that described in these beautiful lines of Moore:

'Tis moonlight over Oman's sea: her banks of pearls and palmy isles
Bask in the night-beam beauteously, and her blue waters sleep in smiles.
All's hushed, there's not a breeze in motion; the shore is silent as the ocean.
If zephyrs come, so light they come, nor leaf is stirred, nor wave is driven,
The wind tower in the Emir's dome can scarcely win a breath from heaven.

The next day we could just perceive the island of Ormus. The only article of export at present from this island (once the emporium of a mighty traffic) is salt, of which the quantity collected here is enormous. Opposite to Ormus, on the Persian main, is the high land of Gamberoon, where, tradition says, the Guebres, or fire-worshippers, made their final stand against the Moslems. The sea now abounded in in snakes: they were all chequered black and yellow, with the dorsal and ventral fins of the common eel. None of them had the paddle-shaped tail of the individual I observed on the Malabar coast, which I am inclined to think belongs to an undescribed species. Vast numbers of *medusæ*, or sea-blubber, floated past the vessel. I caught many of them, and never found two alike; some were of a purple colour, others of an azure hue, and some pink: many of them were a foot in diameter; the greater part had six or eight *tentacula* underneath, with a fringed circumference, and a cross in the centre. We now also frequently caught large pomfret. Several sharks were seen, and once a very large *echineis neucrates*, or sucking-fish, which appeared to be eight feet in length; the tail entire, and the body of a greenish colour.

On the 23d we passed the island of Kishm, which the poet Moore says is celebrated for its grapes, although none have been produced there within the memory of man. His mistake, probably, arose from supposing that kishmish, or the Persian term for raisin, was a grape produced at this island. From the sea there is not a blade of vegetation to be seen on the flat-topped and sandy hills of which Kishm is composed; there is a stunted grass in the vallies, which affords pasture to hares and antelopes. The length of the island is sixty miles, its breadth fifteen.

On the 24th, we sailed over a mud flat, and steered N.E. by E. for Bassadore, a station for cruizers on the N.W. of Kishm, and which is the coolest birth in the Gulf. We anchored in the roads, two miles off shore. Our commander landed, in order to ascertain whether he was to take the despatches to Bushire, or send them by another vessel. He returned with orders to proceed next morning;

morning; we accordingly weighed on the 25th, and stood out of the roads.

There are only two or three European houses at Bassadore, and a small bazar inhabited by Arabs. I observed only a few stunted date-trees and aloe-bushes near the houses. Here are the remains of an extensive Portuguese city. The tanks constructed by that nation are still entire. The ruins of the Portuguese forts, factories, and settlements, are every where to be met with to the eastward of the Cape of Good Hope, along the coasts of Africa, Arabia, Persia, and India. It is difficult to conceive how Portugal could spare from her limited population the number of settlers required for her extensive eastern possessions.

Opposite to Bassadore are Romps and Ras-el-Kaimar, two notorious piratical stations, which were razed to the ground by the force under Sir William Grant Keir, in the beginning of 1820. Near them are the celebrated pearl-banks, where any person is allowed to fish between the middle of May and the middle of September. The divers are Arabs, and the mode in which they collect the pearl oysters is as follows: The diver, having stripped himself, compresses his nostrils with wooden pincers; he then slings round his neck a small basket, capable of containing two dozen shells, and jumping overboard, places his feet on two crossed double-headed shot, attached to a rope, which he holds. His companions in the boat lower him rapidly, and as soon as he touches the bottom he quits the shot and rope, which are hauled up. After having filled his basket, he ascends without assistance to the surface. The divers sometimes meet with springs of fresh water at the bottom: at Bahreen in particular, where the only water used for drinking on

 board

board the cruizers is procured by sending a man down three or four fathoms with a musket-barrel, which he fills and brings up.

Sailing along the Persian coast, the hills of which rose in four distinct series of ridges, to an elevation apparently of fifteen hundred feet, we saw the town of Lingar, notorious for piracy, and inhabited by Arabs, who are almost the only people met with on the coast on the Persian side of the gulf.

Two days after leaving Bassadore, about eleven P.M., I was awoke by a great uproar on board, which I found to be caused by our being taken aback with royals and studding sails set, whilst running at the rate of eight knots an hour. We were now retrograding at the rate of six or seven knots. After carrying away one or two of the studding sails and part of the rigging, the yards were braced round, and the ship delivered from her perilous situation. The Lascars, as usual, were completely "*gabera,*" or confused.

On the 2d of June we hove in sight of Bushire, and next day entered the outer roads. We made signals for a pilot, but without effect for some time; at length one boarded us: he was a stout Arab with only one eye, a very common defect on the shores of the gulf; the excessive glare and the finely pulverized sand, with which the atmosphere is loaded with the slightest breeze, occasion the prevalence of ophthalmia. There is an amusing story told of a Mirza, from the interior of Persia, having been taken-in by a single-eyed beauty of the coast. A lady uncovered part of her face to him, and disclosed a sparking eye: he was so captivated by its lustre, that he went forthwith and demanded her in marriage of her parents; after the completion of the ceremony he found that there was, unfortunately, no match to the eye he had admired so much.

The

The pilots of Bushire are excessively careless. Our's did nothing; he gave no directions for standing over the bar between the outer and inner roadsteads; but, shortly after coming on board, spread out his shawl on the deck and prayed for a quarter of an hour. We anchored off the town.

CHAPTER III.

Bushire......The Sheikh......Preparations for the March......Armenians......Leave Bushire......Chakota......Borazgoon......Dalkee.

THE appearance of Bushire from the sea, although extremely singular, is far from inviting. The town is seated on a sandy beach, and the surrounding country is a dead flat. Towards the eastward are a few date-trees; in the back-ground, and at the distance of forty miles, rises a lofty range of dark blue mountains. The soil of the peninsula on which the town is situated is alluvial, consisting of sand and mud, impregnated with saline matter. From a distance, Bushire resembles a city half-built. The houses are of clay, with flat roofs; above which, dispersed in different quarters, are wind-towers, square, and in height from sixty to a hundred feet. On each side of the towers are three or four longitudinal openings, half way down, by which means every breath of wind is conveyed to the sitting apartment of the great man below.

We proceeded towards the pier, through a heavy sea; a north-west wind having sprung up, the boat grounded several times, and we were a good deal wetted previous to jumping on shore. Staring us in the face on the pier were a dozen long guns, greatly honey-combed, surrounded by a picturesque group of Arabs and Persians; the former wearing turbans and long jackets, and the latter the conical black sheep-skin cap. All had the curved white-hilted dagger in the belt.

Proceeding

Proceeding through the town towards the Residency, two miles distant from the pier, we were followed by about fifty of these idlers, who were passing conjectures as to who we were, the value of our dresses, &c. The lanes through which we passed were exceedingly dirty, and were in breadth about six or eight feet, bounded on each side by the mud walls of the courts which surround the houses. I was always expecting to come to streets, but besides these narrow and intricate lanes there are no other thoroughfares. At last, covered with dust and perspiration, upon turning a corner our eyes were greeted by the flag-staff of the Residency; and passing the guard at the gate, we entered a large court, in the centre of which stood the Residency itself, a large square building of two stories: surrounding it are irregular ranges of outhouses, containing rooms for visitors, stables, &c.

We were very hospitably received by Colonel Stannus, who is peculiarly adapted for the situation which he so ably fills. His disposition being exceedingly liberal, he supports the character of his nation with great *éclat.*

We learned that Colonel Macdonald had left on the 15th of May for Shiraz, where he intended to await our arrival; and that Bushire was threatened daily with a hostile visit from the Imaum of Muscat, in consequence of the infamous intrigues of its Sheikh. The Imaum some time since solicited the hand of one of the daughters of his Persian Majesty in marriage; the Sheikh, through envy, had been using his endeavour to prejudice the king against the noble suitor: added to which, he lately abused and ill-treated the servants of the Imaum, who had repaired to Bushire for commercial purposes. It was supposed that as soon as the Imaum appeared with his fleet in the

the offing, that the Sheikh would betake himself to the mountains, but that very probably he would be intercepted by the army of the Prince Governor of Shiraz (under whose jurisdiction the whole of the low country is), who would without scruple seize on his treasures, and those of the Armenian merchants, who are possessed of immense wealth. One grand article of profit exclusively their's is the manufacture and sale of wine.

The Sheikh had in his service a number of Baloochees, from Baloochistan. These men guarded the gates and manned the walls on the land side, for there are no defences towards the sea. For some trifling offence five of them were ordered to be *fulluked*, or bastinadoed, on the soles of the feet. They remonstrated, and said the punishment was unjust, and that they could not submit to it: however the Sheikh would not relent, and ordered his servants to seize and throw down the men. The first man they laid hold of started back, drew a concealed sword, and made a cut at the Sheikh's son: the blow was received on the arm of a servant, which it severed, and the rest of the attendants of the Sheikh immediately rushed on the unarmed Baloochees and cut them down. The other Baloochees immediately left Bushire.

On our arrival we found Lieutenant Macdonald, of the Bengal Cavalry, commandant of the envoy's escort, and G. A. Malcolm, Esq., of the Bombay Civil Service, who had arrived just before us. We anticipated a pleasant trip to Shiraz in their company.

We had not been many hours in the place when it blew a furious north-wester. The whole air was filled with minute particles of sand, and at dinner in the evening it was excessively annoying: our heads were completely powdered, as were also the viands.

There

There was a party of twelve sat down to dinner, principally marine officers. After the desert, consisting of apples, most excellent Persian raisins, dried apricots, &c., caleoons, or Persian hookahs, were introduced. It was truly ridiculous to witness the awkward attempts of the new-comers to produce smoke, or even to hold the pipe steady. One pulled away at a furious rate, without producing any smoke; another, in attempting to raise the sirpoosh, in which the tobacco is contained, and which is a signal that the smoker has had enough, drew the whole of the tube out of the bottom; and a third, in endeavouring to hand the pipe to the servant in attendance, upset the whole concern, strewing the live charcoal in every direction, to the no small discomfort of his neighbours, and attended with exceeding detriment to the carpet and mats. At night I slept on a terrace: but it was some time before I could close my eyes, owing to the howling of the wind, the baying of the dogs, and the incessant call of the sentries from their watch-towers.

I arose next morning with my eyes completely filled with sand, but which was not half so annoying as the innumerable flies and mosquitoes which swarmed about our faces immediately after sunrise, which compelled us to rise with the great luminary. During the day we employed ourselves in making preparations for our journey, by purchasing horses and hiring mules. An extraordinary character, well known in Persia by the epithet of *Rogue Allee*, to distinguish him from his counterpart in cunning, *Honest Allee*, was very officious in shewing off his stud. However, though my companions dealt with him, I chose rather to purchase a capital steed from the Colonel, for which I paid the very moderate sum of three hundred Persian rupees, or two hundred and twenty Bombay, at which

which presidency the same steed would have realized seven or eight hundred. Horses throughout the whole of Persia are exceedingly good and cheap, and this season in particular, as the jo or barley on which they are fed had been destroyed by a small worm, which ate the seed in the husk, previous to the cutting of the grain. A splendid charger, five years old, might be purchased for three or four hundred Bombay rupees, which would cost three or four thousand in India.

The *Nautilus* stood out of the roads with difficulty, carrying the overland peace despatches to Bussorah. In the evening we rode out on the plain to the eastward of Bushire, and were attacked by a host of fierce dogs, which after a furious encounter we routed with great slaughter. I observed the Arab women returning from the wells, three miles off, veiled, and laden with their sheep-skin *muschuks* or water-skins. They carry them on their backs, and are obliged to perform a diurnal journey of six miles, as no good water is found nearer Bushire. The Arabs, who form the greater part of the population of this place, are an exceedingly strong race. The higher ranks are distinguished from the Persians by wearing turbans, and the lower orders have commonly the sleeves of their loose vestments tucked up by cords, which cross at their backs.

In the Residency stable-yard there was a tame water-hen *(fulica chloropos)*; the plumage was blueish black above, and when any one approached, it pursued, uttering a shrill cry, and flirting up its wings, shewing white feathers underneath. It had hardly any tail: the bill was very strong, the *armilla* red, and the toes of a very great length.

I strenuously endeavoured to form a party to visit Rushire, sex miles

miles off, for the purpose of procuring one of the urns which contain human bones, and which are found in rows close to an antient wall at that place; but the spirit of laziness prevailed, and I could get no one to accompany me. These interesting remains are accurately described in Colonel Johnstone's work.

On the 8th, the day on which we quitted Bushire, we engaged with a muleteer for mules to carry our effects to Tehran, at the rate of forty-eight Persian rupees per mule, which was exceedingly moderate: a short time ago the hire for the same distance was eighty. I engaged three; one for my two portmanteaus, one for my servant, and one for my horse-keeper. It is really quite provoking to observe the laziness and insolence of the servants and mayters, or horse-keepers, in Persia: the commonest fellow will not march with you unless you mount him. The utmost load which a muleteer will allow his beast to carry is three hundred pounds each animal, which shews that they are capital beasts of burden. On the mules of our servants were our cots. The manner in which we intended to march was this: To leave our ground every evening an hour and a half before sunset, strike the tent, and pack up all our things; march on with one servant and a horse-keeper; complete our march, generally of sixteen or eighteen miles, by ten o'clock; sleep on the ground till sunrise, at which time our tent would always be ready pitched for us, as the cafila, or caravan of mules, would arrive an hour or two after us. Sleeping in the open air in Persia, except during rain, which is hardly known, is not attended with any bad effects.

The Resident shewed me several casts which he had taken from the sculptures at Persepolis. He effected his purpose in the following manner. He first made several long shallow boxes of wood, in

 which

which he put quick lime, applied them to the sculptures, and allowed them to remain till thoroughly dry. The case was then taken off and sent to Bushire, containing the impression, from which the cast was again taken in lime. These, of course, are very valuable, as nothing can be more accurate. Processions were the subjects of the casts.

At dinner, Aratoon, a respectable Armenian merchant, his son, and Yacoob Khan, dined with us: the latter is the son of the treasurer to many of the former embassies, and his father obtained the title of khan in consequence. They appeared in Persian dresses. Armenians, in Persia, are generally respectable characters; but mothers not unfrequently sell their daughters, and the men endeavour to persuade the Persians that Europeans are vastly inferior to them, saying that *they* are the heads of the Christian religion, and that our doctrines are heterodoxical. No Persian will take a caleoon from the hands of an Armenian servant; and as this is the first and last compliment to be paid to visitors, Armenians are not commonly engaged on this account, though they are faithful and willing servants.

In the evening we bade adieu to our hospitable entertainer, Colonel Stannus, and having mounted, we took the direction of Shiraz. The manner in which we were equipped was as follows: round hats, surtouts, long loose riding trowsers, Wellington boots and spurs, armed with swords and pistols, with a mounted servant armed with fusee and sword. Each of us sported a formidable pair of mustachios; and along with us were our mayters, mounted on mules, with our bedding and horse-cloths. Our servants carried at the saddle-bow a box containing a caleoon, tobacco, &c., and on the off-side, swinging from the kantle of the saddle by a long chain, a

round

round iron bucket, containing fire for the pipe; from the near kantle hung a skin of water. Our party consisted of about twenty, including servants.

Our cafila, or caravan of mules, had set off before us to await our arrival at Chakota, distant six fursungs, or twenty-four miles. Our trunks and beds were packed in *mafruches*, or cases of waterproof striped carpet, bound and fastened with leather. The cost of a pair of these invaluable covers is twenty Persian rupees.

After leaving Bushire we travelled in a north-east direction, and crossed an extensive tract of salt-marshes, which had the appearance of snow, from the crystallized sulphate of lime which covered the surface of the sandy soil. After wending our way over this uninteresting desert for three hours, at the rate of four miles an hour (or one fursung), we arrived at a small village called Chakaduck. Here we refreshed ourselves with water drawn from a well in the centre of the road, which is a common occurrence in Persia, and attended with extreme danger to wayfarers. Several cafilas of mules, laden with cotton, passed us here, the leading mule of each of which had bells round his neck: several large rough dogs kept the mules from straying. After leaving Chakaduck our guides lost the way, and we wandered about till daybreak, and got involved in extensive fields of ripe bearded wheat. At last we discovered the four towers of Chakota; before we arrived at which, several beautiful Indian grouse, erroneously called rock-pigeons, were shot. These birds are totally different from pigeons in every respect, for besides having only three toes and the legs feathered, the beak is strong and convex. The plumage of those we killed was of a light ash colour, spotted with black, and two long delicate black feathers issued from the tail.

 On

On arriving next day at Chakota, distant from Bushire twenty-four miles, we were obliged to put up in a stable, where we were tormented with flies, &c., as our tent had not appeared, and was not pitched till ten, A. M.: thermometer at noon 110°. But the excessive heat was not our only annoyance, for two or three Moollas relieved one another during the whole day in shouting aloud their prayers, it being Friday. At this place we saw several people who had their eyes put out, as a punishment for robbery.

New Chakota is surrounded with a good wall of fifteen feet in height, built of sun-dried bricks, with four round bastions, thirty feet in height. Old Chakota is a mile nearer Bushire. In the plain the natives from Bushire hawk with the large brown falcon: the antelope and the bustard are commonly the quarry. Sheikh Sala, the chief of Chakota, is very fond of the sport, and particularly attentive to Europeans. When the chief man of a village and district happens to be an Arab (as was the case here), he is termed Sheikh; and when a Persian, Khutkhoda.

From Chakota we proceeded onward to Borazgoon, distant sixteen miles. We went in advance of our cafila, taking with us only our cots on the horse-keeper's mule, and a mounted servant each.

This part of the country has long been in a very unsettled state, principally occasioned by the grasping disposition of the Sheikh of Bushire, who is endeavouring to get under his jurisdiction the whole of the low country, commonly termed *Gurm seer*, or region of heat. Some time ago he sent a body of troops to force the people of Borazgoon to comply with some exorbitant demand: they resisted, and fifteen of the Sheikh's people were killed.

After traversing an undulating tract for four hours, we arrived at Borazgoon

Borazgoon at ten, P. M.; and finding that the caravanserai had been destroyed by the earthquake—which nearly levelled Shiraz with the dust, in July 1824,—we threw down our sleeping paraphernalia, and slept soundly till sunrise outside, when rising, we proceeded to the shelter of the tent pitched ready for our reception. I strongly recommend travellers in Persia to adopt the same plan, especially when they can have the benefit of a bright moon, as was the case with us. I have marched a great deal in India, and always in the morning; but I found the marching in the evening (leaving an hour before sunset) attended with much less fatigue. In Persia the country between the places of halt is generally monotonous and uninteresting. Extensive stony plains, bounded by barren hills, is the character of the country; so that nothing is lost by marching in the evening, and the moon will shew sufficiently the nature of the region you traverse.

Borazgoon is a populous and thriving town: the walls can hardly be seen for the numerous stacks of grain which surround them. If a European happens to put up in the mehman-khana, or guest's-house, in the town, the chief of the place, Sheikh Suleem Khan, will provide him with every necessary, *gratis*. The origin of this custom was as follows: the life of an ancestor of the chief was saved by the interference of a European, and he strictly enjoined all his descendants to treat Europeans in general as above-mentioned.

On going to examine the caravanserai I met a woman (a traveller) in the gate-way. Seeing that no one was near us she threw off her veil, shewed a lovely smiling countenance, and talked with me. I had studied Persian in India, but I found a great difference between the pronunciation in the country itself, and that to which I had

had formerly been accustomed: for instance, *nan*, bread, is pronounced *noon; khuberistan*, a burial-place, *khuberistoon; Iran*, Persia, *Iroon;* and so on.

Having relieved one or two lame and blind beggars during the day, a score or two of the same fraternity issued from the town and importuned us, in the evening. Many of them were strong and able-bodied men. A woman came boldly into the tent, and would not quit it until we had relieved her. Thermometer 105°.

On the 10th we marched in the evening, as before, for Dalkee, distant twelve miles.

A short distance from Borazgoon we observed the corpse of a murdered man by the road side. The road to Dalkee is exceedingly stony, and at eight miles from it is a capital sporting tract, with a date jungle and swamp on the left. Our olfactory nerves were assailed by an insufferable sulphurous effluvia. Shortly after we crossed several naphtha and sulphur streams, which issued from the hills round the bases of which the road winds. At the fountain-head the water is lukewarm. The streams leave on their margin a whitish grey earth, which is of an acid and saltish taste: it is termed *gil-i-toorsh*, or sour clay. The taste is probably occasioned by a mixture of alum and sal-ammoniac: it is used in acidulating sherbet. I brought away a small quantity of this substance for my esteemed preceptor, Professor Jameson.

The petroleum is collected in shallow pits, and is used medicinally, being applied to the sores of camels and other quadrupeds. The timber of which the roofs of the houses are constructed is dipped in it, to prevent the attacks of insects, &c.

Some distance from Dalkee a man was observed reconnoitering us

on

on the left flank. Upon seeing him, half of our party went in advance of our servants and bedding, and half in the rear. Seeing we were fully prepared for a hostile attack, he galloped off. We held on our way, and shortly heard the furious barking of the dogs at Dalkee, where we bivouacked on the roof of a caravanserai, in which we found the Baloochees who had left the service of the Sheikh of Bushire.

Dalkee is an inconsiderable place. Near it are some interesting remains of a fire-temple and fort. We were here regaled by delicious melons and *moss* (acidulated milk); the bread which we lived upon was wheaten, rolled out into large cakes as thin as wafers. The thermometer this day (the 11th) was 100°.

CHAPTER IV.

Konartukht......Illyants......Kumeredge......Devist......Visit to the Ruins of Shapoor ......Kazeroon......Perizun......Dustiajun......Khonahzunnion......Arrival at Shiraz.

MARCHED for Konartukht, distant sixteen miles. Immediately after leaving Dalkee we entered a narrow gorge in the hills, composed of sandstone and clay slate. The hills increased in height as we advanced, from two hundred feet to eight hundred; their upper parts presented the appearance of perpendicular scarps; the dip of the strata towards the north; the angle of inclination 40°. On rounding a corner we came suddenly upon a rapid river, called the Shoora, from its brackish waters. The road continued for some distance parallel to this impetuous and noisy torrent, which was divided into several deep streams. On the other side of the valley, and over the principal stream, a bridge was observed, one or two of the arches of which had been carried away; we were consequently obliged to cross at a deep ford higher up. When we attained the middle the water was over the saddle-flaps. We got over luckily without accident, with the exception of two of our dogs, which went howling down the stream.

In the first part of the pass several rock-partridges were shot; they differed from others in plumage, which was of a greyish pink colour, and also in being smaller. The *capra ibex*, or wild goat, abounds here, but it is of an inferior size to that of the Alps. Wild sheep are occasionally found: they have long legs, and hair instead of of wool. On the road-side, in many places, small recesses were cut in the rock: these are for the shelter of the Tabunchees, or matchlock men, who accompany cafilas through the pass to protect them from Bactiari robbers.

After crossing the river we commenced ascending the pass of the Kootul Moolah. The narrow path wound amongst huge stones and rocks, and it required constant attention to prevent ourselves from being knocked off our horses and hurled down precipices two and three hundred feet deep. It was interesting to observe the sagacity of the mules where there was any thing of a descent: they drew their hind legs under them, and slid down the smooth ledges of rock, and occasionally leaped from one ridge to another. After we had proceeded for some time along the side of the mountain, which was calcareous, with precipices on our left, and a stream gurgling far below us on our right, we began to ascend in an almost straight line the face of the mountain. We were obliged to hold firmly by the manes of our horses to prevent our slipping over the kantle, and in the middle of the ascent we were obliged suddenly to dismount, as our steeds began to slip backwards with us. On coming to a most dangerous part of the ascent, one of our companions, who had been here before, said that he had seen a mule dashed from this spot to the bottom of the mountain, by striking against one of the mules of another cafila which was descending. After attaining an elevation of twelve hundred feet, we arrived at the Rhadar, being a solid piece of masonry with a wide Saracen arch in the centre. At the sides were recesses for the accommodation of the Rhadarees, or protectors of the road. It was with no small satisfaction that we passed through the arch and found ourselves on a

table-

table-land on the other side, being the fertile vale of Kist. The air was here delightfully cool, and our olfactories were regaled by the delicious odour of a *convolvulus*, but which I was unable to discover. Lions with short manes are frequently seen in this plain and on the surrounding mountains.

Journeying merrily along for about a fursung, we arrived at the capital cavaranserai of Konartukht on the 12th.

This village is noted for its excellent caravanserai: it is the best we had yet seen, and it may not be out of place shortly to describe it. It is surrounded by a wall twenty feet in height, with four round towers at the angles. Over the gateway are three rooms, which being open on all sides, catch every breath of wind. Around the walls, in the inside, are arched recesses for the accommodation of wayfarers: these extend half-way to the outer walls, and the vacant space consists of long rows of stabling, which are entered by the four angles. In the centre of the square is a platform, raised three or four feet from the ground, which is used for sleeping on in hot weather. Below this, and under ground, is a lofty vaulted room, in one corner of which is a well of good water. This caravanserai, and others of this country, possess several advantages over those which I had seen in India. There is no stabling in the latter, and no platform in the centre of the square. In Persia, stabling for the mules and horses is indispensable in the winter months.

We here found an extensive establishment of horses belonging to Noor Mahomed, a very *honest* horse-dealer belonging to Kazeroon. He keeps half of his stud here, it being cheaper than in his native place. In the fertile plain of Kist there is most excellent hare and partridge-shooting: several brace were killed by our party. The

hares

hares were smaller, but have much longer ears than those of Europe. The partridges were of the species called painted. The male was a beautiful bird: the feet and bills were red, the breast black spotted with white, with a black ring round the neck; the sides were ferruginous, marked with black. The females and young were brown with black spots. Thermometer 90°.

Left for Kumeredge, distant fourteen miles. On quitting Konartukht, after a mile's ride, I observed, on the hill to the right, an upright stone or small tower, and across and along the road extended the foundations of buildings. In a field I saw several holes made by porcupines, who had been digging for bulbous roots. After traversing three miles of plain, we entered the hills, between which we crept along by a tortuous and narrow path, with a rapid river on our left, which we were told by Noor Mahomed, who intended accompanying us to Kazeroon, was the Shapoor, which name it acquired after passing the far-famed ruins of the city so called. Shortly after this, passing through hills impregnated with salt, it is termed the Shoora, which we had already crossed. The stones in the bed and sides of the river seemed to be indurated sandstone. After winding amongst the hills for some time longer, and crossing several small mountain torrents, we suddenly found ourselves in a deep and narrow glen. The *tout-ensemble* was here of the grandest and most sublime description; steep mountains of sixteen hundred feet in height, seemingly tumbling on our heads: the strata were within a few degrees of being vertical. The moon, appearing from behind one of the loftiest peaks, threw half the scene into deep shade, and mildly illuminated the other half. A complete stop seemed now to be put to our further progress; but oui guides suddenly turning

 to

to the left, commenced ascending one of the loftiest mountains called the Kootul Kumeredge, by a steep zig-zag road. After scrambling up the ascent on horseback for some time, I looked over the side of the path, and found my right leg hanging over an awful abyss of six hundred feet in depth; and on my left was a lofty and bluff rock of amygdaloidal limestone. This occurred three or four times during the ascent. Down one of these precipices a mule of the Envoy's, laden with liquor, was dashed. We were separated from the lofty mountain on our right, consisting of pointed and vertical strata of limestone, by this tremendous gulley. At one or two of the most dangerous turnings there were ridiculous little parapets, of a foot in height: they might be of some small service to descending cafilas. After scrambling and slipping for an hour, we reached the Rhadar, which was a cave on the right side of the road, across which was built a wall with a narrow opening in the centre. Out of the cave issued a savage-looking man with a skin of water in his hand, which we quickly emptied.

Shortly after passing the Rhadar we entered the plain of Kumeredge, bounded by an amphitheatre of mountains, and three miles in length by one and a half or two in breadth. On the right a small encampment of the Illyauts, or wandering peasantry of the country, was observed, consisting of five or six black tents. In the seasons for sowing and reaping the grain, these tribes (some of which are very strong, and have one of their head men at court as a hostage for the good behaviour of the rest) descend from their pastures, of which each tribe has a limited district, and cultivate the valleys. The dress of the men differs from that of other Persians, by the more frequent adoption of a high and white cap of felt,

felt, instead of the conical black sheep-skin. The dress of the women is generally blue; consisting of a loose pair of trowsers, a chemise open half way down in front, and descending above the drawers to the middle of the thigh; on the head is a three-cornered veil of chequered blue and white cloth.

The caravanserai at Kumeredge having been deserted for some time, and in ruins from having been frequently attacked by robbers, we bivouacked in a field near the village.

In the morning of the 13th the head-man of the village presented us with a sheep, for which he received a present of a tomaun, or eight rupees. The price of a sheep here was a rupee and a half, but this fellow would have gone away grumbling if he had not obtained a handsome present. The people of this place are much more deserving of assistance than any where else. The situation being retired, it was selected for the scene of an extensive robbery several years ago. Some men from Scind were on their way to the Prince-Governor of Shiraz with presents; they were attacked here by Bactiari robbers, who plundered them of every thing; which so irritated the Prince of Shiraz, that, having first given the villagers a certain time to recover the presents, he afterwards imposed a heavy fine on them, and killed a man every day till it was paid. After several executions the villagers fled. A year or two ago a party of a hundred Bactiaris on foot and twelve on horseback, plundered the villagers of every thing, stripping them of their clothes; in consequence of which a Rhadar tower has been built at the other extremity of the vale. The villagers have now been induced to remain by being taxed very lightly, *viz.* at the rate of one per cent. Every bullock or cow is computed to sow by the drill (one of which

which is fastened on each side of the animal) one hundred maunds of grain in a year, and twelve pice, the usual price of one maund, is charged on every hundred. The usual tax throughout the country is, I believe, one-fifth. Thermometer 87°.

In the evening we left for Devist, distance twelve miles.

In proceeding along the vale, the hills nearest were stratified after the manner of trap, and were two or three hundred feet in height: these were backed on the right by mountains apparently two thousand feet high, with square summits. The colour was that of red sandstone, but I am inclined to think the basis is limestone. Further on the range was decidedly calcareous, and very cavernous. In passing through the narrow and rugged defile which led into the extensive plain of Kazeroon, the road in one place was nearly blocked up by a huge mass of rock, which had been thrown down by the earthquake two years ago. On the side of the path I observed the *amygdalus Persica*, which being wild is of course a bitter almond. Some distance further on we came to a Rhadar, the chief man of which was excessively insolent, and lied abominably. He presented Captain Campbell with a draught of water, in return for which he was offered two rupees. This he told us to keep to ourselves, saying it was a poor recompense for all the trouble he had taken on our account; positively asserting that he had sent matchlock-men to the low country to protect us on the way up, and also that he had constantly forwarded supplies of snow for us at every stage. Now both of these assertions were infamous falsehoods. I may here remark that snow is found in the clefts of the rocks throughout the whole year.

Before we reached Devist we heard several shots fired by two of our

our party in advance. We galloped up to see what was the matter, and found them engaged in destroying a large rock-snake, the colour of which was a greenish yellow spotted with black. We arrived at Devist, where Mr. George Malcolm and myself intended to sleep, preparatory to visiting the celebrated ruins, sculptures, and cave of Shapoor, distant two fursungs. The rest of our party proceeded to Kazeroon, distant from Kumeredge twenty-four miles.

On applying to the Kutkhoda of Devist for guides to Shapoor, he declared that less than fifteen or twenty armed men would not accompany us, as the hills about Shapoor swarmed with Muhumud Sooni robbers, who the day before had killed on the plain the head-man of a neighbouring village. We retired to rest on the top of the Kutkhoda's house, which was half under ground, almost the whole of the village having been destroyed by the earthquake of 1824. The thermometer till two in the morning was under 40°.

On the 14th June, at two o'clock, we rose, mounted, and proceeded towards the eastward, along the foot of the limestone hills which bounded on each side the long valley of Kazeroon. We were accompanied by eight matchlock-men and two Illyauts armed with spears; four horsemen also strengthened the party. Having marched four miles, the guides requested us to dismount, as they could not proceed for the cold. We had crossed several streams, on the banks of which were juniper bushes, and our legs had got wet; we therefore complied with their request, and halted on a threshing-floor, circular, and the bottom of hard beaten clay. Our conductors lighted a large fire, and having warmed themselves for half an hour, we remounted, and after an hour's ride found ourselves amongst the ruins of Shapoor. We first crossed a broad ditch, through which a

stream

stream of water flowed, and scrambling up the face of a decayed curtain, found ourselves on the top of the antient rampart, and saw the extensive remains of stone-built houses below us. At this moment I experienced the shock of an earthquake; it seemed to pass from south to north, accompanied by a long rumbling noise among the hills, and a sudden oppressive heat in the atmosphere.

We now proceeded along the wall, with the remains of round stone bastions at intervals, in a southerly direction. I observed that very few of the walls of the houses were standing, and from the few that were erect the cement had been washed out from between the stones. Upon reaching the south-west angle of the city wall, the matchlock-men fired several times, and loading with ball, preceded us through a narrow gorge between two hills. On our left ran a clear and rapid river, called the Sasoon, which, after passing the ruins, acquires the name of Shapoor, and after crossing the saline bed, as before mentioned, is termed Shoora. This information we derived from Noor Mahomed, who accompanied us: as to the authenticity of it I cannot answer. On the left bank of the river, and behind some high reeds, appeared several sculptures on the rock: these we intended visiting after returning from the cave. Proceeding further, on our right, we passed a sculpture very much effaced: it represented a bull, and one or two men seemingly in procession. Beyond this is the large group of bas-reliefs of which a plate is given in Malcolm's "Persia." The hill above these sculptures, on our right, seemed to have been the citadel of Shapoor, as the remains of enormously thick walls were visible all over it.

Having advanced about half a mile into the valley of the cave, which resembles an isoceles triangle (the upper part of the valley on the

the right, or apex, being opposite to and a mile from the cave in the centre of the base of the triangle), we crossed the river. Here our guides proved themselves to be excellent marksmen, by killing three large grayling, with their matchlocks. I never saw a finer stream for fly-fishing than this; it seemed completely alive with fish. Proceeding along the left bank (but, more correctly speaking, the right bank, as we were going up the stream), we found ourselves under the cave, and began to ascend, still keeping on horseback. It is here necessary to remark, that the hills which surround this triangular valley are, as usual, calcareous. The base of the triangle, or hill in which the cave is situated, is apparently one thousand feet in height: four hundred feet is a naked and perpendicular scarp; one hundred feet from the bottom of the scarp is the cave; from the bottom of the scarp to the river the angle of descent is seemingly not far off forty-five degrees. The strata of the hills dip backwards from the valley in three different directions; the dip of the strata of the hill in which the cave is situated is apparently towards the north-west: angle of inclination eight or ten degrees. I do not pretend to be correct in either the height or directions, as I was unprovided with a quadrant and compass, having been hurried off from India so suddenly.

We ascended about a third of the way to the bottom of the scarp on horseback, when, wishing to save our steeds, we dismounted and proceeded on foot. However, Noor Mahomed scrambled up on his unfortunate horse the whole way, sending down showers of stones at every step. Persians are very merciless, especially in regard to the inferior animals. They ride their horses furiously over the roughest ground and along the sides of hills, without the least concern. They

 are

are not generally better horsemen than Englishmen. It is almost impossible to fall from a Persian saddle: the pummel terminates in a wooden handle, surmounted by a carved ornament, resembling a *fleur de lis*; of this they make use when in danger of falling. Place a Persian on a hunting saddle, and desire him to gallop over a plain, he would be sprawling on the ground in five minutes.

After scrambling up the steep ascent for about twenty minutes, we attained the bottom of the scarp. I here found abundance of wild oats, bitter almonds, white hollyhock, abundance of the true Scotch thistle, and several varieties of moss, with a few lichens. Proceeding along the foot of the scarp for some distance, we came to a rock twelve feet in height; up this we mounted, with the assistance of our guides. Thinking that we were now close to the great cave, and wishing to be the first to enter it, I turned to the left, and found an arch under a rock. I called out to the rest to follow, but the guides said that the great cave was much further up. Accordingly, after ascending some distance, we came to the mouth, which is upwards of one hundred and thirty feet in length (across), and fifty in height. Standing at the entrance, the appearance is very striking; for the cave seems to diminish from the entrance to a small black spot, but it does not diminish in height. There is a great descent, and in the centre lies the mutilated statue of a king, supposed to be the only statue in the country. We did not stand long to contemplate the interior from the entrance, but ran down the slope in search of water. Passing the prostrate king, we found a square tank on the left, but no water. Immediately opposite to us was a large stalactite, called the Lamp of Shapoor; this overlooked a deep pit, forming the floor of a lofty hall, one hundred feet in height.

height. The sides of this circular hall, as well as of the long gallery of entrance (where we were obliged to light torches, though directly opposite the entrance) were entirely covered by a thick coating of stalactite: no part of the rock was visible. In some places the stalactites stood out from the sides, like trunks of trees, and forming many fantastic figures; from the roof several hung in a threatening position. The floor was covered by a rich mould, arising from the dung of birds, for several pigeons were disturbed by us. We also found traces of Muhumud Soonee robbers.

Having got down to the bottom of the circular hall, we observed galleries running in different directions. We, of course, inquired particularly for the passage that would lead to the water, and were told it was straight forward: we accordingly entered another lofty chamber, and found a large elliptical tank, but not a drop of water in it. What rendered our case worse was, that we heard water dropping on every side of us. Though the place was delightfully cool, our thirst was intense, and we had expended the small skin we had brought with us from the river in the ascent. We now proceeded directly forward, and entered another large hall, and then a chamber resembling a Hindoo temple. The stalactites bore the appearance of stout square pillars, on which were laid architraves. After this we penetrated to the end of a chamber, but had to crawl on our hands and knees. We now returned to the elliptical tank, and turning into a hall opposite to it, with our cheeks adhering to our jaws, to our great joy we found on the floor beautifully cool and transparent water, sufficient for a herd of elephants. After allaying our thirst, we went into several other galleries and chambers, the sides, roofs, and floors of which were entirely covered

 by

by greyish white stalactites and stalagmites, we returned to the entrance.

The tradition regarding the statue of the king, in the centre of the gallery of entrance, is as follows: it was evidently hewn from an immense block of limestone in the place where it now lies, with the head in the dust, and the stumps of the legs resting on the pedestal; before it was thrown from which it must have been fifteen or twenty feet in height, consequently presenting a formidable object in the cave. Two brothers hunting on the mountains, one of them entered the cave, and seeing this tremendous object staring at him, was so overpowered by fear that he fell down and died on the spot. The other brother coming to the cave shortly after, and seeing his brother lying dead at the entrance, guessed the cause, and threw down the statue.

It was now eight A.M.: we descended to our horses, and mounting them, proceeded to the large sculpture, which is quite entire, crossed the river, and sat down under the ledge of a rock which protects it from the weather. We saw snow from hence on a distant hill. In proceeding to the ledge, it was disgusting to observe the cruelty and insolence of our guides. We met two or three poor travellers proceeding through the valley, and our rascals rushed at them in a body, with drawn swords, threatening to kill them if they did not give their shoes and other little articles they had about them. We had some difficulty in putting a stop to their infamous attempts.

After having recruited ourselves under the *bas reliefs*, which represent a king on horseback, with a globe or balloon-shaped crown: beneath him is the prostrate figure of a man. These two are supposed to represent King Shapoor, who subdued the Roman Emperor Valerian, and used him as a step by which to mount his horse.

Behind

Behind the king is a short figure, probably the son of King Shapoor. Three figures (apparently Roman) are approaching them in a supplicating attitude. Between the head of the nearest one and that of the horse is an inscription in the Pehlevi. Behind the king, in several compartments, are many mounted figures of Persians, and opposite, those of Roman foot soldiers all the figures as large as life.

We crossed the river to view the sculptures on the other side, and attaining the foot of the mountain, we found that we had to proceed along the bottom of an aqueduct to reach them. This was in some places breast high, and overhung with brambles and reeds: where it was carried under the rock, we had to crawl on our hands and knees. The first sculptures we came to were exceedingly beautiful, being cut in a semicircle: they consisted of many rows of small figures, seemingly in procession, with offerings. The next were busts of men and a camel. The third and last displayed a very spirited representation of King Ardashir resigning the circlet of royalty into the hands of his son Shapoor. They appear to be approaching each other on horseback; the father is much larger than the son, and wears the globe-like crown.

We recrossed the river, the banks of which were clothed with myrtles, willows, and splendid rhododendrons, and wandered amongst the ruins of the city, which was attended with great danger, from the numerous wells communicating with the subterraneous aqueducts, or kanauts. We came to the remains of a Guebre burial-ground. It was a large square pit, the sides lined with stone, and the highest part of the wall rising ten or twelve feet above the surface of the ground; on this there were three cows' heads, between which the ends of beams probably rested, supporting a roof, which covered

the

the whole. On this the bodies were exposed; and when the bones had been picked clean by birds, they were thrown down a hole in the centre of the roof into a well below.

We now bent our steps towards Devisht, with the thermometer in the shade 103°, being a rise of 63° from the time we set out. It is really wonderful how Europeans are able to stand such changes of temperature. We pursued for some time a lion, but lost him amongst the brush-wood.

Some distance from the village the two Illyauts came up, salaamed, and were going away without receiving any thing. We called them back to receive a present, for these two were the only men who had made themselves at all useful; they accompanied and assisted us up to the cave, when the others sat below with the horses, and did nothing. By the advice of Noor Mahomed, we gave six tomauns to the brother of the head-man of Devisht, who had accompanied us, to distribute among the guides, or guards, as they termed themselves. Out of this he was to reserve a handsome present for himself, two rupees per man being the proper allowance for the guides: but he grumbled exceedingly, was very discontented, and encouraged the rest also to make a disturbance. He had even the effrontery to say that there were thirty men along with us, when there were really only fourteen, including himself: but, knowing well the utter impossibility of satisfying Persians (for if you give a man a coat he will return for a shawl to tie round it; and if you give him a horse he will ask for a saddle: they are the most shameless race I ever saw in this respect), we turned them off, having first made a separate present to the quiet Illyauts.

We marched for Kazeroon, distant from Devisht twelve miles: the road

road was good, but the heat and glare were excessive. At five we arrived at Kazeroon, a long and populous town, but half in ruins from earthquakes. The tent was pitched near tobacco-fields, and at the door of a beautiful garden, close to which was a tank filled with grayling, of which we caught many dozen with the rod, several of three pounds weight. The garden abounded with apples, apricots, cherries, plums, grapes, &c. We purchased as much ice as we could consume for a couple of *shys*, of which there are twenty-five in a Persian rupee or real: of this our servants made delightful sherbet, with the addition of a syrup and water. We feasted nobly on capital fish, fat mutton, and abundance of fruit and ice.

We halted till the evening, when we marched from Kazeroon for the caravanserai of Perizun, distant twenty miles.

In passing through the town of Kazeroon we did not find a single upper story standing, and the lower ones were so hidden by the ruins of the upper, that the houses appeared buried underground. Leaving this town (which, by the way, is one of the hottest in Persia), we marched along an excellent road, and constantly passed runs of water on the surface, and innumerable kanauts below it. The soil seemed to be uncommonly rich, and extensive fields of ripe gendoom, or wheat, were seen in every direction. The sides of the road were lined with the white caper. We passed several cafilas of dromedaries laden with fire-wood. I may here remark, that both in India and in Persia the camel and dromedary are always confounded. These would have been called camels by Europeans, though they had only one hunch on the back.

After some time we crossed a long and dangerous causeway, leading across a marsh, in which there is excellent duck-shooting.

Turning

Turning to the left, and passing under a bluff cavernous rock, we commenced ascending the precipitous Kootul, called the Dokhtur, or daughter. The path is a zig-zag directly up the face of a mountain of eight hundred feet in height, the upper part defended by a low wall. We got up ourselves without accident; but one of the mules striking against another at one of the turns, the unfortunate animal was precipitated with its load down the mountain, and dashed to pieces. Arrived at the top, we saw an extensive salt-lake.

On coming to the Rhadar at the commencement of the beautiful little valley of Dustaburd, six matchlock-men came running to meet us, with their matches lighted. They ran on in a line in front, and at a turn of the road discharged their pieces; then loading, ran on again, and at another turn repeated the salute, and then came up, salaaming for a present. They were well content with a rupee each, at which I was surprised.

This valley was the most pleasant we had yet seen: it was one fursung in length, and a mile in breadth. Generally it was clothed with the baloot or Persian oak, which was not above twenty or thirty feet high. The difference between this and the English oak consists in the leaf being jagged, the acorn and cup being much longer, and the branches not being so gnarled. The leaves at some seasons of the year are entirely covered with the white deposit of an insect, the taste of which is bitter.

At the end of the valley we commenced ascending the mountain of Perizun, or Old Woman, which is seven thousand feet above the level of the sea. This mountain is called "the Old Woman" for several reasons: it has commonly a white head, being covered with snow for many months in the year; the ascent is like the crooked and

and perverse temper of an old woman, &c. After ascending for four miles, during which several hogs and deer crossed our path, we came to a good caravanserai, where we stopped.

We spent the 16th here very comfortably, the people of the caravanserai bringing us apricots, ice, and honey. Saw at a distance goldfinches and green fly-catchers. In front of us was a long serrated ridge of hills. Left in the evening for Dustiajun, distant fifteen miles.

In ascending to the top of the Perizun it is very difficult to keep in the right road, as it winds so much among stones and trees, of which the common hawthorn and oak are the principal. The fruit of the hawthorn differs from that of the British in being rounder. I observed great quantities of *laburnum* in ascending. Holes had been burnt in the stems of many of the oak-trees, for the purpose of getting at the wild honey.

Not a sound was heard all over the mountain; the deepest silence reigned around, interrupted only by the melancholy and peculiar notes of the bird, which constantly calls *huk! huk!* "Oh, God! oh, God!" This, it is said, was a great sinner, who was changed into a bird, and is continually calling on the name of the Almighty.

Having reached the top, we looked down upon the valley of Dustiajun, which was almost entirely covered with a lake. We now experienced a very great exhilaration of spirits, of which our horses and cattle partook: we went gaily forward, and in a very short time reached the lofty willow trees at Dustiajun. A very copious spring issues from a perpendicular and cavernous lime-stone rock behind the trees, which turns several flour-mills, and then rushes impetuously into the lake. We slept soundly on its banks.

The whole of the 17th was spent in fishing in the lake, and many large grayling were caught. There was also a little duck-shooting.

In the evening we went up to the rock, and passed through a fissure, the performing of which feat is a proof of legitimacy. We had to crawl on our hands and knees for twelve or fifteen paces. The sides were quite smooth and shining, shewing that it had been often used. We all passed the ordeal without much difficulty. Near the fissure are several old Persian inscriptions.

Below the fissure, and under the willow trees, is a small building, in which are shewn four holes, said to be the marks of the hoofs of Muhummud's horse Dooldool. He gave him to Allee, who in riding past this spot was attacked by a lion, which he slew. The spirit of the lion visits this place every Friday evening, to prostrate itself before the marks of the hoofs, and the villagers pretend that, during the time the spirit of the lion remains there, no cafila is able to pass. We were obliged to take off our shoes before we were permitted to see the impressions of the hoofs.

I next visited the mills. They are strong substantial stone buildings. The upper mill-stone is set in motion by a wooden horizontal wheel, which communicates with it by means of a spindle. The grain is received into a hole in the stone, which, being inclined at an angle of a few degrees, throws the flour on the floor of the building. Acorn bread is occasionally eaten by the villagers in this district.

On making inquiries regarding the taxes paid by this village, I received the following account: Total amount per annum, twelve hundred tomauns; for each male, four tomauns; for each horse, half a tomaun; each mule, half a tomaun; each ass, a quarter tomaun; each

each cow, a quarter tomaun; a yoke of oxen, four tomauns; a thousand vine-plants, five tomauns.

There was abundance of clover here, canary seed, water-cresses, common rushes, &c. There being excellent shooting the next march, it was determined to sleep here all night, to enable us to shoot along the road in the morning. We accordingly all put our cots into a bechoba-tent; but the musquitoes annoyed us so terribly, that in the morning (not having got a wink of sleep during the night) we rose in a complete fever, from the irritation occasioned by our virulent tormentors.

On the 18th we marched at four A. M. for Khonahzunnion, distant twelve miles.

The road was a romantic one. There was a considerable quantity of low jungle the whole way, and it was a continued series of small ascents and descents. Many cupks, or large brown partridges, were seen, and several shot. I saw for the first time a magpie; also crows with white breasts. Several juniper bushes adorned the hollows, in which hares in great numbers were skipping.

The caravanserai at Khonahzunnion seemed to be several centuries old: it was decidedly the worst we had yet seen; the accommodations were most wretched. The village also was poor in the extreme.

Yacoob Khan, of whom mention was made at Bushire, here joined us. He was only four days from Bushire, and travelled in the Persian mode, night and day.

We marched in the evening for Shiraz, distant twenty-eight miles.

The road lay between low hills, which were very bleak, and divested

vested of vegetation. There was a good deal of water on the road, and we passed the ruins of an ancient bridge. At eight miles from Shiraz, and at the entrance of its fertile valley, is a capital Rhadar and excellent bridge. Here we slept; and on the morning of the 19th we started for the far-famed city.

CHAPTER V.

Shiraz......Effects of the last Earthquake......The Palace of Tukht-i-Kudjur......Tombs of Saadi and Hafiz......Visit to the Minister......Audience of the Prince...... Sculptures......Bazar......The Garden-Palaces.

The valley of Shiraz is twenty-four miles in length and twelve in breadth; it is bounded on each side by hills of no great height, which are bare of vegetation. The trees in the plain are the chinar, or plane, the cypress, and poplars in the gardens round the city.

Shiraz does not now present an imposing appearance: there is not a single dome or minaret standing; they were all levelled by the earthquake in 1824. The walls are of a good height, defended by round bastions at regular distances; the gates are distinguished by having a couple of towers to flank them. There is, as usual, a rampart and parapet. The ark, or citadel of Kureem Khan, is square, with four bastions; it is within the walls of the city, and surrounded by a deep wet ditch. The population of Shiraz is at present computed at thirty thousand.

Since the last earthquake, the climate of Shiraz has very much changed from its former salubrity. The water in the wells has risen very near the surface. Where formerly there were ten and fifteen yards of line there are now only three or four; therefore the increased evaporation has, it is supposed, been the cause of a deleterious atmosphere in the plain.

We were met at some distance from the city by the Envoy, Colonel Macdonald. In proceeding to the Tukht-i-Kudjur, a palace belonging

belonging to the Prince of Shiraz, and which he allowed Colonel Macdonald to occupy, we passed the lofty pole to which, at the *No Roz*, or new year's day, a popinjay is attached, at which the prince and nobles fire.

The party now consisted of the Envoy and his lady, Major Willock, Captain Campbell, Captain Jarvis, agent for horses, Sir Keith Jackson, Bart. H.M. 4th Dragoons, Military Secretary to the Governor of Bombay, Dr. Reoch, Mr. George Malcolm, Lieutenant McDonald commanding escort, Lieutenant Strong, and myself.* The escort consisted of fifty men of Spiller's horse, under the control of a jemadar. Their full dress was a long yellow coat with a red sash, turban, breeches, and long boots; the greater part armed with spears, the remainder with matchlocks; the undress dark blue and red. Their appearance was exceedingly shewy, and well calculated to please the eye of the splendour-loving Persians.

The Tukht-i-Kudjur is built on a small rock, under a hill to the eastward of the city, overlooking a large garden filled with fruit-trees of every description. The hall of audience commands a beautiful and extensive view of the city and valley. It is about twenty feet in height, open on one side; the opposite side filled up by a large window of stained glass.

The Envoy did not propose to start for Ispahan for four or five days, so that we had abundance of leisure to see all the objects worthy of notice in and around the city. The Envoy had already visited the Prince, Houssein Allee Mirza, his prime minister, Zachee Khan, &c. His lady had also visited the wives of the Prince.

* The Envoy having politely requested me to attach myself to his suite.

Prince. Whilst she was engaged in conversation with them, she observed the Prince himself sitting in a balcony observing them, and smoking with the greatest coolness: however, as soon as he caught her eye, he stooped down, and an attendant threw a cloak over his head. This he constantly repeated whenever Mrs. Macdonald looked at him. The lady was naturally provoked at his rudeness, and revenged herself by continually turning round towards him: which interrupted his smoking, and caused him to be half-smothered with the cloak, so that he at length was forced to retire. The princesses were very anxious to obtain many of Mrs. Macdonald's jewels, and urged her to part with them; of course their unreasonable requests were not complied with.

We went on the morning of the 21st to visit the tomb of Saadi, &c. It is about two miles and a half from the Tukht-i-Kudjur, and to the south, situated in a small garden surrounded by high walls. The tomb itself is under cover, and of marble. Inscriptions cover every part of it, being passages from the Koran and from his own works. At the head of the tomb are a pair of nightingales. Outside the garden is a well, with steps to descend to it. It is of octagonal shape, with recesses. Here Saadi used to sit and compose, screened from the heat. The water is beautifully clear.

We next proceeded to the garden of the Dil-i-gooshah. On entering it you are introduced into a little octagonal porch, in which is a cistern of water. Here was painted in very brilliant colours Roustam, the Persian Hercules, throwing himself off his horse, and plunging his dagger into the Deeve-i-Sufeed, or white demon. Down the centre of the garden from the house is a shallow stone channel of water, interrupted every ten or twelve paces by small cascades.

We

We could not gain admittance for some time into the house, as the Prince's women were in it: however, they went to the upper story, and we were allowed to visit the lower apartments. We found them painted and gilded in the most extravagant manner. The ceilings represented furious combats between the Persians, Russians, and Turks; the royal princes were represented larger than the rest, and cutting men down from the crest to the saddle-bow. As usual, no regard was paid to perspective.

We then went to the tomb of the Persian Anacreon, Hafiz, which is about a mile only from the Tukht-i-Kudjur: it is in the midst of other tombs, in a burial-ground enclosed with a wall: but vulgar bones do not repose near him; men of rank alone were allowed that privilege. His tomb is distinguished above the rest by its superior dimensions. The marble, like Saadi's tomb, is covered with inscriptions, beautifully cut. Shiraz is deservedly famed for stone-cutting, enamelling, and seal-engraving. Near the tombs is an open building, in which resides a venerable Fakir, who has charge of a complete copy of the works of Hafiz: this he produced, and we opened the book at random to see what would be our fates, by the *fal*, a kind of divination, like the *Sortes Virgilianæ*.

In the evening, Captain Campbell, Lieutenant McDonald, Lieutenant Strong, Mr. George Malcolm, and myself, accompanied Colonel Macdonald to be introduced privately to the Prime Minister. We went in undress: round hats, blue surtouts, sashes, and trowsers; on our feet we wore red cloth boots with slippers. We proceeded on horseback through the Ispahan-gate, and rode along several streets, in which the accumulation of dry mud and dirt was so great, that the level of the court-yards of the houses on both sides

was

was several feet below that of the streets. Arrived at the door of Zachee Khan's house we dismounted, and walked through the garden to the house. In the outer room we left our slippers, and were received at the door of the inner by the Minister, standing, who graciously shook hands with us, upon each being presented to him. We then all sat down in a row, close to the wall, on soft nummuds, or pieces of felt. The hall of audience was open on one side, as usual, looking into the garden. The principal topic discussed was this. A bugalow, or large gulf-boat, had left Bombay for Bushire laden with six chandeliers, intended as presents for the King; it had also on board china, and a variety of articles belonging to Colonel Macdonald. In the north-wester which prevailed during the time we were at Bushire, it grounded on the Persian coast, about sixty miles to the eastward of Bushire, and three hundred armed men went down and plundered her of every thing. This subject was fully discussed by the Envoy and Minister during our visit.

One of the women of the Prince was delivered of twins in the morning of this day, and the Minister mentioned it as a remarkable circumstance; but he was quite astounded to hear that in Europe women had been delivered of five at once.

Zachee Khan is very corpulent: his age is about fifty. He became a great favourite of the Prince by sitting up and drinking with him whole nights. On this occasion there sat beside him a very intelligent-looking man, Hussun Khan, Mehmandar, related to the royal family, being of the Kudjur blood. To shew to what straits a man of his rank was reduced, the Envoy having sent him presents, consisting of broadcloth, arms, watches, &c., altogether to the amount of sixteen hundred or two thousand rupees, he, upon receiving the presents, requested that they might be exehanged for their value in money, as he was greatly in want of that indispensable article.

Caleoons were first introduced. The servants came into the room with socks on their feet, and entering a few paees, made a low obeisanee; then went up and presented the caleoon on their knees. Coffee was then brought in: small china cups, surrounded with silver fillegree-work, to prevent the hand being burnt, contained the strong beverage, which was drank without milk or sugar. Caleoons followed again (the flavour of which the coffee greatly improved); then ieed sherbet, and finally ealeoons for the third time, which was the signal for departure.

Next day, the Prince (who got presents and money to the amount of thirteen thousand rupees, besides six thousand being given to his Minister) sent khilaats, or dresses of honour, to those who had formerly been introduced to him. He asked Colonel Maedonald how many he should give. The Colonel replied, only to those whom he had seen. To this he answered, "I know that five more gentlemen "have joined you, and do you think I'll grudge giving them dresses "likewise? No; they shall all have dresses." However, after all his boasting, he only sent five, and the new comers got none. The Envoy's consisted of a rich silk dress with a considerable quantity of silver lace and buttons on it, two shawls, and a sword: the others consisted of a silk dress and two shawls eaeh, some of them very paltry.

We went in the evening of the 23d, in state, to take leave of the Prinee. We were all in full dress: those who had got dresses of honour, wore one of the shawls as a sash. The order in which we went was this: first, the Envoy, in full staff-uniform; then nine gentlemen,

gentlemen, two and two; then came two European serjeants of the Bombay horse-artillery, who were proceeding to Azerbijan to drill part of the troops of the Heir-Apparent; the whole of the escort followed in their dashing yellow dresses. Arrived at the citadel, we heard the beating of a drum and an ill-played fife on our left, when a disorderly band of musketeers ran out from a house, and drew up in an irregular line close to the gate at which we were to enter. We dismounted, and were received inside by the master of ceremonies, who bore a wand of office, and had on a large and high turban, with a profusion of sables about the upper part of his garment. He introduced us into the garden in which was the palace of the Prince. When we came within sight of the hall of audience, and first obtained a view of his Royal Highness, we halted and made a profound obeisance: this was repeated three times as we advanced. We passed several mutes and men bearing iron maces, and entered the outer apartment, where we left our slippers. Entering the hall of audience, we bowed again to the Prince, who was sitting, and then sat down in a row at some distance from him. The hall looked like a palace of steel, as every part of it was covered with mirrors to within three feet of the ground, when slabs of white marble, painted with flowers, finished the decorations of the apartment: three large chandeliers were suspended from the ceiling. The master of ceremonies and Zachee Khan remained standing during the whole conference. The Prince's age is about forty: he is of the middle size, and has nothing pleasing in his countenance. He wore on his head the common black sheep-skin cap; his dress was red silk, with a vast profusion of jewels, and the hilt of his dagger glittered in a splendid manner. His conversation was common-place.

Caleoons were introduced, then coffee; caleoons again, and then we departed. When we got outside, there was considerable delay in making the obeisance, as a fellow thought fit to conceal my slippers, and I was obliged to come to blows with him before I could recover them. I then fell into the ranks as quickly as possible, and bowed with the rest. After bowing three times in the garden, as before, we mounted our horses and rode off. In mounting, Lieutenant Strong was struck on the breast with a stone. This was the only insult that was offered to us, though the Shirazees are notorious for rudeness to Europeans.

In the morning of the 24th we visited some new sculptures executing by order of the Prince on the Ispahan Road: they are on the face of a rock on the left hand side, and the celebrated Rock-nabad flows past them. The subject of the first is his Majesty, Futteh Allee Shah, seated on his throne, with the Heir-Apparent standing near him. The second sculpture is Roustam on horseback, killing a tiger with an arrow: the tiger has a man underneath. The workmanship is by no means despicable. Near the sculptures is a gateway across the road, in the upper room of which there is a Koran seventeen maunds in weight, or a hundred and nineteen pounds.

In the evening we visited the bazar of Kureem Khan: it is very extensive, and the finest that I had yet seen. The whole is arched in; the height of the arcade is thirty or forty feet. The shops on each side are completely sheltered from the sun and rain; light and air are admitted by windows along the top. Over each shop is the name of the occupier. As is usual in Oriental bazars, the different trades are assembled together. From the bazar I went to the

Juhan

Juhan Noomah Garden. There is nothing remarkable about it, except its being the place where the late lamented Resident of Bagdad, Mr. Rich, was interred, and also Dr. Taylor. They were not allowed to rest in peace by the Shirazees; their grave-stones were broken, and it was thought advisable to take up their bones, and transport them to Ispahan for re-interment in the Armenian burial-ground. They were accordingly disinterred, under the superintendence of Dr. Reoch, and carefully packed in boxes. I next went to the Baugh-i-No, or New Garden. There is nothing particular here, except a drawing in the house, representing Sir John Malcolm having an audience of his Majesty.

The heat of the weather was now very great; the thermometer in our tents rose daily to 103° and 104°. We were pitched amongst great quantities of liquorice and camel-thorn.

On the 26th I went to the Baugh-i-No to take the hot bath. I was first introduced into an outer room, where I undressed, and then proceeded to the bath-room, which was filled with steam from a great body of hot water contained in a cistern in one corner. I had no sooner entered than a man came up to me and threw half a dozen buckets of hot water over me, which nearly deprived me of breath. I then sat down, and he soaped my head; then taking my hands, he rubbed them with a hair glove: he did the same to my feet; then more hot water was thrown over me, whilst stretched at length on my back upon the stone floor. He next applied the colouring matter, being the pulverized leaves of indigo, which he laid on in a thick paste upon my mustachios and eyebrows: he then shampooed me, and rubbed me with the hair glove, which cleaned me most effectually. My hair was then washed with a scented clay; I

was

was soused again with hot water, and the operation being completed, I found myself quite supple, with my eyebrows, &c. dyed a beautiful black. I was very careful not to catch cold after coming out of the heated room. A couple of tomauns is the usual sum to give to the dullak or operator.

CHAPTER VI.

Zergoon......Bund Emir......Ruins of Persepolis......Sculptures...... Futteabad. .... Mayen......Imaum Zada Ismael...... Oojan...... Aspas......Kiosk-ki-zurd......Deygurdoo......Yezdikhurst......Muksoodbeggee......Pigeons...... Ghomesha......Ma yar ......Ispahanek.

On the 27th June we marched from Shiraz for Zergoon, distant sixteen miles: the road was a very bad one, and Zergoon an insignificant place. Fevers now began to appear in camp; they were of an intermittent character, and prevailed chiefly amongst the Indians. The appearance of the camp was very respectable; besides ten large tents, there were a great number of small ones for servants and followers. The Envoy had five hundred mules; and the whole number of horses and mules was a thousand.

Next day we marched to Bund Emir, distant sixteen miles. I cannot refrain from inserting the following beautiful lines on the Bund Emir in *Lalla Rookh*:

> There's a bower of roses by Bund Emir's stream,
> And the nightingale sings round it all the day long;
> In the time of my childhood 'twas like a sweet dream,
> To sit in the roses and hear the bird's song.
> That bower and its music I never forget,
> But oft, when alone in the bloom of the year,
> I think, is the nightingale singing there yet?
> Are the roses still bright by the calm Bund Emir?

We neither saw rose-bowers, nor heard the soft warbling of the bulbul.

bulbul. Weeping willows hung over and dipped into the stream, which dashed with a loud rushing noise through the arches of the bridge, sending up clouds of vapour from the white spray and foam of its broken waters.

There is here a large and strong stone dam across a deep stream: on the top of the dam is a substantial bridge of a dozen arches, without parapets. The purpose of the dam is to give a fall to the water, in order to turn mills. Fish are so numerous here that ten thousand graylings were caught in a few hours, in nets, many of a large size. Bund Emir is in the plain of Merdesht: a small stream, dignified by the appellation of the Cyrus, and which Strabo mentions that Alexander crossed in going to Persepolis, joins the Bund Emir stream at the village. Several pelicans were seen here, though I was not fortunate enough to obtain a sight of one. A wild sheep or kooch, which had been shot in the hills, was brought into camp: it had the horns of the common English sheep, but instead of wool it was covered with hair, similar in colour and texture to that of the deer; the tail, likewise, was hairy and not woolly, and the legs were longer than those of the common sheep.

We left in the evening, intending to march to the celebrated Tukht-i-Jumshed, or Persepolis, fourteen miles distant. I was in company with another officer, but we had not proceeded far before we lost our road. We went to a village in order to procure a guide. After a great deal of intreaty one was persuaded to accompany us, with the promise of a reward; but he had not preceded us far when a large body of the villagers pursued us, calling on our guide to go back, and not to shew us the road. We of course would not allow him to return to his companions. The villagers, seeing this, ran up, seized

seized him, and were carrying him off: we remonstrated with them; they abused us grossly and threatened us: we charged them, and a considerable scuffle ensued: however, we succeeded in carrying the guide with us; but, as may naturally be supposed, he proved a faithless one, and led us into the midst of water-courses, from which we could not extricate ourselves. After wandering about for an hour or two, we were at last obliged to throw down our cots and betake ourselves to sleep.

It is the river Kur (Cyrus) which forms these water-courses: its stream is divided into innumerable channels, for the purpose of irrigating the plain of Merdesht. A beetle, called the *seen*, had this year proved very destructive to the crops in the plain, and the ignorant peasants said that it was occasioned by the Europeans having broken a talisman which existed amongst the ruins of Persepolis, and which used to preserve the grain from injury. Colonel Stannus, the year before, disinterred a number of sculptured stones, capitals of columns, &c.: a flight of locusts appeared a few days afterwards, and the peasants immediately set to work and carefully covered up what the Colonel had taken so much pains to reveal. This shews to what ridiculous causes ignorant men sometimes attribute their misfortunes.

On awaking we observed the pillars of the palace of Persepolis rising grey in front of a dark hill, and about a fursung off. We quickly mounted, and attempted to ride towards them and the tents; but it was a couple of hours before we reached them, being impeded by the swampy ground.

The ruins from the plain have a very imposing appearance, rising on a platform fifty feet in height, which is built of huge stones.

 The

The length of the platform is fifteen hundred feet. Towards the northward of the platform is a double flight of easy steps, of blue marble veined with quartz. At the top are four walls, two pillars between them, and the bases of two others. On the walls are the figures of winged bulls, of colossal size. The whole may have formed part of a gateway. Near is a stone cistern for water. Proceeding onwards is another double flight of steps, on the front of which are sculptured an immense number of figures, with high caps, in procession. Having surmounted the few steps leading to the highest part of the platform, we got amongst the pillars, thirteen of which only are now standing: there are the traces of forty. Those which exist are very elegant and lofty, with a fluted shaft; they exhibit the appearance of very great antiquity, and are composed of greyish marble, which takes an excellent polish, and yields easily to the hammer. These pillars, some assert, supported a roof of wood, which was consumed when Alexander wantonly set fire to the building, at the instigation of the courtesan Thais. The Khutkhoda of the neighbouring village said that the tradition was that the roof was a net-work of iron. Proceeding to the southward are seen the remains of apartments: they are square enclosures; the sides of the doors are sculptured. There are four figures of a king stabbing a horned lion in the belly. Near the hill there is an immense square enclosure, which seems to have been the principal residence. Through different parts of the platform run narrow subterranean passages, originally perhaps aqueducts. The marble of the square enclosures is jet black. In many parts of the ruins are square tablets, inscribed with the arrow-headed characters, which have hitherto defied interpretation.

To

To attempt to describe more fully these ruins and sculptures, an office which has been so often and so ably performed by former travellers, would be superfluous: the above is merely a short general sketch, to explain the accompanying print. Behind the ruins, on the platform, are two sepulchres on the hill, a considerable portion of which has been scarped, and the smooth rock sculptured: at the bottom of the scarp is an opening in the rock, into which having crawled, I entered a small apartment, wherein I perceived oven-shaped recesses, which probably contained the bodies. There is a third round to the southward, which has never yet been entered.

All along the crest of the hill above the ruins are seen the remains of fortifications, consisting of dilapidated stone walls. Many travellers assert that there could have been no city of any size within many miles of the palace, from there being no remains of buildings in the plain; but the peasants are constantly turning up immense quantities of bricks in every part of the valley, from the hill fort of Istakar to the northward as far as Bund Emir: consequently there must have been an immense city here.

On the 30th, a party proceeded to Nukshee Rujub and Nukshee Rustum, to view the sculptures and sepulchres. The first is about a mile and a half from Persepolis. Here are sculptures on the rocks, similar to those at Shapoor, of one king delivering to another the circlet of royalty: other sculptures represent kings mounted on horseback, with attendants on foot behind them, &c. Nukshee Rustum (which, by the way, is the general name throughout the country for sculptures of any sort) is a fursung from Persepolis. Here are several sepulchres similar to those at Persepolis, but more difficult of access. Several sculptures represent a combat between two horsemen, but unfortunately they have been very much defaced: the execution is very spirited. Here is also the Shapoor sculpture of the two mounted kings, one presenting the ring to the other.

Colonel Macdonald employed people in clearing away the earth from a staircase, and made the interesting discovery of a chimerical figure representing a lion or dragon winged, with a human head, resting one of its paws on a lotus-flower, supported by a stem like that of the date tree. No similar figure had ever previously been discovered at Persepolis. Four figures mounting steps were also brought to light: they seem to be employed in carrying viands requisite for a feast. The first bears two cups, the second a covered goblet, the third a lamb, and the fourth a skin either of water or wine.

The sickness in camp to-day increased to a most alarming extent. Every instant there was a fresh patient: not only the Indians, but also many Persians were taken ill. Bilious and intermittent fevers were the prevailing diseases. Most of the Europeans were likewise laid up. In attempting to sketch a sculpture which had been exposed by Colonel Stannus, representing nine men with high caps, curled hair, and armed with spears, bows and arrows, marching from one side towards a tablet of arrow-headed characters, and nine similar figures advancing from the opposite side towards the same tablet, I found that my hand trembled so much that I was unable to hold the pencil: I was consequently forced to desist, and in the evening was so ill with a slow fever, that I could not sit on horseback, and was obliged to proceed in a *cajava*. These are panniers made of wood, with plank bottoms, and covered with cloth: a mule carries

PERSEPOLITAN PROCESSION.

carries two of them. They are four feet in length, therefore the person carried is forced to remain in an upright sitting posture during the whole journey, with the constant risk of getting his head broken against the sides of the conveyance, than which a more disagreeable one I never travelled in. The *tukt-i-rowan* is comparatively a pleasant vehicle: it consists of a frame similar to that of the *cajava*, with a round top, and is covered with cloth; it is carried by two mules on a couple of poles. Spare mules accompany it, to change as occasion requires; on one of these the driver rides. A man walks by the side of the vehicle to steady it where the road is rough. We had only one of these in camp, and three sets of cajavas.

On the 1st of July we reached Futeabad, distant from Tukht-i-Jumshed three fursungs, a miserable village.

Next day we arrived at Mayen, six fursungs; on the road to which we passed a good bridge, near the ancient and impregnable fort of Istakar, at the foot of the perpendicular rock of which numerous flocks of sheep were grazing, the property of the Prince of Shiraz. It is usual in Persia for a proprietor of sheep to give the charge of five hundred, if he possess that number, to one shepherd, who pays yearly to the owner a maund (or seven pounds) of butter for each sheep. In Persia butter is prepared from the milk of ewes.

Mayen is much superior to the usual character of Persian towns: it is surrounded by numerous gardens, in which was abundance of fruit. The approach to it is also very romantic; the road winding along the foot of beautiful hills, below which were extensive rice-fields. Thirty-five pounds of rice were sold for one real, little more than a shilling.

We halted next day, the sickness increasing.

On

On the 4th we marched to Imaum Zada Ismael, three fursungs, a small town in a narrow valley, distinguished by a dome. Here are ten families of Syeds, which number causes the place to be exempt from taxes, as they are considered particularly sacred, being descendants of the Prophet. The town, or village rather, is not obliged to provide the *Sursát*, or supply provisions, which all the other places had done through which we had passed. Instead of snow we now got beautifully clear ice from the hills to cool our liquors. What a luxury in a hot climate, to have snow or ice throughout the most disagreeable months of the year, and that in such abundance, that even our servants were enabled to indulge themselves with it! Fruit, too, was almost every where to be procured in the greatest plenty. Apricots were a drug, they were so common; the same may be said of melons and plums. It is incredible what quantities of fruit a Persian will eat: many will devour sixteen melons before breakfast.

We marched on the 5th to Oojan, distant four fursungs. Surmounted a not very steep kootul, called that of Imaum Zada Ismael: the air at the top I found exceedingly bracing and refreshing. I rode a mule for the first time, it being thought preferable to a horse for a patient (I had not ventured into a *cajava* after the journey from Persepolis to Futeabad). I found its paces very pleasant, but it was extremely difficult to guide; and the only mode in which I could manage it was by hitting it on the side of the head with a large stick, striking according to the direction in which I wished it to go. Riding-mules in Persia fetch as high prices as horses. I have seen a white mule which cost a thousand Persian rupees: white is the favourite colour for a riding mule.

We descended into the Vale of Heroes, the favourite hunting-field of of King Byramghour, &c. By the road-side I observed a tree very similar to that which produces the gum mastick. The village of Oojan is completely uninhabited, and of course in ruins. We were agreeably surprised at finding a part of the dilapidated caravanserai occupied by an English traveller, Mr. Giberne, of the Bombay Civil Service, who was proceeding overland to India.

We halted next day on account of the sick, whose numbers unfortunately did not decrease. The attentions of the Envoy's lady to the sick were unremitting; and it was quite distressing to see the hard duty our most attentive doctor had to perform, running about the whole day, exposed to the baneful influence of a powerful sun (in a large tent the thermometer rose to 105°), to administer to the distressed; and the moment he approached his own tent, he was surrounded by a crowd of Illyauts, many of whose encampments were near us. We found the Mehmandar to be particularly disobliging: it was with difficulty he could be induced to halt. He was desirous (for reasons best known to himself) of hurrying on at a furious rate, seven and eight fursungs per day, which would have killed half of the invalids in a march or two.

On the 7th we marched to Aspas, three fursungs. Here is the fatal pool, or rather fountain, in which King Byramghour was drowned, whilst in pursuit of the wild ass: two serjeants who accompanied the last mission of Sir John Malcolm lost their lives in the same place. The pool seems to be of considerable depth, but there is only a small part free from sedges and flags.

Next day we marched to Kiosk-i-zurd, or Yellow Palace, five fursungs, which completely knocked up the sick. However the thermometer was lower here, probably owing to the great quantities of snow

snow on the hills around us. There is here a most excellent caravanserai.

We halted on the 9th, and next day marched to Deygurdoo, or the village of walnuts, seven fursungs (twenty-eight miles). This was a most terrible march. I was myself now fortunately convalescent; for after lingering with a slow fever for several days, I had three smart attacks of intermittent, of which I was cured by that invaluable medicine *quinine*, so that I did not feel it so much as the rest. This we owed to our *considerate* Mehmandar, who pretended that he could get no supplies nearer, though he might easily have arranged to take them on half way from Kiosk-i-zurd.

On the 11th we marched to Yezdikhurst, thirty miles. The sick were now reduced to such extremity that the doctor pronounced them incapable of proceeding farther; it was therefore determined that they should be left here, and brought on by easy stages to Ispahan, if they recovered. Four Europeans were very dangerously ill.

Yezdikhurst is a very remarkable place; its site is singular in the extreme. The town and fort are built on an insulated rock, which is seated in a deep valley, dividing the provinces of Irak or Media, and Persia or Fars, the original kingdom of Cyrus. The rock consists of conglomerates, being rounded pebbles of quartz, serpentine, and limestone, united by a calcareous cement. The soil round Yezdikhurst seemed impregnated with iron. At the bottom of the rock are an immense number of subterranean chambers. The town and fort are entered by a narrow bridge thrown across a deep ditch: the former consists of a single street, and is partly covered in; the houses are generally of three stories, with small staircases and

galleries.

galleries. There is here an ancient church, in which is preserved a round piece of marble, representing the sun, which had been an emblem worshipped by the Sabians. In the extensive burial-grounds in the vicinity of the town are many sepulchres, on which are a lion and a sword. These are the graves of Persian puhilwans or heroes.

There is a saying in Persia, that to live happy, a man must have a wife of Yezd, eat of the bread of Yezdikhurst, and drink of the wine of Shiraz.

A horrible tragedy was acted in Yezdikhurst in 1779. The usurper, Zackee Khan, entered the place and made a demand on the inhabitants for a large sum of money. They were unable to comply with his exorbitant claim; upon which he ordered twenty of the principal inhabitants to be thrown from a lofty window, and they were instantly dashed amongst the rocks below. The attendants, conceiving a sudden disgust at the horrible cruelty of their master, despatched him with their daggers.

The valley of Yezdikhurst is cultivated throughout, and there is excellent shooting along its sides. Here died Mr. George Malcolm, of the Bombay Civil Service, a young man of first-rate abilities and the most amiable disposition: also Mr. Steuart, treasurer of the mission.

On the 13th we marched to Muksoodbeggee, twenty-four miles, on the road to which we saw the *oshauk*, or gum ammoniac plant, the stalk of which was three feet in height, and jointed like that of the sugar-cane. Muksoodbeggee is a ruinous village, but on a very rich soil. There is a large pigeon-house here, a round tower fifty feet in height, on the top of which is a small one with orifices for the entrance of the pigeons. The inside of the large tower is perforated with holes, which form comfortable nests.

Persians

Persians never eat pigeons: they are kept in these immense dove-cots for the sake of their dung, which is used in the melon-grounds. All the way to Ispahan from hence, and round that city, pigeon-towers are to be seen in every direction; but most of them are now tenantless. The Persians say that formerly it was extremely dangerous to approach a pigeon-tower; for if a person happened to cough near one, such crowds of pigeons rushed out, that the intruder would instantly be knocked down and stunned.

Next day we reached Ghomesha, twelve miles, on the road to which we met Major Hart (the generalissimo of the army of the Heir-Apparent), and Mr. Clarke, of the Bengal Civil Service, who had accompanied Mr. Giberne overland from England.

The former of these gentlemen came down to meet and accompany the Envoy to court, and was attended by twelve begzadas, who are sons of men of rank, and serve as cadets, in expectation of commissions in the regular battalions. We heard now for the first time that the King was determined to go to war with Russia, on account of the old dispute respecting boundaries.

Ghomesha was one of the largest and most flourishing towns we had yet seen; the walls and bastions were in excellent order, and the country around was highly cultivated. Here, in a garden, is the tomb of a saint, by name Shah Reza, who has reposed here for seven hundred years: in the garden are several tanks of sacred fish. Some delicious nectarines were brought us by the head-man.

On the 15th we came to Mayar, sixteen miles; where the lime-stone rock disappeared, the hills being composed of red sand-stone. Here we were met by Nujuf Coollee Khan, who had been sent by the Governor of Ispahan to escort us to the ancient metropolis.

His

His office was that of Nasukchee Bashee, who is similar to our Earl Marshal, and an officer of primary importance.

Next day we reached Ispahanek, twenty-four miles: this was a most disagreeable march. In descending a dangerous kootul, near the bottom I had a very narrow escape, my horse slipping and falling on its side upon a smooth ledge of rock; I had just time to throw myself off before he touched the ground.

We marched next day for Ispahan, distant two fursungs. Shortly after leaving Ispahanek, we passed old Ispahanek, an inconsiderable round fort, but with a very broad and deep wet ditch. This place, however, inconsiderable as it seems, was defended successfully against the Affghans, under Nadir Shah, and more recently held out for several months against the whole Persian army, upon the following occasion. A year after his present Majesty ascended the throne, a brother of his, Hussain Coollee Khan, rose up in rebellion against him. He, however, first placed his wives and treasure in Ispahanek, as a place of greater security than Ispahan, where he happened to be living; he then took the field against his brother, but having met with reverses, fled for refuge to the asylum at Koom, the tomb of Fatima; but after some time he gave himself up to Futteh Allee Shah, who several years afterwards deprived him of sight.

CHAPTER VII.

Arrival at Ispahan......Istakball..... Khoosroo Khan......Visit to the Prince......Visit to the Governor......The Califa......Dined with the Mehmandar.

At the distance of a fursung from Ispahan, which we saw dimly stretched out below us, we heard symptoms of the approaching *Istakball*, or deputation sent out to meet the Envoy, *viz.* the firing of matchlocks and the rushing noise of horsemen: by-and-bye we observed large bodies of horse and foot advancing towards us, and upon drawing nearer we found regular streets formed of matchlock-men, drawn out in very regular order. After we had passed them they discharged their fire-arms, ran forward, and formed another long street. Every horse in Ispahan had been put in requisition; steeds of all sorts and sizes, from the stately *Toorkoman* * to the miserable *yaboo*. The crowd, dust, and noise were tremendous: *furashes* running about in every direction, and using their sticks, with very powerful effect; pieces discharged close to one's ear, with a thick canopy of dust overshadowing us: really the honour was too great. We were met by the master of the ceremonies and many khans. We

* The Toorkoman horses have frequently wounds in the neck, arising from the following cause: the Toorkomans, in their marauding expeditions, often run short of provisions; to guard against which, they carry a bag of flour, and when reduced to necessity they bleed their horses in the neck, and mix the blood with the flour, which they form into cakes on the fire.

We passed close to one of the walls, and found a body of Armenian priests in their holiday clothes and high-peaked black caps, standing ready to salute us. They had richly-gilt standards, representing the crucifixion; and altogether the sight of these men, who were using their best endeavours to do honour to their fellow Christians, was most gratifying.

Passing through a gateway, we entered a beautiful avenue of plane-trees, planted in four rows. On each side were lofty walls, in which were arches of open brick-work: on the other side of the walls were gardens. The roads in the avenue had been watered, and there were basins and tanks of water at intervals. Passing through another gateway, we dismounted at the palace of Saadatabad. This is a lofty edifice, with twelve pillars in front of the hall of audience, which is composed almost entirely of looking-glasses. In the centre of the twelve pillars is a tank of water, into which lions (supporting the pillars at the four corners of the tank) disgorged water. Numerous piles of fruit, interspersed with bouquets of flowers, surrounded the water, and carpeted the floor of the Diwan Khana.

We passed on to the Huft Dust, or seven suites of apartments, which was destined for our residence; the appearance of the place, and coolness of the atmosphere, were quite refreshing, after having been half-roasted under canvas. The Huft Dust is a large square with suites of apartments on three sides, and a palace on the fourth: they all face inwards, as is the case in caravanserais. In the centre was a garden, in which were some ancient chinar trees and very lofty pine-firs. Tame antelopes bounded through the little glades formed by the fruit-trees, and small canals of water ran along the centre of the walks. The rooms were lofty, and the walls being of of great thickness, the thermometer very seldom rose many degrees above 80°. What a change from 105° in tents!

Shortly after our arrival, a deputation from the merchants of Ispahan came to wait on the Envoy. Many of them were men of highly respectable appearance; they mostly wore large white shawl turbans: they complained that last year they had suffered heavy losses; they had sent down considerable investments of silk to India, and had brought up indigo, in both of which, they said, they had been no gainers.

In the evening we performed a very melancholy but sacred duty, consigning to the earth the mortal remains of Mr. Rich, Dr. Taylor, Mr. George Malcolm, and Mr. Steuart. The bodies of the two last had been brought from Yezdikhurst to be deposited with the bones of the former in consecrated ground, *viz.* in the Armenian burial-ground, in the square of the cathedral in Joolpha, or the Armenian suburb of Ispahan. We left the Huft Dust, and proceeded along the south bank of the Zainderood river (the fish of which are poisonous, and seemingly the water also, as our horses would not drink of it), which flows close under the walls of the Huft Dust. We passed under the arches of an aqueduct which crosses the river, and after riding three-quarters of a mile, approached a noble bridge of thirty-three arches, with arcades on each side for foot passengers. We entered Joolpha, which formerly was a city of itself, and owed its origin to the illustrious Shah Abbas, who transferred the inhabitants of Joolpha in Armenia to this new Joolpha, in order that by trading they might attract a greater resort of merchants and wealth to the capital. Where there were formerly thousands of families, there are now only three hundred; which, estimating the

number

number of souls in each at five, gives fifteen hundred. Lofty sun-dried brick walls, narrow streets, and strong doors, was all we saw of Joolpha, until our arrival at the cathedral. This is a lofty edifice, surmounted by a dome, in a small square; opposite the entrance to the cathedral is a handsome belfry, in which is a chime of four bells.

The graves were in one corner of the square, near to that of Doctor Jukes, who died at Ispahan of fever, whilst proceeding to court on a private mission from Bombay. Besides his we did not discover the grave of another European in the enclosure. There were in attendance at the solemn ceremony one califa or archbishop, twelve bishops, and forty priests, besides boys bearing candles, &c.: for all which, of course, a very handsome present was given, and also a donation to the church.

At six A. M. on the 18th, Khoosroo Khan, the Governor of Ispahan and its dependencies, visited the Envoy. He is a Georgian, thirty years of age, strong made, and with a frank open countenance. He has not been a year governor. His history is as follows: He is of noble parentage, and was at fifteen a cadet in the Russian service. At this age he was taken prisoner by the Persians, and emasculated. The king took him into his service, kept him near his own person, and finding him brave and trust-worthy, advanced him to the important situation which he now holds.

In the evening of the ensuing day we crossed the Zainderood by a small bridge near the Huft Dust, but built on the same plan as the long one formerly mentioned, and passed down for a considerable distance one of the splendid avenues of chinar trees. It being Thursday, when most of the inhabitants free themselves from their occupations,

occupations, we were met by crowds of men on horseback, rattling over the stones at a furious rate, and leaving the dusky walls of the town for the gardens and cool avenues outside. We passed through several small arched bazars, covered in with lofty arcades, in the same manner as that of Shiraz. As usual, the quantities of fruit exposed for sale were enormous: we observed some very fine pears amongst the heaps.

At a sharp turn we came unexpectedly on the grand Meidan-i-Shah. This is a very large square, or rather parallelogram, formed by buildings of two stories high, formerly used as barracks for the troops. In the centre of the west side is the splendid and lofty gateway of Allee Copee, in the bala khana, or upper story of which, the mighty Shah Abbas used to sit and witness the evolutions of his troops below, and the dexterity of his nobles in firing at the popinjay, which was suspended to the pole in the centre of the Meidan. On the south side is the Musjid-i-Shah, or king's mosque, surmounted by a dome covered with blue enamelled tiles; on the east side is the mosque of Lootf Ulla; and on the north, the entrance to the large bazar, extending for several miles, and all covered in. It was sunset, and the enamelled covering of the mosques was glittering from the evening rays, when all of a sudden the awakening sound of trumpets and drums attracted our attention to a gallery near the entrance to the great bazar. On inquiry we found that it was the King's band, which plays here every evening at sunset.

We left the Meidan-i-Shah, and passing through several streets and alleys, entered another noble avenue, the trees in which were of great size, and one hundred and fifty years old. We drew up at the entrance to the palace of the Husht-i-Behisht, or eight paradises, so called

called from its being an octagon with eight doors. This was the palace first destined for the accommodation of the mission. We found it to be a beautiful building, in the midst of a garden thickly planted with trees, with great abundance of water, the canals being large and overflowing. I observed in the garden trees loaded with black and white mulberries. There were no outhouses, and no accommodation except for the Envoy and his lady, which was the reason of the Huft Dust having the preference. We then went to the Mudersa, or college. We found it to be a square surrounding a garden: on one side was a large and beautiful mosque. Round the square were the apartments for the professors and students. One of the latter I observed attentively perusing a manuscript: I went up and asked him what it was, and found it to be a translation of the Pentateuch! Upon inquiry I learned that physic, theology, logic, astronomy, astrology, &c. are taught here, and that a great part of the students are from Mazanderan. Leaving this oriental Alma Mater, we passed down the long and shady avenue, crossed the splendid bridge of thirty-three arches, and returned to the Huft Dust.

On the 20th we visited the Prince of Ispahan, a favourite son of the King, named Sultaun Mahomed Mirza. We were prevented from setting out till near eight A. M., in consequence of a great dispute regarding the place which the Envoy was to occupy during the audience. Khoosroo Khan, the governor, and prim e ministerto the Prince, the master of the ceremonies, and other of his advisers (for the Prince himself is only fourteen years of age, and of course is directed in every thing by them), were desirous of seating the Prince in an inner room, the Envoy and suite in an outer, with a window between us and his Royal Highness, which would have been excessively degrading to the Envoy. Of course he would not listen for a moment to such an insulting proposal, but insisted upon sitting at the corner of the same numud, or painted felt carpet, on which the Prince sat, in the same manner as he had done at Shiraz; and if this were not conceded he positively declined visiting the Prince at all. At last, after a great deal of trouble and delay, Major Hart, who was well acquainted with all those in authority at Ispahan, prevailed upon them to give up the point, and we left in state for the palace of the Imarat-i-no, or new residence built for the residence of his present Majesty, whenever he visits the ancient metropolis.

On our arrival at the garden-gate we were received by the master of the ceremonies, and conducted through long and well-ordered files of musketeers, matchlock-men, men bearing iron maces, nasukchees (or executioners) with high shawl turbans, &c., to the front of a most splendid hall of audience, in which, on a high musnud or cushion, was seated the young Prince. We bowed, as at Shiraz, and were conducted into his presence. He was a handsome young man with a florid complexion. We had neither smoking nor coffee-drinking, as it seems they are always dispensed with at Ispahan. On two sides of the Diwan Khana, which far exceeded in size and splendour of decoration any thing we had seen at Shiraz, were hung large green curtains, covering pictures of Futteh Allee Shah. These curtains had been put up for the occasion, in order that we might not sit in the actual presence of his Majesty. We staid but a brief space, and returned through a burning sun to our comfortable quarters.

In the evening I rode through two or three miles of the large bazar: truly it was a most extraordinary scene. The quantities of of merchandize exposed for sale were immense, and the hum of so many voices under the lofty arcade, with which the whole extent was covered, securing the traders from the sun and weather, had a very peculiar effect. But not now, as in the days of Shah Abbas the Great, and until the Afgan invasion, were there varieties of costume indicating merchants from foreign countries. The black Persian cap universally prevailed, and I did not even observe an Arab amongst the throng. What must attract the notice of every stranger in visiting this bazar, is the peculiar mode of beating out the cotton, which is done by means of a large and thick bow and string: the operation causes a loud buzzing sound. Ispahan is the great mart for the turquoise, which is procured from the mines at Nishapore.

We entered from the bazar the house of the native agents to the mission, where we were regaled with fruit and sweetmeats. The two old men, brothers, devoured no small quantity of opium whilst we sat with them.

On the 21st we visited Khoosroo Khan, the governor. We found him seated in a most delightful private room, in which a *jet d'eau* cooled the air. In the court were files of matchlock-men and musketeers, and in a corner lay a large ibex, just killed. We were received by Khoosroo Khan in his usual frank and engaging manner, and, contrary to the stiff formality and ridiculous ceremonies attending common Persian visits, we laughed, talked, and joked with him for a couple of hours. He was very anxious to become a freemason, but time could not be spared to initiate him in the mysteries of the craft. Alluding to the dispute between him and Major Hart regarding the audience, he said at parting, that he would settle it by

 fighting

fighting the Major with either sword or pistol. Another observation the Governor made in the course of conversation was this: he said there were four things which constituted happiness in this life; good sense, a good horse, a good sword, and the fourth (which, he added with a sigh, I can never enjoy) a good wife.

From the palace of the Governor we repaired to that of the Chehel Setoon, or forty pillars. This is certainly a splendid edifice, but the time to view it to advantage is at sunset: the rays strike at that time directly into the hall of audience, and produce the most beautiful prismatic colours, from the innumerable mirrors, &c. with which it is covered. There are in reality only twenty pillars; but these are reflected in a square tank in the midst of them, at the corners of which are lions, as at Saadatabad. Behind the hall of audience is a magnificent banqueting-room. In this there are six large pictures painted in fresco, representing battle-scenes, feasts, &c. In the foreground of one of the battle-pieces is an old man expiring from a wound in the chest, the expression of whose countenance in the last agonies is so far superior to the usual productions of Persians, that it is highly probable it was painted by an European artist.

We had now frequent occasion to use the bastinado, our servants playing a number of tricks which required the fuluk. The operation is peculiar, and is performed as follows. The culprit seats himself on the ground, elevates his feet, which are put into a loose noose in the middle of a fuluk, or stout stick, held by two furashes, or carpet-spreaders; the stick is then twisted, which effectually prevents the offender from withdrawing his feet, and exposes the soles to the strokes of willow-rods applied by two other furashes standing

in

in front. They frequently miss the soles on purpose, and break their sticks over the fuluk, especially if the person operated on pays them well; but turning up the heels of one of the executioners prevents a repetition of this. Miserable is the condition of the unfortunate Armenian who may be subjected to this punishment: his toes are seen to hang down after a few strokes, and not unfrequently the nails are torn from his feet! Persians generally endeavour to spare their fellow Musselmans, if they can do so with impunity; but to a Christian no mercy is shewn. So little sense of shame the Persians feel, that a person even of rank and family does not consider himself disgraced by having his soles turned up. His Majesty punishes his nobles frequently in this manner.

On the 23d we visited the Califa, or Armenian Archbishop, in Joolpha. When the Afgans invaded Persia, and took and sacked Ispahan, in 1720, Joolpha fell first; they then got possession of the bridges, and lastly the city. Though it at that time contained a million of inhabitants, twenty thousand Afgans obtained possession of it without much loss. The present population of Ispahan is two hundred and fifty thousand.

We first inspected the cathedral, which is very lofty: the walls are adorned with pictures of our Saviour, the Apostles, Saints, &c. There is here a very ponderous bible, to visit which Armenians perform long pilgrimages. We went in rear of the cathedral, through a small garden, in which was abundance of marygolds, pinks, and carnations, to the house of the Archbishop. We found him in a small room, in the centre of which was a table loaded with fruit of every kind. I observed several shrines round the room, with curtains before them, containing images probably. The Archbishop

bishop was a grave and mild-looking personage, about forty-five years of age. He and his fellow priests spoke in bitter terms of some Armenians who two or three days before had become renegades to their religion, and turned Musselmans, from worldly motives.

On the 24th the young Prince was taken seriously ill with fever. Forty sheep were sacrificed on the occasion, to allay the violence of the disease.

In the evening of the next day we partook of a splendid collation of fruit and sweetmeats, with the Governor, in the palace of the Husht-i-Behisht. Trays were placed before every two, and after smoking, tea and coffee-drinking, most delicious ices were brought in. They were in square and oblong cakes, of every variety: cherry, cream, nectarine, rose-water, &c. The Persians excel in the preparation of ices.

On the 26th we dined with our Mehmandar, Mirza Abool Cassim. In proceeding thither, a Persian salaamed to us in a very respectful manner, and not thinking we observed him, immediately turned to some of his companions and made grimaces. A few cuts from Major Hart's whip gave a different expression to his features. This is not an unusual practice in Persia. We got to the Mehmandar's house, situated at the opposite extremity of the bazar, about six or seven miles off, at six. After an hour spent in smoking, fruit-eating, &c. (for the Persians always eat the fruit and sweetmeats before the more substantial part of the meal, and which is probably the most wholesome way), the fruit, &c. were removed, long coloured cloths were spread before us, seated cross-legged on the ground, with our hats on or off as suited our convenience, and water was brought in for us to wash our hands. Then two cakes of bread were placed before each; one

one a large and soft one, to serve as a plate, and the other hard baked, to eat. Large wax candles were set in a row in the middle of the floor, and round trays, containing iced sherbets of rose-water, milk, zegunzabeen, with large pear-tree spoons to sip them with, were placed between every two persons. Pillaus, rice, kababs (or roasted meat kept warm between two cakes), and fowls over-roasted, in order that we might pull them in pieces with ease, were then introduced, with a profusion of other substantial fare; and at the bismallah, or a signal from the host, the feast commenced. All the viands were excessively greasy, yet they seemed to please the palates of the Mehmandar and three or four Persian friends of his. I must say, I was well pleased when at last the cloths were drawn, and hot water was brought in wherewith to cleanse our right hand and mouth, for the left is not permitted to assist. After some more smoking, we left at half-past eight.

CHAPTER VIII.

March from Ispahan......Fire Temple.......Nujufabad.......Teiran.......Askeran...... Domina......Wo Nishan......Proneness of the Persians to falsehood......Ill behaviour of the Mehmandar.......Komin.......Gilpacgah.......Hoormabad........Amarut....... Dancing boy......Khooshbajan......Insolence of the Mehmandar......Khoondab...... Sickness......Kurdahoor......Bactiari Robbers......Affray with the Townsmen of Kurdahoor......Gallantry of a Tailor......Barwund.

On the 28th of July we marched from Ispahan to Nujufabad, distant twenty miles, on route to the royal camp at Sultaneah.

We passed through Joolpha, and endless avenues, lanes, and gardens. About two fursungs distant from the Huft Dust we arrived at the Atush Gah, or fire temple; it is seated on the top of a small and very steep hill, three hundred feet above the level of the fertile plain of Ispahan. We dismounted and ascended to inspect it. We found on the summit a number of ruinous edifices, built after the Babylonish mode of large sun-dried bricks, with a layer of reeds between. The temple itself was a small circular building surmounted with a dome, and having nine doors. We disturbed a number of jackalls on the top of the hill, which commanded a beautiful view of the city, its numerous suburbs, and highly cultivated environs. The rock on which we stood was indurated sandstone.

The road from hence to Nujufabad was intersected by ravines, water-courses, and dangerous kunauts. On our arrival at Nujufabad we found it to be a large and flourishing town, and the Kutkhoda's house,

house, or rather palace, he gave up to the Envoy. Nujufabad contains four thousand families, or twenty thousand inhabitants. Its history is as follows: Shah Abbas was sending a camel-load of treasure to Nujuf, where repose the bones of Allee. The camel, with its precious burden, got as far as the site of the town in question, where it lay down, and could not be induced to rise again. The circumstance was reported to his Majesty, who the same night had a dream, in which an angel appeared to him and commanded him to found a city at Nujufabad, where the camel had lain down with the treasure which it bore, instead of sending it to the tomb of Allee. He did so, and also brought from a great distance a large stream of water, which abundantly supplies the town and neighbourhood.

We here were presented with very fine black grapes, pears, &c.

We arrived at Teiran, in the district of Karwan, on the 29th, fifteen miles. What a delightful change in the climate from what we had experienced on the other side of Ispahan! At eleven A.M. the thermometer was at 70°, and in the mornings and evenings the air was bracing and invigorating. I felt myself quite alive, after several years of languor in Hindoostan.

Next day we reached Askeran, twenty miles, situated under some very remarkable primitive peaks.

To-day a *cased*, or messenger, brought the news from the royal camp of war having been actually declared between Russia and Persia, and of his Majesty's march for Oojan, nine fursungs from Tabreez, whither it was now our lot to follow him.

On the 31st we arrived at Domina, twenty miles, a small ruinous village. We passed the ruined caravanserai of Mader-i-Shah, at which is a guard of Bac.iaris. The mountains inhabited by this

 savage

savage and untamed race, and forming the frontier between us and Louristan, a country almost wholly unknown, extended on our left from north-west to south-east. If Mr. George Malcolm had been spared, it was the Envoy's intention to have sent him with another person by way of the Koh-i-Zurd, or yellow mountain, through Louristan, by a route untrodden by Europeans, to collect information regarding the internal government, manners, and customs of the Bactiaris. This would have been a most perilous enterprize; but if achieved, a great store of valuable information would have been acquired. The royal treasury receives little or no revenue from the Bactiari tribes.

On the 1st August we were conducted on to the village of Wo Nishan, twenty-eight miles, instead of halting at Konsar, which we passed, on account of the Mehmandar's fear of offending the proprietor, Allee Khan, a son of the King, by causing a deduction of revenue on account of sursat for the Envoy's camp. The village and valley of Konsar are really beautiful. The former is of considerable extent; it principally consists of gardens, in the midst of which are lofty houses. The head-man, with a large retinue, came out to meet the Envoy, and regretted much that he was denied the pleasure of entertaining him. He said that he had sent one thousand tafünchees, or matchlock-men, to join the Royal army (though we learned afterwards that he had not sent one); and that one thousand had gone from Feredoon. We did not need this instance to convince us that lying was the great and national vice of the Persians.

In passing under the walls of the numerous gardens, branches of apple and apricot trees, laden with fruit, hung temptingly over. The

The vine, too, displayed its black and green clusters, but they were not thoroughly ripe. The gowan plant, or that from which the zunzebeen, or manna, is collected, is found in abundance in this neighbourhood. I did not see the plant myself, but it was described to me as two feet in height, with a fan-shaped head, the leaves spinous. The insect which deposits the manna on the leaves and stalks, is said to resemble the musquito. It remains forty-five days feeding on the plant, in the months of August and September: it then vomits on the plant, and leaves a white deposit, which the Persians collect and make a sweetmeat of, called zunzebeen, by boiling it with sugar.

From Ispahan to the northward and westward, Turkish is generally spoken in the villages: the natives hardly understood a single word of Persian in some of the villages which we passed.

The behaviour of our Mehmandar was now quite unpardonable. Although the country in every direction was covered with cultivation, and we were surrounded with plenty, we could procure no barley for our horses, our servants got no rations, and had had none for several days. He evidently took advantage of the forbearance of the Envoy, who was very averse to quarrelling with him, through fear of defeating the object of the mission by raising up enemies at court. He chose, rather than have any altercation with him, to purchase what he wanted. Not only were we deprived of sursat for several days, but our servants were prevented, through the intrigues of the Mehmandar with the Khutkhodas, who of course bribed him handsomely, from purchasing necessaries in the villages. The Envoy at last sent to the Mehmandar (for he was too mighty a man to wait on the Envoy for orders), to endeavour to get some explanation of all

 these

these extraordinary proceedings: the answer returned was, that the Envoy and himself had hitherto been friends, and he hoped they would continue so. His behaviour on our leaving Ispahan was insufferable: he remained two days after the Envoy had gone, without signifying his wish or intention to do so, and sent privately to the Kutkhoda of Nujufabad (the first stage), to endeavour to make us halt there a couple of days.

We reached Komin, in the district of Kumara, distant twenty-eight miles, on the 2d. We passed the village of Imaum Zada, where is the tomb of a saint; and also a large river, in which there is excellent fish. We crossed the river by a good bridge. Gilpaegah we passed on the left; it is the principal town in the district, which is governed by a prince, Hyder Coollee Mirza, who is addicted to the worst vices of the Persians.

Gilpaegah derives its name from having been built in the dried-up bed of a lake (*Gil*, mud; *pae*, the foot, and *gah*, place); for when the people were engaged in the erection of the town their feet were in the mud. The most ridiculous specimen of etymology is exhibited in the alleged derivation of the name of the last village, Wo Nishan. The proprietor of this village ordered it to be built on the banks of a stream which runs past it: after the builders had commenced operations he came to view the progress of the work, and finding that they were not building on the side of the stream, which he intended, he pointed to the opposite side, saying "*wo nishan*," there is the spot; from whence the village derives its name.

Around Komin the country was exceedingly fertile: villages appeared in every direction, attesting sufficiently the productiveness of this wide valley. Twelve hundred men had just left for the Royal camp.

camp. I observed here extensive fields of grain, and considerable quantities of palma christi, or the castor-oil plant.

On a dry grassy ridge a serjeant stated that he had seen a rabbit-warren, but it was found to consist of only a few brown jerboas (*jaculus*), about a foot in length, with white bellies. These animals seldom injure the grain, preferring waste and dry plains to cultivated spots.

Next day we came to Hoormabad, five fursungs and a-half: it was somewhere near this village that Nadir Shah defeated the Afgans. We passed Leihan, an Armenian village, of which there are many in this part of the country. Near Hoormabad herds of antelopes crossed the road, and we heard quails in every direction. That beautiful game-bird the bagaree-kara, or black-breast, one of the varieties of the Persian grouse, constantly winged its noisy flight over our heads. I observed in this neighbourhood great quantities of *echinops*, or globe-thistles, which the Persians call khoja-bashee, or *head-eunuch;* they grew to a very large size. The *centaurea cyanus*, or common blue-bottle, also appeared at every step.

On the 4th we arrived at Amarut, ten miles. The view of this village, and the highly cultivated plain below, is beautiful in the extreme, presenting the very picture of fertility and abundance. Standing on a small hill overlooking the town, and on which were the remains of a citadel, a considerable stream, which seemed to take its rise at the bottom of the hill, was seen to wander amongst the fields. Descending, we found a moordashor, or house for washing the dead, with a long cistern of water in it. Close to this building innumerable springs bubbled up from the ground, and were collected in a pond; in which hearing there were large fish, those provided

provided with rods commenced operations, and quickly caught several dozens of capital dace and tench.

Yega Balakh, or the fountain of the horse, was the ancient name of this village. The tradition explaining the origin of this appellation is as follows. A water-horse formerly inhabited the fountain, to which the people of the surrounding country brought their mares, and the colts afterwards produced were the finest in the world. This reminds one of Sinbad the Sailor, in the "Arabian Nights," when he came to an island which a sea-horse visited for a purpose similar to the above.

The Envoy was now visited daily by the Khans, or lords of the districts through which we passed. Asud Oollah Khan was one of them; a fat merry old fellow, constantly joking and laughing. In riding a stage along with the Envoy who was inquiring regarding the resources and revenue of his district, he replied: "Of what use "is it to tell lies to Europeans? myself and a neighbouring Khan "contrive every year to cheat his Majesty out of a great portion of "the revenue, *ulhumdullilah*, thanks to heaven!" Immediately after, recollecting himself, he said: "For God's sake, do not mention "this to that ugly rascal of a Mehmandar of your's, for the *gorumsak* "would certainly inform the King: he is going about the country "as a spy on the governors of districts, in order to ingratiate him-"self with Futty Allee Shah."

A *baziger*, or dancing boy, exhibited before us at this village: he was dressed in a short jacket, from which depended a profusion of ribands; he wore also a loose gown. He kept time with castanets to the songs of three men (beating tambourines and drums), and danced very gracefully.

We

We arrived at Khooshbajan (pleasant to life), distant twenty miles, on the 5th. We were told that it was on the banks of the river Zurenrood, which flows past this village, that Cyrus (Kai Khoosroo) was born and bred, and that he disappeared from mortal sight on a mountain which lay directly opposite the encampment, called Shah Zinda; and Herodotus distinctly mentions that he was born near Hamadan, the ancient Ecbatana and capital of Media, from which we were only a few marches distant.

The greatest attention and civility were shewn us by the Khan of this district, Hajee Alee Khan, who resides in a delightful upper-storied house seated in the midst of a large garden, close to which we were encamped. He invited us to breakfast. After partaking of delicious fruit, piled up in a very neat manner, trays were introduced, containing pillaus, kababs, different preparations from milk, as moss or acidulated milk, clotted cream, curds, cream-cheeses, and milk sherbet, besides six lambs, roasted whole and brought in on the spits, and a variety of other delicacies. For fifteen people there were one hundred and fifty dishes and thirty different kinds of food, amongst which were some excellent preserves.

Our Mehmandar came in, and, as usual, we all rose to receive him, with the exception of the Envoy, who did not observe his entrance, happening at the time to be looking into the garden. Mirza Abool Cazim sat down with a countenance black with rage, and was in the worst of humours during the whole meal, which lasted from ten till twelve, refusing to eat; and at last when we took leave, he turned his head away without rising. Nobody could divine the cause of his ill-humour at the time: but the Envoy in the course of the day learning the reason, hesitated not to send him an apology

for

for the unintentional affront. To this he had the insolence to return for answer: "Just wait till we get to camp, and you shall see who "I am, and with what honour I shall be received. I have no expec- "tations from the Envoy: I never came down for the sake of lucre, "but I at least expected civility." To this impertinent message the Envoy replied, that he wished to have no farther communication with him, and desired that all intercourse between them might cease. However, next day the Mehmandar, either repenting of his conduct and bearing, or more probably acting by the advice of some friend, sent a most humble apology; premising it, however, by a gross falsehood, *viz.* denying *in toto* that he had sent the above answer to the Envoy's apology for not rising, and concluded by trusting that good fellowship would in future subsist between them. The Envoy answered, that he accepted his apology; and that as this dispute had originated in his not rising on his entrance, he took the opportunity of telling him that amity would exist between them, provided in future he received the gentlemen in his suite with a little more respect than he had done at Shiraz: alluding to three officers who went to visit the Mehmandar in his tent, upon which occasion he assumed a royal privilege, never rose from his numud, but merely pointed to where they were to sit.

In the river there is excellent sport for the fishermen. Roach of three and four pounds were caught with the rod, and loach and barbel of very fine flavour.

Next day we came to Khoondab (signifying in the Pehlevi, much water), twenty miles. The same river, the Zurenrood, flows under the walls of this town, and we had abundance of fish again. The Kaimokam, or second minister of the king, is the proprietor of

Kazeroon,

Kazeroon, a large village which we passed on the road; the hills, as we proceeded, presented a very different appearance to almost all we had hitherto seen, and sufficiently attested an improvement in the climate: instead of arid and sun-burnt ridges, verdure now clothed the hills to their summits.

Sickness again attacked our camp; all the serjeants were laid up with severe bilious fevers, almost all the Indians, and many of the Persians. We learned that the last stages are considered dangerous on account of the water of the river. Great quantities of rice are cultivated, which is irrigated from the hills; the water from the rice fields afterwards flows into the river, carrying with it a slime, which renders the water very unwholesome.

Kurdahoor, the next stage, sixteen miles, we reached the following day. On the road we passed the tombs of four of the royal servants murdered by the Bactiaris, whilst proceeding on a mission to them. The roads are here exceedingly dangerous, on account of this savage and predatory race. We passed an extensive Illyaut encampment, the whole of the inhabitants of which had turned out, and were welcoming the return of their flocks from pasture with prolonged shouts. Near Kurdahoor is an extensive salt lake, and the surface of the ground near it is so saturated with saline matter, that it presents the appearance of a recent fall of snow. The change of temperature was here very great: from 45° an hour before sunrise, the thermometer rose to 100° before mid-day.

In the evening a serious affair occurred, which arose from the following circumstance: The Mehmandar had sent a *bulud*, or guide, to accompany the treasury. The people of the town were not inclined, for some reason unknown to us, to let the man go; accord-

 ingly

ingly a party of them forcibly seized him, and carried him off. One of the escort went after them to bring back the guide; he was attacked with missiles: our party then went to his assistance, when a large body, armed with matchlocks, spears, and swords, issued from the town, and a desperate conflict ensued, which lasted some time. At length the town's-people were driven back and routed, after losing one man killed and many wounded, with a loss on our part of a dozen wounded, three of the escort very severely with spears, and several horses. Our surly Mehmandar, in riding past during the affray, to the great joy of us all, received a blow on the head which unhorsed him.

Mrs. Macdonald's maid had a serio-comic adventure after we had left the ground. A tailor (a Hindoo) and she were riding on a mule in cajavas: they were separated from the rest. Three Illyauts came up to them, thrust their hands into the cajava in which was the fair one, and attempted to pull her out. The valiant tailor slunk back in dismay into a corner of his pannier, and though called upon by the distressed damsel to fire a pistol of a couple of feet in length, which he had got for their mutual defence, he endeavoured to conceal himself as well as he could. The lady defended herself with a tin kettle, until the appearance of some of the muleteers caused the Illyauts to decamp. The tailor, upon being afterwards reproached for his cowardice, swore that he courageously jumped from his cajava and cocked his piece, upon seeing which the Illyauts instantly fled. After he had finished his oration, a muleteer came in and contradicted every word he had said.

The next stage, Barwund, sixteen miles, we reached the ensuing day. We here entered the territory under the jurisdiction of the Prince Royal.

CHAPTER IX.

Arrival at Hamadan, the ancient Ecbatana......Remains of the Palace of Sushan...... News of the war with Russia......Coins......Jews of Hamadan......Tombs of Mordecai and Esther......Tomb of Avicenna......Visit to Prince Buhman Mirza...... Ancient Sculptures and Inscriptions......Shevereen......Moran......Kaboot Rahung Gaosowar......Tousley......Hissar...... Bool Mulledge......Fountain at Hyder Pyghumber......Sultanea......Zunjan......Visit to Prince Abdoollah Mirza......Zohra..... Skirmish with the Villagers of Koorkundee...... Armaganah...... Achkund...... Mamoon......Copper Mines at Shaikh Durah Bad...... Kureem...... Arrival at Ardebeel.

On the 9th we arrived at Hamadan, fourteen miles, the ancient Ecbatana, the present population of which is twenty-five thousand. We were met at some distance from this extensive city, above which the lofty mountain of Elwund lifts its majestic and hoary head, by a large Istakball, headed by Allee Khan, the Nasukchee Bashee of Abbas Mirza. The body of irregular cavalry which accompanied him exhibited various feats of horsemanship before us, turning out by two's, a spear-man pursuing a matchlock-man, who, upon the approach of the former, quivering his lance, threw the reins on his horse's neck, and turning round, fired at him. Others hurled the jureed, which the person at whom it was darted avoided by throwing himself down on his horse's neck.

We passed under an eminence surmounted by the remains of a palace and fort. This may have been the castle mentioned by ancient authors, which was surrounded by seven walls, rising one

 above

above the other, and probably is the site of the palace of Sushan,* mentioned in the book of Esther. We proceeded to the encampment situated between the city and Elwund, where we found a body of three hundred Russians drawn up opposite the Envoy's tent to salute him. They form a part of Abbas Mirza's army, and were dressed in green jackets with red facings; the common sheep-skin cap on their heads, and loose white shulwas, over which were pulled black boots. They made a very respectable figure, and were commanded by a major, a noble-looking Georgian. The privates receive a tomaun a month, and daily rations of bread and meat, with a small quantity of spirits. There is no other reason to be assigned for these men quitting their country and service, but the scanty pay and rations they receive from their own government, namely, one ducat a-year (or *six shillings*), black bread, and salt-fish.

Despatches arrived from the Royal camp this day, stating that the Russian Ambassador, Prince Menzichoff, who had arrived there on the 10th, had left on the morning of the 24th ultimo, and that the King was to leave Sultanea for Ardebeel, towards which we were now to direct our steps.

Our camp was daily visited by great numbers of Jews, bringing coins and gems for sale. The coins consisted principally of Sassanian, Shapooree, Bactrian, and a few Alexanders and Seleucuses. The best silver coins may be purchased for a Persian rupee each, little more than a shilling, and copper ones for a quarter of a rupee: very few gold ones were brought, and I tried in vain to

* Others think Susa to be the Sushan of Scripture.

to procure cylinders. Hamadan is the emporium of coins and antique gems; Bagdad of cylinders, &c.

The Jews in Hamadan are obliged to wear a piece of red cloth on the breast of their garments: in other respects they are dressed similar to the Persians. It is disgusting to see the way in which the Persians abuse and oppress the unfortunate Israelites. When a Persian wishes to have the snow cleared from his flat-roofed house, he goes into the street and catches a Jew, and obliges him to perform the office. For the murder of a Jew a Persian has only to cut round a finger, so as to draw blood, and the offence is expiated.

In the evening a number of them accompanied me to point out the tombs of Mordecai and Esther. After passing through streets along which, four hundred centuries before the Christian æra, the haughty and cruel Haman conducted the humble Mordecai, the man whom the King delighted to honour, we arrived at an open spot, and on the summit of a small eminence rose a brick building surmounted by a dome, on the apex of which a stork had constructed its nest. The door was of one stone. On entering, the Jews reverently kissed it, and I was conducted into an outer apartment, in which were a number of lamps. From this a low door led to the lofty apartment, where, under two carved wooden arks, seven feet in height, reposed the remains of Mordecai and his niece, the favourite Queen of Ahasuerus (Ardashir Diroduste of the Persians). The walls were covered with Hebrew inscriptions. On inquiring the cause of several fractures on the arks, I was informed that the Persians had broken in and wantonly injured them. I did not neglect to purloin a relic from each.

The

The tomb of the celebrated physician, Abou Avicenna, is in a sad state of neglect; it is in an exposed spot likewise, and is open on all sides, with a small dome. It was a long time before I could discover its site; nobody could tell me any thing about it. Most of the common classes had never heard of such an individual; at last a Mirza pointed it out.

A furash was sent up Elwund to collect specimens of the rock forming the basis of the mountain; he brought down quartz, crystallized and in mass; quartz in grain, in which were hornblende and small particles of mica, and hornblende in mass in considerable quantities. The limestone is here particularly fine and pure: the quarry is a fursung from Hamadan. From the superiority of it, and the fine polish it takes as plaster, when mixed with whites of eggs, the palaces here are mostly finished with white, instead of being covered with painting and gilding, as we had hitherto seen.

In the forenoon of the 11th we visited Prince Buhman Mirza, the brother of Mahomed Mirza, who is son of the Prince Royal, and governor of Hamadan. The Russian guard were drawn out before the palace gates (in the new fort) to receive us. The young Prince whom we visited governed in the absence of his brother in the field with his father; he was about thirteen years of age. In the evening we visited the Minister, Mirza Hussun, and Allee Khan before mentioned: the former is a man with a calm and very pleasing expression of countenance. He was dressed in black, the emblem of mourning, as were all the respectable Persians in Hamadan, it being the Mohurrum: all the shops were shut, and the people are supposed to mourn for ten days for the grandsons of Mahomed. The Minister treated us with ices and fruits. Allee Khan is a merry, noisy old

old fellow, constantly joking and laughing. The roofs of all the houses round the square of his palace were covered with women to gaze at the Furingees: they were not very scrupulous about shewing their faces.

A short distance from Hamadan, on the Mulaer road, is the colossal statue of a lion, cut out of the mass of rock which forms its pedestal. It is highly deserving of being visited, and I think is unnoticed by former travellers. The gunj namah, or "account of the (concealed) treasure," an arrow-headed inscription on a rock, a fursung from our encampment, is interesting to those who may not have seen the tablets at Persepolis, &c.

Hamadan is celebrated for its beautifully painted numuds of felt, manufactured at Yezd, and for its carpets.

On the 13th we marched for Shevereen, four miles. At Hamadan we were obliged to leave another detachment of sick (consisting of all the serjeants, a great number of the Hindoos, and many Persians), under the charge of Major Hart, who had received orders from Abbas Mirza to superintend the raising and drilling of a new battalion there.

We lived at Shevereen with Mahomed Wullee Khan, son of Rustam Khan, formerly governor of Hamadan. We were received at the gates of the fort (one of the best we had seen in Persia) by two hundred and fifty recruits of his own tribe, the drums and fifes playing Scotch tunes. We were most kindly received and hospitably entertained by the Khan. The whole establishment seemed that of a feudal chief surrounded by his clan.

The Khan, after receiving a handsome present from the Envoy, of a saddle, gun, cloth, &c., offered in return a colt. The Envoy did not

not wish to take it, as he had always avoided receiving presents. He declined it, saying in the Persian form of speech, "*mal-i-ma mal-i-shuma ust o mal-i-shuma mal-i-ma*;" "since my property is your's, and your's mine, keep the colt in your stable till it is fit to ride, and then, *inshallah* (if it please God), I will send for it." The Khan replied, "*mohubut kurdeed*," "you have done me a kindness;" "*shufkut-i-shuma kum ma shŏud*;" "may your favour never be less!"

In the evening a ghoolam-i-shah, or one of the royal body-guard, arrived from the King, charged with the news of a victory over the Russians.

On our arrival at Moran, sixteen miles, on the 14th, we were joined by Dr. McNeil. We proceeded next day twelve miles, to Kaboot Rahung. It is wonderful how the number of patients increased after the arrival of the doctor. Men in high health an hour before his arrival, and after eating hearty meals, fell suddenly sick: however, when they found that they were obliged to swallow nauseous draughts, before quitting his tent they speedily recovered. It is a continual trial of temper for a European doctor practising in Persia. It frequently happens that, after giving medicine to a man, and asking him next day if he had taken it, he replies with the greatest coolness, "No, for that an old woman had given him something else, which would have a better effect." After prescribing to another patient, and attending him for weeks, he at last becomes so ill that you are obliged to go to his own house to see him; you there find all the medicines you had given him carefully piled up in one of the nches.

Though the cultivation was now much more extensive, and further removed from the villages than we had hitherto seen it, yet the state

of

of the country may be easily imagined, when we never saw the peasants go singly or unarmed from one village to another. The general features and character of the country were still the same as we had been accustomed to (with the exception of the terrific Kootuls) from Bushire to where we were; arid and grey coloured plains, of greater or less extent, covered with a peculiar rose (the *rosa uniflora*), in which here and there was an oasis of green, indicating a village; no where had we seen the line of the horizon unbroken by hills. For its extent, Persia is perhaps the most mountainous country in the world.

Travelling in Persia I found to be monotonous in the extreme; passing through the same scenery every day, and not meeting with a wayfarer for perhaps weeks together. After the first march from Bushire we had not seen a single cafila of mules the whole way up.

Our next three stages were Gao Souar, twenty miles; Tousley, sixteen; and Hissar, twenty-six, where we arrived on the 18th.

A short distance from the last encampment, we passed a village, near which was a large tumulus, evidently artificial. This village is built on the site of a Guebre town, and (like all the others which we now saw) presented the appearance of rows of large bee-hives, or rather nests of termites or white ants. There being a great scarcity of timber in this part of the country, they cannot construct their houses with flat roofs, they are therefore each surmounted by a small dome.

We now frequently observed tumuli. They are supposed by some to have been those on which the fire-temples were built: others again maintain, that from the quantities of brick and pottery, and not unfrequently coins and pieces of cloth, which are met with in digging into them, they are formed by the falling in and ruins of two or three of the ancient many-storied Guebre houses; but if this were the case they would appear in rows, according to the direction of the streets, and not singly and insulated, as they now appear.

At Hissar there is excellent bustard shooting; also many storks were seen at a distance, starlings, larks, &c.

Despatches arrived this day from the Royal camp, announcing that a battalion of Russians, twelve hundred strong, with four field-pieces, had been attacked by the Heir Apparent, and defeated.

On the 19th we travelled to Bool Mulledge, distant twenty miles. We passed the village of Hyder Pyghumber: here a dome covers the remains of a person, who some say was the grandfather of Mahomed, others the grandson of Abraham through Ismael. We were told we should here find a beautiful fountain, which issued from the ground several yards in height, forming a natural *jet d'eau* of the thickness of a man's body, and capable of supporting a person sitting on the top of it. We proceeded to examine it, and found, in a small enclosure, under a limestone-rock, a beautifully clear stream of water, a few inches in diameter, issuing from the ground, but not rising above it, as had been described to us, though perhaps it rises higher in winter.

Next day we reached Zunjan, five fursungs distant, a city and capital of a province. We passed through the valley of Sultanea, in which is the palace, the summer residence of the King. Here a magnificent mausoleum covering the bones of Sultan Khooda Bunder, towers above the plain; the dome is accounted the finest in Persia. This was intended to be the last resting-place of Hossein, but the King above-mentioned died before he had time to remove the bones

of

of the saint hither, and it became afterwards the depository of his own remains. The plan of the city of Sultanea was extensive and magnificent, being a series of squares; but it never was completed, and there are now but few inhabited houses on its site.

A few years ago a peasant, whilst hunting on the range of hills above Sultanea, found several very large pearls. He went to Tehran and offered them for sale in the bazar; but the pearls were of so fine a quality, and so large, that it was thought they could have belonged to no one but the King, and that they must have been stolen. The peasant was accordingly seized, and on being interrogated as to where he got them, a party was sent to the spot, which he pointed out. There, partly concealed by rubbish, was found a stone coffin, in which were the bones of a female, with jewels to a great amount.

Zunjan, seen from the top of a pass above it, has a beautiful appearance. The rocks of grey wacke in the foreground,—the city gradually opening out (with an extensive and undulating plain behind it) as we descended the steep road, at the bottom of which were numerous gardens filled with lofty trees,—these altogether formed a charming picture, on which the eye could rest with pleasure, already sufficiently tired with the daily monotonous scene of arid plains and hills.

We passed through the city to the palace of the Prince Governor of Zunjan, Abdoollah Mirza, a son of the King. At every corner men were running out with baskets and trays of fruit to present to the Elchee.

We arrived in the square of the palace, and were received by a considerable body of disciplined infantry, with a flourish of trumpets.

 We

We passed through the front apartments of the palace, and in a garden-house found the Prince seated at a large open window. He was one of the finest-looking men I ever saw: a noble and commanding countenance, with a fine aquiline nose, and a complexion clear and ruddy; his age about thirty-five; his frame stout and vigorous; he looked a prince: but his disposition is exceedingly grasping and tyrannical. His peasantry are the most oppressed in Persia, and, as a natural consequence of this, they are the most insolent, and very much addicted to plundering. How different the condition of the cultivators under the mild government of Casveen! In that province the inhabitants are contented and happy; the meanest peasant has a carpeted room, and a plentiful meal to offer the stranger. Civility and hospitality are there every where met with; whereas you are extremely fortunate if you pass through the country of the Prince of Zunjan without being plundered of every thing you possess, and probably beaten into the bargain.

The manners of the Prince were extremely agreeable. His dress was of the most splendid description; a scarlet robe, on which were closely embroidered large golden laurel leaves: he smoked a magnificent karanai, or Turkish caleoon, composed (with the exception of the cut-glass bottom) of gold and gems. I sat within a yard of him, so that I had a full view of all his splendid accompaniments to a fine person.

Our next stage was Zohra, twelve miles, where we arrived on the 21st. Captain Campbell and myself, in journeying to this village, had an adventure of rather a disagreeable nature the previous evening. We had got into the high road to Zohra, which we had been told was a fursung shorter than the low one. After ascending

and

and descending the steep banks of numerous ravines, in a narrow glen amongst the hills, we at last lost all traces of the path. The moon, obscured by clouds, from which vivid lightning darted at intervals, shed an uncertain light over the scene, which was one of peculiar wildness. We were completely at a loss which way to bend our steps. We had got to the top of a ridge, when far below us we heard the baying of dogs. We proceeded towards the sound, and found in a nook of the glen a village: we got into the middle of it, and found one of the inhabitants at his door; all the rest were buried in sleep. He inquired gruffly what we wanted there? We told him we had lost our road, and requested him to point it out to us. He replied, "You are the Furingee Elchee's people, I suppose; your "tents are beyond the hills." After a great deal of intreaty to make him point out the proper road, at last, after promising him a present, he walked slowly along in front of our horses. A servant (we had only two with us, and a furash mounted on a mule which carried the beds) used violent and abusive language to the villager, to make him quicken his steps, when he stopt, and pretended he wanted to go back for his shoes, although he had them actually on his feet. We urged him to proceed: he set up a loud cry, when instantly a large body of villagers issued from their houses and attacked us most furiously. We called to them to desist, and for one of them to come forward who spoke Persian: they answered, "We speak Turkish, and know nothing of your Persian." With loud shouts they continued to assail us: the whole village was up in arms. After Captain Campbell had received a severe blow on the head, which stunned him, and I had sustained a cut on the right hand, which nearly disabled me, we used our arms, and sending the

mule

mule to the front, covered the retreat as well as we could. The people followed us for two miles, keeping up a sort of running fight, and abusing us the whole way. We fortunately had struck into the right road, and after an hour's ride arrived in camp. The name of the village in the hills is Koorkundee.

The above occurrence shews the necessity of travellers being always well-armed and mounted in journeying through Persia, and also of moving in large parties. If we had been a more numerous body, these villagers would not have dared to attack us; as the case stood, it was extraordinary that they did, especially as we used no violence to the guide.

Next day we arrived at Armaganah, twelve miles. Here we could get no sursat, or provisions. The Kutkhoda of the village is noted for his unaccommodating behaviour and insolence to Europeans; both Sir Hartford Jones and Sir John Malcolm were obliged to complain of him, and he was severely punished on both occasions. However, the head-man had a good excuse this time, as the King had halted here on his way to Ardebeel. His people, as usual, had turned their cattle loose in the grain-fields, and had ruined most of the young crops, the horses and mules destroying the grain, and the camels the cotton: the inhabitants were consequently cursing his Majesty, and consigning him to the lowest pit of *Jehunnum*.

The climate of Armaganah was delightful. It might well be said of it:

> " *'Na gurmish gurm, o na surmaish surd.*"
>
> " Its warmth was not heat, its coolness was not cold."

Achkund, twenty-eight miles, was our next stage. The features of the country before us were now exceedingly rugged and wild:

hill

hill rose above hill, backed by lofty mountains; the whole crowned with a canopy of dense clouds. On the road to Achkund large masses of mist, heaped on one another, rolled across our path, driven from the Caspian by the Bad-i-mai, or wind of mists, which set in strong and cold every evening: it sunk the thermometer to 40° at six P.M., and at eight to 33°. After the sun rose the mists disappeared from the tops of the hills, and then from the valleys, and in the distance disclosed the mighty range of the Kafilan Koh. Heavy dews now fell every evening, which were not altogether pleasant, as we bivouacked at night.

We reached Mamoon, eighteen miles, on the 24th. We passed, within a fursung of this, a salt-mine in limestone. The salt was crystallized in four-sided prisms, and was very pure: a large rock of it was exposed.

Mamoon is a beautiful village surrounded by trees, and rising up the side of a small hill, on the summit of which is the citadel. Below the village flows the Kiziloozun River, which empties itself into the Caspian, and is one of the best fishing streams to be met with. Trout and whitings were caught in great numbers with the hook, and we had good duck-shooting. The water of the river is brackish.

Near to Mamoon, and within two fursungs of the town of Miana (supposed by D'Anville to be the Atropatina of Alexander's geographers, and well known from its being infested with poisonous bugs), is the village of Shaikh Durah Bad. Here are, perhaps, the richest veins of copper in the world: silver and lead are also found in considerable quantities. The soil is ferruginous. The veins are at the bottom of a range of hills running from north-west to south-east,

in

in front of the Kafilan Koh. The river Gharangoo, which is a branch of the Kisiloozun, runs through the district where the veins are met with: an unusual rise of its waters discovered the precious ore a short time back.

Three fursungs from Shaikh Durah Bad is a small forest of pine and baloot (Persian oak), the wood of which the villagers are prohibited by the Prince Royal from using as fuel, as he contemplates working the mines, which would not be a difficult undertaking, as the ore is found close to the surface, yet of some depth. The price of labour is low: in summer one panabad, or sixpence, per day; in winter ninepence each man. Instead of smelting at the mines, it would be more expedient, perhaps, to convey the ore to a large forest, fourteen fursungs to the eastward of Shaikh Durah Bad, which extends to the Caspian, and is inexhaustible. Coal is, however, said to exist close to the veins, which might obviate the necessity of transporting the ore from the place where it is found.

Iron is obtained here in great quantity; and the oxide of lead is found on the surface of the ground. The latter is melted by the villagers into bullets.

If ever an European colony were to be established in Persia, I know not of a better situation for it than this: the climate being good, the soil fertile, rich ores being in abundance, and as it is at a distance from the frontier, the colony would not run the risk of being disturbed during war.

Our

* I am indebted for the above information to my friend Mirza Sadik Beg, agent in England of his Royal Highness Prince Abbas Mirza, who has long zealously promoted the English interests in his own country.

Our next stage was Herees, twenty-five miles; on the way to which we ascended a steep pass, but with an excellent road. The wind blew with great violence, endangering the mules; it was so sharp and cold, that it seemed to cut us in two. At a small village on the road we passed three hundred Russian prisoners; they were going down to Ispahan to enter the service of Khoosroo Khan: they did not seem at all concerned at their change of masters. They were comfortably clothed in Arab brown and white cloaks and foraging caps, with good shoes on their feet. These had been furnished them by their new master, as they had been stripped of every thing, with the exception of their shirts and trowsers, by the Persian soldiery, when brought into the Royal camp.

Kureem, the next stage, twenty-five miles, we reached on the 26th. We were now daily subjected to thick fogs, accompanied by drizzling rain. Two of us, after getting completely soaked, and our guide leading us out of the road, were obliged to bivouack amongst some wet grass, the mist and rain continuing till after sunrise. Near Kureem we met several parties of horsemen from the royal camp. When we first came in sight of one another, on opposite ridges, they unslung their long guns, drew together, and prepared for action. We were informed by the first we met of the King's march from Ardebeel for Achar the previous evening. Our informants added, that, *Ulhumd ullilah!* 'God be praised!' it was all up with the Russians now; that Teflis and Sheesha were all that were left to them in Georgia; and that, *Inshallah,* 'God willing,' these too would shortly fall.

Mr. Henry Willock, late *chargé d'affaires,* and now Secretary and First Assistant to the Envoy, arrived in camp and confirmed the intelligence of the King's march: Lieutenant Shee accompanied him.

Our next day's march brought us to Ardebeel, where we arrived on the 27th.

CHAPTER X.

The City of Ardebeel......The Chowal Mogam......Humaum......Visit to Prince Shaikh Allee Mirza......Tombs of Shaikh Suffee and Shah Ismail......Fort of Ardebeel......Russian Prisoners......Pillars of Heads......Muleteers.......Ascent of Mount Sevelund......March from Ardebeel......Talib Kishlak......Furukhabad...... Ahmedbegloo......Mizan......Arrival at the Royal Camp at Achar.

THE ancient city of Ardebeel stands on an extensive plain, the Chowal Mogam, and possesses a climate nearly assimilated to that of England. The lofty Sevelund attracts all the clouds from the Caspian, so that there are always dews on the plains around it, mists, and frequently rain. The winter is colder than ours. Ardebeel was formerly the capital of the Turkomans of the Kara Kousloo or black sheep; but it is principally celebrated for having been the birth-place of Shah Ismail, the founder of the Suffavean dynasty, who was descended from Shaikh Suffee, from whom are the Soffees, and who was a lineal descendant of Moussah, the seventh Imaum. Shah Ismail was the first who established the Sheah as the national religion: he died and was buried at Ardebeel in 1519.

The plain of Mogam is the winter resort of the Illyaut tribes: it is celebrated for having impeded the march of Regulus, whose army was attacked by a monstrous snake; and it is well known in Persia, and I was assured of the fact, that some parts of the plain are still infested with immense numbers of these reptiles. The soil about Ardebeel is white and calcareous; and towards Tabreez, porphyritic, containing hornblende.

In

In márching to our encampment, we observed a large *tip* or body of horsemen crossing the plain before us. First there appeared five or six yedducks, or led horses; then came an Arusbeggee, or receiver of petitions; then four Shatirs, or running-footmen; alone, and apart from the rest, rode a person of rank, whom we found to be Shaikh Allee Mirza, a son of the King, who was proceeding, with what he called a thousand horse, to join Abbas Mirza, engaged with the Russians in Karabaugh. Before the Prince walked the crier, proclaiming his titles; behind him, and at some distance, three hundred horse extended over the plain in a long irregular line; several of them dashed out at intervals and skirmished. Their tents were not far from ours. They were Zunds, from the province of Mullach, the Prince's government. Kurdahoor, where we had had the skirmish on the 7th, is in that province.

We lost no time in repairing to the Humaum after our arrival. We found it, though old, to be the largest and best we had yet seen, to be a private one. In it there were two cisterns of water, each forty feet by fifteen; one of hot, the other of cold water; the depth seven feet. After the dullaks, or barbers. had done their office, we had a delightful swim in the latter. After dinner we waited on his Royal Highness Prince Shaikh Allee Mirza. He was seated in a Persian double-poled tent, which differs little from an English one, except in having no ridge-pole, and in being divided into a number of small apartments. He asked a great many foolish questions, displaying great ignorance, and telling innumerable lies; one of which was, that certain intelligence had just arrived of a great battle having been fought between the two brothers, Nicholas and Constantine, in which five thousand officers alone had fallen. It was ridiculous

ridiculous to witness the shouts of exultation of the Prince and some of his satellites outside, when talking of the recent successes over the Russians.

On the 28th we proceeded to visit the tomb of Shaikh Suffee, and his illustrious descendant, Shah Ismail. Their remains repose under lofty domes; four swords surmounting the apex of that of the latter. The ark over the grave of the saint is fenced off by a silver grating. The rooms are highly ornamented. In one is a large collection of china (amongst which I observed some beautiful agate cups and dishes), and a library of splendidly bound and valuable books, one of which is remarkable for its weight. All of them had been presented by Shah Abbas the Great, as offerings at the tombs of his ancestors. We next proceeded to the fort, which is square, with four bastions at the angles, and ravelins to protect the two gates, with a fausse-bray round the whole. It was coustructed by Major Monteith, of the Madras Engineers, surveyor in Persia. We crossed a deep dry ditch, and found the fort inside to be clean and well kept. It was garrisoned by a detachment of the Janbaz, or his Majesty's disciplined infantry. We visited sixteen Russian officers who were confined here: one thousand rank and file were prisoners outside. We found the officers in a comfortable apartment within a court-yard; they consisted of one Lieutenant-Colonel, a Major, twelve infantry and two cossack officers. Two of them were wounded; one in the hand, which wound he received from the pistol of that savage, the Sirdar of Erivan. This officer, having been on detachment, with a company, on the frontier of the Sirdar, was attacked by a large force, against which he defended himself gallantly for some time until overpowered. When brought before the Sirdar, the

the latter drew a pistol and fired at him. The Colonel, Mizemooski, when asked the cause of defeat at Kunjeruk (for he was the commandant of the battalion of twelve hundred men with four guns which the Prince had vanquished), replied, that they had fought for nine hours in the heat of the day, at a spot where they could not procure a drop of water; that, totally overcome by heat and thirst, after four hundred had been killed and wounded, one gun dismounted, and a tumbril blown up (which last Serjeant Dawson, an Englishman in the service of the Prince, had effected), they were obliged to throw down their arms. They were dressed in the clothes which Mr. Willock had liberally supplied them with. When brought into camp, they were stripped by their rascally guards of every thing except their shirts and trowsers. Seeing that they still wanted many necessaries, particularly the privates, we subscribed amongst ourselves such a sum as provided caps, comfortable cloaks, and shoes for all the men, and what little necessaries the officers stood in need of. They requested the Envoy to use his influence with his Majesty to get them removed to Tabreez, where they would be under the eyes of Europeans. A Russian officer taken at the commencement of the war had turned Musselman, and obtained the appellation of Abdoollah Khan. Many attempts had been made to induce some of those we saw to do the same, but they had not been successful. We breakfasted with Secunder Khan, the governor of the city and province of Ardebeel.

About a mile and a half from camp was a singular monument of barbarity. On a small hill on the plain were erected five kellah-i-minar, or pillars of heads. The pillars were built of brick and lime, and into nitches were thrust the heads of about one thousand Russians,

J. E. A pinxit

Tᵗ M. Baynes litho del.

PILLARS OF HEADS.

near Mount Sevelund.

sians, which had been sent to the Royal camp; they had been all pickled, and were placed round the pillars in rows. A more disgusting sight can hardly be imagined: into the mouth of one of the heads a pipe had been insultingly stuck. The price of Russian heads at this time was five tomauns. The custom of making a pyramid of the heads of enemies has existed in Persia from time immemorial.

The insolence of our *katirchees*, or muleteers, now exceeded all bounds: although they had been paid most liberally, yet they now demanded in future a rupee per day for each mule, else they positively refused to move another step. This was most exorbitant. One of them using abusive language, the Envoy ordered him to be bastinadoed. The furashes, in attempting to bring the culprit to the fulluk, were attacked by the other muleteers, who rushed to the rescue: a violent scuffle and fight ensued. Hearing the noise, two or three of us ran from our tents to the scene of action, and quickly succeeded in putting the muleteers to flight with our fists, they neither being accustomed to, nor relishing that species of attack. The offender then underwent the punishment which he so richly merited. His companions immediately had recourse to the *punah be-shah-zadah*, taking refuge in the Prince's stables, who was pitched near us. This is a sacred asylum, from which the Prince himself (unless acting against the established customs of the country) could not drive them. However, next morning they came and humbly asked forgiveness. Four horses were stolen here. The thieves were discovered before they had time to escape: a pursuit ensued; three were recovered, but one was irretrievably lost.

The lofty mountain of Sevelund towered before us in hoary majesty,

jesty, a third of its height (which is computed at seven or eight thousand feet) being covered with eternal snow. I was extremely anxious to ascend it, but as the excursion would have required three days, I was obliged to relinquish the idea. However, I shall now subjoin the account which was furnished me by Mr. Willock of his expedition to its summit, in company with Lieutenant Shee, a few days before our arrival at Ardebeel.

On the 10th of August these gentlemen left the royal camp at eleven, A. M., in company with a Mirza and a Khan. After a pleasant ride, they arrived, at four, P. M., at an obeh of Illyauts, which was still six miles from the base of the mountain. Here they determined to remain all night, and to commence the ascent next morning. Whilst waiting for their dinner, a party who had been to the top of Sevelund joined them; the chief personage of which was the Moollah Bashee, or Chief Priest of Tehran, who had been sent by the Shah to visit the mountain. He told Mr. Willock that it was not worth his while to proceed, as there was nothing to be seen; that after surmounting the greatest difficulties in ascending, he had found nothing at the top to repay him for the immense labour he had undergone; and that, *Ulla kureem*, 'God was merciful,' in having permitted him to return alive.

The appearance of the Moollah and his party not being at all that of men who had suffered from fatigue, and Moollahs not being particularly famed for adherence to truth, the Chief Priest's advice was disregarded, and he returned to camp.

At three, A. M., on the 11th, having procured two guides, they mounted in order to ride up Sevelund as far as was practicable. At sunrise they were obliged to dismount; and leaving their horses, they commenced

commenced the ascent on foot, which at first did not seem a matter of any great difficulty; but they soon found their mistake, and had to pass over four distinct ridges on the E.S.E. side, each of which deceitfully led them on with the hope of its being the summit, which by great perseverance they at last reached, at eleven, A. M., having been five hours in performing the task, and being excessively fatigued with their exertions.

The summit of the mountain was amygdaloidal, and was chiefly green-stone and grey wacke, in which there was iron. Even before arriving at the snow and ice, not a plant of any kind was seen, with the exception of some small daisies. The air at the summit was so rarified, that several of the party felt an oppression in the lungs, and one or two vomited, probably from over-exertion.

On first reaching the top a tomb was discovered, consisting of stones neatly put together. A few at the head had been displaced, which disclosed the body of the frozen prophet, who has lain here from time immemorial. He was lying on his right side. The parts visible were the skull, the left collar-bone, and the left arm, from the scapula to the elbow, and four ribs; the remainder of the body was buried in ice and earth. On the arm there was a considerable portion of dried flesh, and part of the winding-sheet enveloped it. Ten of the front teeth had been knocked out of the skull, and were lying in the tomb; the remainder were even, and beautifully white. The body appeared to be that of a young man. Before the stones at the head were removed, it is probable the body was perfect, and also that the remainder is still so, which had not been disturbed. An ancient rosary was found near the body, offered probably by some pious Musselman.

Having satisfied their curiosity, the party proceeded to view a most extraordinary stone which distilled oil, and which contained, in a hole at the top, a diamond. So they had been told by some Persians in camp; but which proved to be as true as what a man reported to the King the day before their departure, *viz.* that he had seen the prophet (so called from being imperishable) sitting bolt upright in his tomb, and wearing a long beard. The party having crossed a plain of two miles in length, covered with snow and ice, came to an amphitheatre, six hundred yards in circumference, in which was a small lake of the purest water; round it were hanging large and beautiful icicles. The water was very pleasant to the taste, and had evidently been frozen in the night; but the ice had been mostly dissolved with the meridian heat. To the right of the pool was a square enclosure, surrounded by a wall three feet in height: this the guides called the musjid, or mosque, In this was a stone about three feet and a half high, and rounded at the top, on which oil appeared to have been sprinkled; and a hole in the centre was probably the receptacle of a wick to form a rude lamp. In the hole was a piece of lead, which was the Persian diamond! Offerings were placed round the stone, consisting of rags twisted round sticks, and a piece of copper money. Near this was another stone, on which were three arrow-headed characters. From the appearance of the place, it is probable that the Illyauts (who in this province of Ardebeel are of the Shah Savund tribe, and all speak Turkish) perform some religious ceremony here at a certain period of the year, and make the first-mentioned stone their lamp. It will be a matter of interest to trace the origin of this custom, and of what religion it is the remnant: not unlikely that of the Sabians. Kai Khoosroo, according

according to tradition, built a fire temple at Ardebcel, of which this is probably the site.

A ludicrous occurrence took place at the musjid illustrative of the Persian character, and of the little regard which some of them pay to, at least, the forms of the religion to which they all pretend to be so much attached. The Mirza took up the copper coin before-mentioned, and regardless of the remonstrances of the guides, put it into his kullumdan, or pen-case (which all Mirzas wear in lieu of a dagger in the girdle), saying that he would preserve it as a relic. The guides urged him to restore it to its place, or else to leave another offering; but the Mirza was obstinate and would do neither, saying, "Do you think me such a fool as to leave a rupee for you to come "and take it?" The party then sat down on the ground to rest themselves, the Mirza placing his kullumdan before him, and when he was not observing, the Khan slyly abstracted the coin from the case, and put it into his pocket. A call was then made for the kullumdan to make a memorandum. The Mirza opened it, and lo! no coin appeared. The Khan immediately cried out, "a miracle! a miracle!" The Mirza, in the extremity of terror at the sacrilege he had committed, fell prostrate on the earth, as did all his attendants and those of the Khan, and commenced crying, "*heh wohee! heh wohee!*" "alas! alas!" praying and knocking their heads against the ground, in order to avert the misfortunes which threatened them. The cunning Khan, laughing at their beards, did the same, prayed louder than any, and knocked his head on the earth as vehemently as the rest, sobbing most bitterly, but every now and then holding up his hand to Mr. Willock and his companion, and shewing the coin in it, and winking and grinning at his deluded fellow Musselman.

 The

The barometer in boiling water stood at 83° of Reaumur; but it was thought there was some error in the experiment. The wide expanse of the Caspian, distant thirty-five miles, was dimly visible: heavy fogs were hanging over it. Talish, behind a range of hills, stretching north and south, was covered with forests, in which roams the royal tiger.

After remaining two hours at the top, the party descended, and passed six large pools of water; some of them covered with recent ice, though it was the height of the dog-days. After three hours' walk over rocks and deep gravel, formed by the debris of the amygdaloidal rocks, they reached their horses, greatly exhausted, having walked five fursungs, or twenty miles. After refreshing themselves with tea, they mounted, and at sunset reached the Illyaut encampment, and from their own feelings were fully impressed with the idea that the Moollah Bashee had never ascended the mountain. Before coming to the obeh, the guides ran on before and told the Illyauts of the miracle, and the whole of them turned out to gaze at the unfortunate Mirza, who, in their opinion, and probably in his own, was doomed shortly to give up the ghost. The deluded man afterwards applied to the Shah to erect a goombuz, or dome, over the tomb of the prophet, in consequence of the miracle.

The party slept at the encampment, and on the morning of the 12th descended to the plain to visit a hot sulphurous spring twelve miles from the royal camp. A bath has been constructed here, four feet in depth; the temperature of the water is 130° Fahrenheit.

Some time ago a gentleman visiting the bath found an old woman in it in a state of nudity, and standing up to the breast in the water; greatly annoyed at being thus intruded on, to improve the matter,

she

she jumped out, pursued and threw stones at the gentleman, abusing him in the grossest manner.

We again mounted in pursuit of his Majesty, whom we had so much difficulty in coming up with. From Ispahan to this place, with the exception of the two days' rest at Hamadan, we had not made a single halt, and had marched altogether, from one extremity of the kingdom to the other, nearly thirteen hundred miles.

The Envoy was now constantly receiving highly complimentary letters from the Shah's ministers, which led us, of course, to hope that the mission would be well received.

On the 30th we marched to Talib-Kishlak, twelve miles, crossing the Kara Soo river by a good bridge. At this village there was excellent sport both for the rod and gun; gudgeons in abundance, with wild geese, bustard, &c. There were extensive encampments of Shah Savund Illyauts near us, residing in circular felt tents, which are highly requisite here, the cold in winter being much greater than in England, and the ground for four months constantly covered with snow.

Next day we reached Furukhabad, twenty-four miles, passing some beautiful villages with extensive gardens, situated in a very wild-looking and broken country. I observed by the road-side a diminutive species of the flower, called "Love lies bleeding," and great quantities of globe-thistles. The rocks were now profusely covered with lichens, attesting the moistness of the climate. Forty camels laden with powder for the Royal camp passed us this day.

We arrived at Ahmedbegloo, twenty-four miles, on the 1st of September. Our road lay through plains covered with high grass, in which the Illyauts were tending their horses and sheep: the vegetation

vegetation was most luxuriant. Near the village we were met by a Khan from the Royal camp, bearing in his cap a *futtah namah*, or letter announcing victory, from the King. He dismounted to present it to the Envoy, who received it on foot. The *futtah namah* intimated the fall of Herat, in Khorasan, inhabited by Afgans, who not being prompt in the payment of their revenue, a force had been sent against them under the command of his Royal Highness Hussun Allee Mirza. After investing the place, he heard that the Afgans intended to beat up his camp: he accordingly marched out with the greater part of his troops, and posted himself in ambuscade in a narrow defile, leaving his camp-fires burning, and a body of men in rear of, and at some distance from, the tents. The garrison, as he had been warned, marched through the defile to attack the camp; finding it deserted, and hearing a body of men charging them, they precipitately retreated, but found themselves at the defile between two fires. They were completely routed, and the place fell.

His Majesty's poet laureate, who had been deputed by the Shah to conduct the mission into camp, now joined us; also Major Monteith and Dr. Cormich, in the service of his Royal Highness Prince Abbas Mirza. We had now a party of ten besides the Envoy.

On the 2d September we reached Mizan, ten miles. We now left the district of Miskeen, and entered the mountainous province of Karadaugh. The hills were now wooded, and altogether the scene was most romantic and beautiful; the face of the country presenting the appearance of the ocean under the influence of a mighty storm, it was so broken.

At Mizan is the finest sporting in Persia: game of all kinds abounds.

abounds. On the wooded hills are *maral* or noble stags and the wild sheep. On the plains, hares, foxes, pheasants, quail, English partridges, bustards, snipes, &c. in the greatest plenty. We had some excellent coursing, and our sportsmen returned with full bags.

Next day we arrived at the Royal camp, near Achar, twenty miles.

CHAPTER XI.

Approach to the Royal Camp......The Istakball......Visit to the Ministers......Audience of the Shah......His Character......Anecdotes of his Majesty......The Taj-i-Dowlah......Hunting Excursion......Presents to the King and Queen......Arrangements for Departure.

In approaching the camp we had a delightful ride through a most romantic valley. It was very narrow. At the bottom rushed a tumultuous stream; the banks were clothed with low jungle, and in many places were little millet-fields. We passed a mill, close to which was a high tower, intended, in case of the mill being attacked, as the place of refuge for the miller, and those who might have come to get their corn ground.

The glen widened into a broad valley. At a distance was seen a white mass of tents stretching quite across the valley, and overshadowed by lofty mountains: nearer us was a black line of horsemen. They formed the Istakball, and advanced in line; six hundred of them, with the Nasuckchee Bashee in their front, accompanied by other grandees and khans. The Royal standard was displayed in their centre, upon it the device of the lion and sun. We were all in full dress, and the escort, I must say, in their dashing yellow and scarlet, looked infinitely better than the party-coloured and motley group of Persian ghoolams. We proceeded towards the camp, passed the Royal tents, surrounded by a lofty serai purdah.* The tents were

* The serai purdah is a tent-wall of canvas, surrounding the tents of the king and nobles.

were white with red stripes. In front of the enclosure was the tent in which the King holds his salaam or levee, and sits daily in public on his judgment-seat, to hear complaints, reward and punish. It was distinguished by three golden balls, on the summits of the poles.

In front of, and at some distance from, the royal tent, were the Zambooruks, or camel-artillery, amounting to six hundred swivels (the tents pitched in a square); to the right of the Zamboorukchees, the street of the bazar; to the left, the Envoy's encampment, on the bank of the Achar river. To the right of the royal camp were three regiments of Jan-baz, or disciplined infantry, each a thousand strong; and to the left, three thousand ghoolam-i-Shah, or King's body guards (horse). The Prince's ministers and khans were pitched wherever their fancy dictated; their tents were surrounded by a confused mass of small ones containing their dependants. On a hill to the left of, and commanding the camp, was the park of artillery, consisting of two brigades of guns.

We were received at our tents by a guard of honour, consisting of one hundred regular infantry, with drum and fife. They were dressed in round jackets of green with red facings, loose white shulwas and black boots, with the common Persian cap: their commandant was adorned with the third class of the order of the Lion and Sun. In the last war with Russia, he had belonged to the Prince's army, had run away, got well bastinadoed and had his ears cropped: he made interest with the King and got a commission in his army, as well as the order, although he was a notorious coward. The Envoy's encampment made a highly respectable figure: it consisted of ten large tents, in line, with innumerable baggage and servants' tents

 in

in the rear. To the grand receiving-tent was a large shamiana or vestibule: the lady's tents were of course enclosed by a serai purdah. The lining of the tents was red; the fringes party-coloured, in which yellow predominated. The Persians were highly pleased at their splendid appearance; and the union waving proudly in front gave rise to a report in the bazar, that the Elchee paid to his Majesty one thousand tomauns a day for the privilege.

In the evening, the drums beat to and the gun from the height was fired at sundown, as in a regular encampment. The band of his Persian Majesty played for half an hour on the right of the camp: it was composed of huge brazen trumpets and drums; the crash of the one and the swell of the other had a singular but not a very harmonious effect. Dancing and tumbling boys likewise attended.

On the morning of the 4th we paid a state visit to Saliar (or Mahomed Hussein Khan), the son of the Asuff ud Dowlah, or Prime Minister. His father, the main promoter of the war, had been sent by the King, much against his inclination, to co-operate with the Prince Royal, with an army of ten thousand disciplined infantry, irregular horse and guns. He left two or three days before our arrival. On the left of Saliar, who was a proud-looking young man, sat Mirza Abdool Wahab, Möutim-i-Dowlah (keeper of the seals); beyond him, a very intelligent-looking personage, Mirza Cassim Khan, Kaim-Mukam, second minister of the King and first minister of the Prince. He was now in disgrace: being an excellent satirist, he had been exercising his talents on the latter. He has the best library in the kingdom; and being altogether a very clever and superior man, he will doubtless soon be restored to favour, as the Prince cannot well do without him. On the right of Saliar (the

Envoy

Envoy intervening) sat a corpulent and joyous-looking character, arrayed in flowing scarlet robe (which hardly concealed a fair belly) and high turban. On closer examination we discovered Mirza Abool Hussein Khan, the celebrated Persian ambassador, so famed for his conquests among the English fair. He still retained the same clear healthy complexion which he exhibited in Europe, but had grown enormously fat since his last embassy with the fair Circassian, who is still an inmate of his harem at Tehran. With his overwhelming powers of speech he engrossed the whole of the conversation, talking partly in English and partly in Persian, and loudly laughing at his own sallies. After loading the Russians with every term of abuse, saying *che khak be sir-i-mun amud*, "what ashes have fallen on my head for ever having any thing to do with them!" and characterizing them as faithless and grasping barbarians, he drew odious comparisons between the Russian and English missions. Certainly the former did not shine in their last. His Serene Highness, Prince Menzikoff, had neither tents, horses, mules, nor escort. The King pitched a tent for him, and he came almost without baggage, on the chupparee or post-horses of the country. However, he was a fine looking, very intelligent, and gentlemanly person, and it was the fault of his government that he did not come with a better retinue.

After the Mirza had vented his spleen on the *Pedur sukhtah Roos*, he amused us with sundry stories of himself, one of which was to the following purport: When living in London he was visited at his lodgings by a lady attended by a handsome maid-servant. Pretending to pay devoted attention to the fair dame, he was all the while making love to the handmaid behind her back, which the lady unfortunately discovering, jumped up in a fury, seized a brush that was lying on the table, broke all the mirrors and glass-ware in the room, and left the house in a towering passion. The Mirza always commenced his stories by saying "I'll shew you what a fine fellow I am;" and wound them up by declaring, "upon my honour," that all was true which he had been saying. He holds the office of Moukarij-i-Dowlah, or minister for foreign affairs, and enjoys a pension from the Company of fifteen hundred rupees per mensem, nearly £2,000 a year, which he has the assurance to say is not enough to feed his dogs. He had seen the Envoy's lady ride past the camp on the day of our arrival, on a side-saddle, and had mentioned it to the Shah: however, the old Monarch would not believe that any one could sit a horse in the way the Mirza described, and sent a request to have ocular demonstration of the fact. The saddle was of course sent him, and it is said he made "old fatty," the Mirza, mount and shew him the way in which English ladies ride; doubtless, greatly to his discomfort

The head eunuch of the Queen, Aga Mubarik, called with Mirza Mahomed Allee, the secretary of Mirza Abool Hussein Khan, requesting a visit from the Envoy's lady to her Majesty, the Taj-i Dowlah (crown of the state). The Aga was a Nubian, small, and of a slender build: he said he got his thick lips from the kick of a horse! In the evening we visited the Nasukchee Bashee, and the minister for foreign affairs. The Nasukchee Bashee, a dull and proud old fool, was the first man I had seen behave disrespectfully towards the Envoy. When the coffee was brought in, instead of taking a cup and handing it to the Envoy, as is the custom to an honoured visitant, he took his own cup first, and desired the servant to

hand

hand one to the Envoy, who of course very properly declined taking it.

The 7th being the day appointed for our public audience of the King, we proceeded on horseback and in gay apparel (with the *chackchoors*, or scarlet cloth boots), attended by the escort and a large body of servants, towards the royal tents. Before the first entrance, in three sides of a square, was drawn up the corps of Zambooruk-chees, or camel artillery-men, arrayed in a most fantastic uniform. Scarlet sugar-loaf caps, with an edging of black fur, brass plate and feather, was their head-dress, with a yellow hussar jacket, white shulwas and boots. We dismounted and entered a receiving-tent, where we met some of the first men of the court: the Nasukchee Bashee; the Nudeem-i-Shah, or companion of the King, to whom he addresses himself in public, called by the Turkomans *Bullee Bullee Khan*, from assenting to every thing His Majesty says;—the old man who figures in Hajji Baba, under the epithet of Namurd Khan, and several others. Here we went through the ceremony of smoking, drinking coffee, tea, &c. After waiting some time his Majesty was announced to be on his throne. We rose and passed through the first entrance, the Envoy carrying the letter from the Governor-General enclosed in silk and cloth of gold. We found all the troops in camp drawn out in a large square, who in compliment to us were dressed in scarlet jackets. We walked onwards, passed through the immense tent in which was the judgment-seat, which was a small throne adorned with pearls and precious stones, and then through the entrance to the enclosure formed by the serai purdah. Over this, as over the first entrance, was the favourite representation of the hero Rustum killing the white Demon, and liberating his Sovereign from

from confinement. Within was a line of battle-axe and mace-bearers. At the upper end of the enclosure was a splendid open tent, supported by flowered and gilded poles: we advanced towards it, led by the master of the ceremonies, with wand of office, high turban, and scarlet and furred robe. Half way up the walk we stopped, threw off our slippers, and made a low obeisance towards the tent, from which issued a clear and solemn voice, saying, "*Khoosh* "*amudeed*," You are welcome. We made two other obeisances, passed through a guard of richly-dressed musketeers, and entered by a door in the side wall of the royal tent. The front wall of the tent was open. Opposite to us, on a high and magnificent throne, sat his Persian Majesty, or, as the master of the ceremonies designated him, *Kebleh Alum, Shah in Shah, Zilloollah*, (The centre of the universe, the king of kings, and the shadow of God upon earth).

He appeared a hale man and tall, sixty-five years of age, and had lost some of his front teeth. He had on the usual Persian cap, encirled by the *toorah*, a rich bandeau of jewels, and was clothed in a close red dress; his *bazoo bunds*, or armlets, were splendid, as were his girdle and dagger. All these were closely set with gems of rare beauty and immense value. His beard flowed below his girdle. On his right stood a line of twelve princes of the blood royal, all possessing the fine aquiline nose which distinguishes the Kujurs: below them, and near us, stood several of the ministers; among others our friend Mirza Abool Hussein Khan, adorned with the first and second orders of the Lion and Sun. He marshalled us along the wall, opposite his Majesty, according to our rank. The Envoy was in front of us, near a gilt chair. The letter of the Governor-General was laid at his Majesty's feet. After again bowing low, and

and receiving the *khoosh amudeed*, the Mirza introduced us to the King, who was amusing himself with dangling in his hand a heavy dagger-knot of large pearls. Outside the tent, and on his Majesty's left, splendidly attired, were three young men, the shield-bearer, sword and cup-bearers, all of which insignia glittered with jewels. On the King's right, and on the ground upon a carpet, was the lofty cylindrical crown, on which the plume or *jika* nodded; the *Kara nai* (or Turkish caleoon) and an immense pillow studded with pearls. Altogether there was a great display of pearls; the throne (high-backed and with arms) was one mass of them. It is said that his Majesty has a mule-load of these precious articles in his treasury, besides a vast quantity of jewels and thirty millions sterling in specie: no other monarch in the universe is possessed of so much treasure. His Majesty was in excellent spirits, or "*dumaughish chak bood*," as the Persians express it, and was exceedingly affable and polite. His personal attentions to the Envoy were very marked; he twice pressed him to sit, which the Envoy declined doing. This mark of respect on the part of the latter raised him in the good opinion of the Shah and his ministers. His Majesty's manner to the Russian Envoy, Prince Menzikoff, was cold and distant: he did not ask him to sit, and would not permit his suite to enter the tent; they stood in a line outside. The Russians had themselves alone to blame for all this, for they still insist on wearing their boots.

The Shah said that he had been anxiously expecting the Envoy for some time, and that "his place had long been empty:" the latter replied, that after leaving Shiraz the sickness which prevailed in camp prevented his making such rapid progress as he wished, but that

that after quitting Ispahan he had hastened to the Royal stirrup. His Majesty said, it was fortunate he had not arrived sooner, or he would have been involved in disputes with the Russians; adding, "*poof reskha pur*," I spit on their beards! He then drew comparisons between the English and Russian nations, and was complimented by the Envoy on the successes which had attended the Persian arms. In return to this compliment, he said, "whose dogs "are they that they should attempt to compete with the *Kizil* "*bashees?*" or golden heads, as the Persians call themselves. Upon this Mirza Abool Hussein Khan, who had been long anxiously waiting an opportunity to join in the conversation, exclaimed, "*Aferin!* "*aferin! la illa illulah koorbanut-i-shoomah*, Excellent! there is but "one God; I am your sacrifice. *Mashalla!* God be praised, the vic-"torious army of the Shah has already driven the Russians out of "Georgia." Then turning to the Envoy, he said: "Your face is "whitened, your consequence is increased by the *shufakut* (con-"descension) of his Majesty." The Envoy merely answered, "*Ba-*"*rekullah!*" (Praise be to God!) After the Shah had drank coffee and smoked from a diamond-covered caleoon, brought in by a khan, we took leave (*khoda hafiz*) after half an hour's desultory conversation. The introduction was well conducted and very impressive, and the exhibition grand and imposing.

His Majesty, except where money is concerned, is the most sensible man in his dominions: he is beloved by his subjects, his rule is mild, and he seldom punishes with severity, except unpardonable offenders. He was hurried into the present war by the Mooshtaed (chief priest) and a set of bigots who beset the throne, loudly calling on him, in the name of Allee, to avenge the wrongs of the faithful,

who

who groaned under the tyranny of the Russians. He now sighs in secret for the quiet of his palace at Tehran, and anxiously desires the speedy termination of hostilities; which there is no likelihood of, as the Russians must first wipe out the stain upon their military character, and the Persians cannot in honour withdraw their protection from the Russian subjects who have so ably assisted them and joined their cause. The King, as before observed, is excessively fond of money. It is the custom of the Kings of Persia, on the occurrence of any fortunate event, to receive presents from their nobles; thus, when his Majesty (who is very fond of the chase, and is a capital shot) hits his game, he throws his hand behind him, crying, '*Shabaash! sicca bajoklee*, excellently done! the ducats, if you please.' But it is alleged against him, that even when he misses, he does the same instinctively, so that then also his nobles are obliged to fill his hand to pacify him for his bad success. Amongst other anecdotes of his avarice the following is related: A khan had won a considerable sum from the Shah at chess, and his Majesty was rather long in liquidating the debt; at last the khan, losing all patience, begged one day to remind his Majesty that a month or two before he had lost a hundred ducats to him. "Very true," said the facetious old monarch: at the same time holding up his feet to the khan, "here are my soles, Futty Khan, "beat away as long as you please, but you know I cannot part with "my money."

Whenever the children or the ladies in the *underoon* play, the King's bag is placed in the middle, into which the winner pays ten per cent. of his gains, which all goes to his Majesty, who seldom gambles himself. His favourite wife, the Taj-i-Dowlah, is a very

 sensible

sensible and superior woman; she was formerly a dancing girl of Ispahan, was noticed by the King for her shrewdness, and has reigned sole queen of the harem for the long period of thirteen years. She is exceedingly kind to the other wives and ladies, which is politic on her part, as she is not subjected to the bad effects of their envy and jealousy. She was very kind to the Russian prisoners, and sent them abundance to eat and drink. In his Majesty's harem there are one thousand ladies, and he is the father of one hundred children. The ladies punish their slaves in a variety of ways: one of which is, to make them drink the water from the caleoon after they have smoked; another is, to subject them to be clawed by a cat. Occasionally they beat them soundly with the heels of their shoes, and shave their heads.

The lady of Dr. Macneil, the physician to the mission, was one day in the zenanah, when she observed one of the princes, a boy of ten years of age, with a handkerchief tied over his eyes, groping about the apartment. Upon inquiring what he was doing, he said that, as he knew that when the Shah his father died he should have his eyes put out, he was now trying how he could do without them.

During the night of the 7th there had been a fall of snow on the lofty Sevelund: the wind blew cold and chilly; the thermometer seldom rose above 56° or 60° in the middle of the day. The Persians now began to sport their fur coats.

One evening, whilst I was riding through the camp, a mounted Persian in passing pointed at me in an insulting and taunting manner, saying, "*Roos, Roos,*" meaning "Russian." I made at him, when finding he was getting the worst of it, he threw himself off his horse and took refuge in a tent. I was about to follow him, when several

of

of the *ghoolam-i-Shah*, or King's body-guards, came out and interceded for him, observing that he was a fool for not knowing the distinction between the barbarians and the civilized *Furingees*.

Round our encampment there was abundance of game: one sportsman bagged twelve brace of quail in two or three hours; and five minutes' walk from our tent hares and the English partridge abounded. I obtained a day's relaxation from my daily task of writing public letters and registering the books of former missions, and went out hawking with Aga Bairam, the second eunuch of the harem.

We set out in a large party for the hills at six in the morning, all armed and mounted. When we came near the ground the hawks and dogs led: one of the party rode on the flank, singing Persian love-songs, and assisting the modulations of his voice with a book, which he waved in his hand. The hawks were cast off at partridges and quails, the dogs and horsemen beating the grain covers. We came to steep hills covered with dwarf oak, thorn, and plum trees. It was an animating scene to see how the Persians dashed fearlessly down the declivities and up the rocky ascents, after the hawk in pursuit of its quarry, sending down showers of stone into the torrent at the bottom of the glen, in the retired nooks of which, and far below us, were scattered the black tents of the Turkish Illyauts. The silence of the hills was disturbed by the lively and encouraging shouts of the Persians to the noble falcons, when they had singled out a bird from a covey, then marked him down, and rattled away to secure the plump quarry. When the falcon missed, which he seldom did, he flew over and attacked the small quail-hawk. The partridges, after they had seen their enemy, became so frightened there was no getting them out of the bushes. The horses were sure-footed, and

 the

the Persians most courageous horsemen. My character would have been gone for ever if I had not risked my neck as often as, and wherever they did.

We sat down to breakfast in a deep dell by the banks of a mountain torrent, shaded by dwarf oaks, the ground carpeted with the wild strawberry. Then caleoons were brought : a numud was spread, on which were placed the rich pillaus and game stews, and spits (the ramrods of the firelocks) with kababs, washed down by Sekunjebin and Shiraz wine, of which the Persians drank deeply. Our repast concluded, away we went again in search of game.

On the 9th the Prince of Bokhara, brother of the king Hyder Toorah, and son of the famous Beggee Jan, visited the Envoy. He was a thin spare man, with all the features of the Usbeg Tartars; small nose, prominent lips, and thin goat-resembling beard. The prince was formerly the Governor of Merv: he was now in distress, having fled from his brother, and desiring an asylum in India. He seemed to be deeply versed in astronomy and astrology.

The presents were this day sent to his Majesty; they consisted of the following articles:

Twelve scarlet bags, each containing one thousand tomauns.

Six magnificent chandeliers.

Twelve cut-glass table lustres.

A highly-finished double-barrelled gun, inlaid with gold, valued at 1,600 sicca rupees.

A pair of pistols, valued at 800 sicca rupees.

Eight trays, containing twenty-four Cashmere shawls, of four colours.

A superb alarum table-clock, valued at 2,500 sicca rupees.

A handsome

A handsome telescope, gold-mounted reading glasses, snuff-boxes, and a variety of other articles. Altogether the value of the present was about one lakh of rupees.

What is rather singular, and completely unprecedented, his Majesty made no return for this magnificent present.

The Envoy had a private audience of his Majesty; after which, on the 10th, his lady visited the Queen, and was received by the Taj arrayed in all her jewels: her dress was so loaded with these precious ornaments that she could scarcely walk: two diamond wings adorned her head, and women slaves, in rows, dressed in silks, and ornamented with jewels, stood before her. The King's jewels were also displayed, and the crown, throne, &c. A small string of seed pearls was all the present the Taj gave, though next day she received the following articles:

Four trays, containing twelve very rich Cashmere shawls.

A splendid gold repeater, with chain, &c.

A beautiful breakfast set of Wedgewood china.

Large and valuable work-box and colour-box.

Essences and scents of all sorts; knives, scissors, &c., besides trays filled with cambrics, muslins, rich velvets, longcloths, shawl dresses, silks, &c., and, what will no doubt surprise the fair reader, a very considerable quantity of Hodgson's pale ale; for true it is that the Queen of Persia *malts*.

On the 12th we visited the two eldest princes in camp, Allee Nukee Mirza and Imaum Wurdee Mirza: the former the governor of Casveen, and the latter Sir Kasuckchee Bashee, or commandant of life-guards. They were both exceedingly affable.

His Majesty having, before our arrival, determined on sending a

Persian

Persian ambassador to England, for the double purpose of soliciting the aid of the British Goverment in mediating an amicable arrangement of the differences between Persia and Russia, and to obtain the subsidy, the Envoy was enabled to dissuade the King from this intention and to send Mr. Willock, and it was determined that I should accompany him. At first it was the wish of the King that we should see the Prince at Sheesha (at which I was much rejoiced, as it would have given me an opportunity of witnessing the awkward operations of a Persian siege), and from thence across the mighty Caucasus to St. Petersburgh, to communicate with the authorities there. But this plan was laid aside, and it was finally settled that we should depart on the 20th, and proceed to Constantinople, through Asia Minor: from thence to England, *viâ* Vienna, Paris, &c. This certainly, in contemplation, was a most delightful and interesting route.

CHAPTER XII.

Leave the Royal Camp......Arrival at Tabreez......Fukir......Leave Tabreez...... Murand.......Nukshewan.......Shuheroor.......Erivan......Ararat.......Kuremarchee ....HajeeBairamloo......Enter the Turkish Territory......Nukshewan......Koords ......Armenian Villages......Kars......Visit to the Pacha.......Turkish Dandy...... Contrast between Persian and Turkish Manners......Ben Ahmud......Turkish Delibash......Arrival at Azeroom.

On the 20th, after bidding adieu to the Envoy and his lady, from whom I had experienced much kindness and attention, and taking leave of my other friends in camp, Mr. Willock and myself mounted and marched for Tabreez, where we arrived after a journey of sixty-four miles on the same horses. It is quite surprising what horses can accomplish in Persia. At Shiraz there is now a chupparee (post) horse, which travels between that city and Tehran, on important occasions, in five days, the distance being five hundred miles, with the same rider on its back the whole way. Many of the chupparee horses would beat the celebrated hurkara camels of India, which make most extraordinary journeys. There is a ludicrous story told of one, which arrived at the station of a Bengal regiment in an unprecedented short space of time. One of the officers got up from dinner to try the motion of the camel; he mounted, and the animal set off with him, and carried him the whole stage, seventy miles, without his hat.

The

The country between Achar* and Tabreez has the usual arid Persian aspect. After passing the village of Shaheruk and Khoja, the former half-way, there is much to arrest the attention of the geologist. Many of the hills are entirely white; others are striped red and white, calcareous strata alternating with soft red sandstone. The soil, on which was incrusted salt in considerable quantities, was formed by the debris of clay slate, which appeared above the surface under the red sandstone. This tract of country was very trying for the eyes, the glare being excessive. Near Tabreez I observed granite similar to that of Aberdeen.

Tabreez, the ancient Tauris, and capital of Azerbijan (the region of fire, so called from being the province in which the doctrines of Zoroaster first took root), is in a low situation, surrounded by extensive gardens, in which, besides every variety of fruit, potatoes in great quantities are raised. Coal was lately discovered, in considerable quantity, in sinking a well in one of the gardens. The city is walled, and has an ark or citadel much superior to that of Shiraz: the population is said to be eighty thousand. The winters are here very severe. The European gentlemen enjoy the amusement of skaiting for four months, during which period the ground is never free from snow. A few years ago the cholera committed dreadful ravages here, particularly among the troops of the Heir Apparent, who we now heard had advanced towards Teflis, the siege of Sheesha having been raised.

Just as we were leaving Tabreez, a fukir (a resh-sufëed, or white beard,) came running up to us, blowing a horn, with the usual exclamation of "*huk hu, ullah ho ukbur.*" He presented us with a talisman,

* Supposed to be the ancient Hara.

talisman, which was a paper inscribed with sundry strange characters and devices. On his head he wore a high cap, and a goat skin was thrown over his shoulders. Altogether his appearance was wild and uncouth.

Having put myself in still lighter marching order than before, being obliged to throw away most reluctantly almost all the specimens I had collected, in the afternoon of the 23d my companion and myself, armed *cap-à-pié*, and equipped in wide Turkish trowsers and boots, mounted for a Tartar journey to Constantinople. We were attended by only one servant, not being able to take another from the difficulty of procuring horses. Our first stage was to Murand (passing Sophian), distant forty miles. The horses of the Tabreez Chupper-khana (post-house) were excellent, being cossacks recently captured.

On the 24th we arrived at Nukshiwan, sixty-four miles, passing Gurgur, eight fursungs from Murand. In this day's journey we crossed by a ford the noble stream of the Araxes, or Arras, which Russia is so anxious to make the boundary between herself and Persia. Our fording the river instead of crossing in a boat was very hazardous: the stream was deep, over the saddle-flaps, and rushed past us impetuously. The river was divided into several streams by islands: the banks were clothed with osiers, &c. Along the river there is most excellent sporting; pheasants, and all other varieties of game, abound. Rice is extensively cultivated here. We now entered the province of Erivan.

The march next day from Nukshiwan (where it was rumoured the King intended to winter) to Shuheroor, distant forty miles, was the most disagreeable I ever made. The heat was intolerable, occasioned

 by

by the reflection from the white calcareous soil, and our wretched cattle could with difficulty move under their loads. When we dismounted they fell down, and had not strength to lift their tongues out of the dust. Every thing around us during this horrid stage seemed to glow with a white heat: not a drop of water was to be procured for miles to allay our burning thirst. At last, on ascending a small eminence, we were enlivened by the sight of Mount Ararat; its hoary head, the resting place of the ark, towering above a mass of clouds. Coming to a small clear stream of water, we dismounted to rest the horses, and sitting down under the shade of a ruined wall, a rosy-cheeked Illyaut woman, who was not particular about concealing her bust, brought us a refreshing feast of curds and melons. In the course of our day's march we passed Ilan Daghee, or Serpent-mountain. We observed in the neighbourhood of Nukshiwan blue compact limestone. Arriving at Shuheroor at a late hour, we experienced from the head-man of the village that attention which Englishmen usually receive from the people in travelling through this province. The Khutkhoda gave us his best room, and placed before us an excellent dinner.

We passed the following day through a very feverish district, abounding with streams of water, which produces luxurious crops of rice and other grain. I now saw carts for the first time in the Persian dominions, and very antique-looking ploughs, with wheels, to which were attached four yoke of oxen. At a late hour we arrived at the fort and town of Erivan, fifty-six miles. We had sent on our *fesoul*, or useless old fellow of a Mehmandar, to procure us lodging for the night. On requesting admittance into the fort, we were told to wait outside till an answer should be received from the Killedar.

Killedar. Kicking our heels for an hour at the gate, exposed to a chilling wind after being parboiled during the day, we lost all patience, and expostulated with the guard, but to little purpose. At last the gate opened, and the Mehmandar appeared with the intelligence that the Surdar had issued positive orders that no one should be admitted, as they were making preparations for repelling an attack of the Russians, who in the last war attacked this fort and were repulsed with great loss: we accordingly were obliged to bivouack under the walls without supper.

Next morning we procured a lodging in the house of an Armemenian, and were delayed half the day waiting for the men who were to accompany us across the frontier. In the afternoon, having sent back to camp our Mehmandar, we obtained a guard of three men to accompany us. Passing under the western wall of this excellent Turkish fortress, we crossed a rapid river (the Zengui) and on the other side saw a small and beautiful kiosk in a garden. We passed the three Armenian churches, called Yeuch Kalissa: here the Patriarch and head of the religion (whose authority extends even to Constantinople) resides. In one of them is preserved a portion of the ark, said to have been found at the foot of Mount Ararat (from which these churches are not far distant), having been brought down by the snow. The churches are each of them surrounded by a wall with bastions.

Since the days of Noah, no human foot has ascended to the top of Ararat: I believe not even to the summit of the lesser peak, or Little Ararat. Besides the glaciers and snow with which the mountain is covered commonly half-way down, in approaching the summit there is a wide chasm, which is party filled with ice, and the

 scarp

scarp on the further side is said to be nearly perpendicular. Lions, bears, and lynxes abound about the base of the mountain, and also enormous rock snakes. No vigorous effort has been ever made to attain the summit, although I think there is not a more interesting mountain to ascend than this. There would be little difficulty attending the accomplishment of the task if the proper season of the year were selected. At this time there was not a particle of snow on Little Ararat, and very little on the great peak: this then (the beginning of October) is the best time for making the attempt. The journey through Syria, &c. to Ararat would be short, and extremely interesting.

About the base of the mountain red and trap porphyry abound.

It got dusk before we had accomplished half the stage; our guides lost the road, and we wandered for half the night amongst dreary fens and morasses. The noise occasioned by countless hosts of frogs was tremendous, mingled with the plaintive notes of different species of water-fowl, which resembled children crying. Coming suddenly to the edge of a pool, we were startled by the tumultuous ascent of flocks of wild geese. Our horses got knocked up, and were continually slipping and falling into the mud. In attempting to leap a ditch, the jaded animal which I rode came down in the middle of it, and had not strength to get on its legs again: I was forced to jump off into the mud and water, and pull the beast out. At last we met a peasant, who conducted us to our stage, Kuremarchee, thirty-two miles from Erivan. It was so late that all the villagers had retired to rest, and we could get nothing to eat: I thought I should at least enjoy a comfortable sleep after my misfortunes, but even this was denied me; for the rascals who accompanied

panied us procured a light, and sat up smoking and talking of the war.

Next day our road lay along the rocky and picturesque banks of the Arras. I observed some very pure rock salt, which was carried on mules in large slabs; it is found close to the river in great abundance. To Hajee Bairamloo, the frontier town, the country was rich and well-peopled. At this place the people were very inquisitive; they came up and examined us most attentively, put on our hats, and minutely inspected our arms. There was an unfortunate double-barrelled pistol (with a trigger to shut down when on half-cock) which had no rest; it was cocked, and uncocked, and unscrewed a hundred times. A party of women came up to me, when I was standing out of the view of the men, and began to pull me about. After they had satisfied their curiosity with an attentive scrutiny of the different articles of my apparel (they were not quite so troublesome as the Burman dames, who were not satisfied until they had seen how the European dress was put off and on), they presented me with a handful of cucumbers, and clapping me on the shoulder wished me a pleasant trip to Islambool.* Hajee Bairamloo is eight fursungs from Karamarchee.

Crossing the Arpachaee river (the ancient Harpasus), we entered the territories of the Grand Seignor, being part of Armenia. We ascended a stony and very tedious pass: the postillions tied the halters of the rear horses to the tails of those in front, and drove them before them up the pass. At a late hour, and after having been exposed

* *Islambool*, not *Istambool*, is the name by which Constantinople is called in Turkey as well as in Persia.

posed to an excessively disagreeable storm of wind and rain, the drops falling like pieces of ice on the face, we reached our stage, Nukshewan, having marched fourteen fursungs, or fifty-six miles. We were comfortably lodged in a clean Armenian house; our horses were in the same room with ourselves, separated from us by a low railing. The Soobashee, or head of the village, a Koord, dressed in the Turkish costume, with a large turban, round and loose jacket, and enormously wide trowsers, came in to see us and hear the news. Koordistan extends as far up as this, and most of the heads of the Armenian villages between Hajee Bairamloo and Kars are Koords. They commonly wear the red turban, which hangs in a bag down the back.

In the morning of the 29th September we found all the hills round us covered with fresh snow, and the cold during the day's ride was very severe. We passed many Armenian villages, each having a small stone church, some of them with a sort of low steeple. The rocks, generally speaking, were a fine white sand-stone. We crossed a tract of snow ancle-deep, which to me was a great novelty, and in the evening entered the large and populous town of Kars, distant twelve fursungs. It contains thirty thousand souls. We were taken to a large house inhabited by Armenians, where it was intended we should sleep; but an old lady, who was washing linen at the door, was not at all inclined to allow us to enter. She scolded furiously: and said to our conductors, "If Musselmans come to Kars you bring "them here; if Christians come, you bring them here. I wo'n't open "the door, so take yourselves off." After a delay of half an hour the master of the house appeared, and admitted us, with many excuses for the incivility of the old woman. He took us to a large and comfortable

fortable upper-room, carpeted and cushioned round three of the sides. There were many more Armenians present, dressed in loose and long black robes, with a fur jacket and silk vest underneath: on their heads they wore a black cap, like a hat without the brim. After refreshing with chebooks and coffee, a low round table was introduced, on which was placed a most excellent trout with the best sauce I ever tasted, followed by a vegetable stew, and fruit. The Armenians are most excellent cooks: rich Turks have commonly an Armenian servant in that capacity. We spent the evening very pleasantly.

Next morning the Pacha, who enjoyed the distinction of three tails, requested a visit from us, and sent a horse magnificently caparisoned in white and gold housings. In riding through the narrow streets, with substantial stone houses on each side, the upper stories projecting over the ground floor, and the windows grated with iron, or wood in imitation of iron, I was particularly struck with the great diversity and richness of the Turkish costume. Fierce looking fellows of Janissaries (for these troops were still retained here, it was only in the neighbourhood of the capital that the revolution substituted the new disciplined troops) swaggered about in round embroidered jackets, with chebooks in their mouths and a pair of pistols in their belts. We crossed, by a good bridge, the river dividing the Armenian suburb from the city, which is walled, and overlooked by a castle built on a rock, which the Russians vainly endeavoured to take. We entered the court surrounding the palace of the Pacha. Opposite the entrance were two field-pieces, near which was picketed that species of *cervus* which is known by the name of the horned horse. The palace was a long range of buildings, two storied, the

upper

upper entirely of pine wood, like the generality of houses in Kars, large pine forests being in the neighbourhood. We ascended by a wooden stair-case, and entered a hall filled with soldiers. From this we were conducted into a room, where was seated a grave and respectable looking personage, being the Kaia, or Minister of the Pacha. Round the room were seated several well dressed Effendies (Turkish gentlemen). After smoking a pipe about six feet in length, and having sipped a little coffee, we were conducted into the large room, where, at the upper end, and on the left hand side, sat the Pacha himself (Osman) enthroned on cushions, and clad in very ample robes. A line of servants, richly dressed in red cloaks with silver-hilted daggers in their girdles, extended the whole length of the room, which was hung with small pictures of galleys and portions of the Koran beautifully written. Several antique-looking carbines and long guns were suspended from hooks round the walls. The great man himself was very affable; the whole history of the war had for the hundredth time to be gone over. After smoking, at a signal from the Pacha, all the servants left the room, and there was a little confidential conversation: after which we took leave, much pleased with the gentlemanly demeanour of the Pacha.

Sitting in the afternoon at the door of the munzil khana (post-house), one of the greatest dandies I had yet seen, the Tartar Bashee, or head-courier, came and seated himself by us. On his head he wore an ample yellow shawl-turban; his body was incased in half a dozen different coloured silks; a cloak embroidered with silver-braid and sky blue silk hung over his left shoulder. He lisped and talked in a most affected manner, and held his chebook negligently between his fore-finger and thumb. After we had answered his in-

quiries,

quiries, as to what nation we were of, and what route we intended to pursue to England,—he whispered to a man near him, "Wulla! these "are not what they pretend to be: they are not English; Vienna is "not the road to England; Moscow, which I have twice seen, is "the nearest and only road to England." He then turned round to us, and began talking of the great superiority of our countrymen at sea. This is the prevailing notion all over the East.

I was particularly struck with the contrast afforded by the courteousness and civility of the Persians, and the *hauteur* of the Turks. The former are affable, polite, and anxious to please; the latter are morose and surly, and display a sovereign contempt towards the kaffirs, or infidels, as they term Europeans. Had the Persians enjoyed the same advantages as the Turks, especially in respect to intercourse with Europe, they would have been a much more polished and powerful nation than their neighbours.

We rode that afternoon to the village of Ben Ahmud, three saut, or hours, from Kars. The Turkish mode of reckoning the distance is the space traversed by a camel in an hour, or saut. Now some travellers call the saut three miles, others four. He must be a very slow camel indeed which is not able to accomplish three miles and a half in an hour: I think the general length of a saut is four miles. We slept in a house under ground. The whole of the houses of the village were subterranean; the chimneys only being seen, to which were shutters to close, after the flame of the fire was extinguished and the live embers only remained, so as to throw the heat into the room. The severe cold obliges the inhabitants to construct their houses in this manner. On the roof was built a stack of fuel, consisting of dried cow-dung made into large cakes. The church stood

 outside

outside the village, a square stone edifice. We were unable to march farther than this village, as we were obliged to wait for a guard of Turkish Delibash (horse-soldiers), to escort us to Azeroom, through a forest infested with Koordish banditti, as this is the season when they leave their summer encampments for their winter quarters. Our guard arrived in the night; and next morning, the 1st of October, we could hardly get them to rise. At last we prevailed upon the kettle-drummer to mount his horse. He was a stout fellow, with a cap two feet in height, covered with leopard-skin. After performing three times on his instruments, the rest turned out and mounted, and filing irregularly past us, gave us a rough *oroolla*, or salutation. There were twelve of them, armed with spears, pistols, and carbines, and a few with sabres: they all wore the high black cap, surrounded at the bottom with a small turban. Their aga, or leader, wore a rich scarlet silk jacket, lined and trimmed with fur: he had a led horse. The men wore the common brown Turkish jacket with black cotton lace. We had not been long on horseback before the aga rode up to us, and said, "For God's sake, make haste and bring out the wine." On telling him that we carried none with us on a march of this kind, he answered that it was the very time above all others to indulge, and seemed much disappointed. They were highly pleased with our arms, and were quite surprised at finding priming in my pistols. Neither the Turks nor Persians can make locks which will retain the priming. When I drew my light sabre, and bending it round my body, tied it in my sash, they were delighted with the superiority of the English steel over their own unbending blades. They told me the only thing I wanted was a carbine, and advised me to return from England to Kars with one and become a Delibash, and that I would

would soon be a Pacha. I lent them my Persian *jureed*, and whenever we came to a level piece of ground, they pursued and charged one another, firing their pistols and playing the devil. At last we entered a forest of beautiful fir trees, being the *pinus larix*. Previous to this, after we had proceeded about six saut, the lazy fellows wanted to halt for the rest of the day at a village, and it was with great difficulty we could get them to move on. We travelled for many miles along a valley in this beautiful wood, in which I picked up some fine specimens of obsidian. Suddenly a fire was observed near the skirts of the wood. A halt was immediately ordered: our party shook their heads, and proceeded to prime their pieces; the aga mounted his war-horse, and brandishing his lance, pricked on with three or four to reconnoitre: but the enemy had retired, and we saw nothing of them. A rich prize we should have been to the Koords, for we had money, jewels, and shawls, to the amount of, I suppose, £2,500 or £3,000. At last we arrived at the munzil, being the village of Misingird, to the great relief of the Delibash, who had never made such a long march in their lives, though it was only fifty-two miles, or thirteen saut. The apartment in the munzil khana was a warm and comfortable-looking room, with a large pine fire blazing in one end of it; but when I attempted to sleep I was tormented with vermin of every description.

On the 2d we marched to the city of Azeroom, distant eighteen saut, or seventy-two miles, passing a very ancient-looking town (with a citadel on a rock surrounded with three walls), called Hussun Kella. We refreshed here with milk, honeycomb, and fruit. We entered Azeroom through a large burial-ground, the graves of the men distinguished by a turban, cut in stone, like that which they wore when

 alive:

alive: each rank and profession has a peculiar turban. At the munzil khana we found the Tartar (courier) who had been despatched from the Royal camp at Ardebeel in August. If any thing could surprise a Turk, our appearance at Azeroom ought to have done so; but the old fellow did not seem much discomposed.

CHAPTER XIII.

Visit to the Pacha......Leave Azeroom......Cross the Euphrates......Askalar...... Karakulukh......Posting in Persia and Turkey......Sheitan Dura......Recent Earthquake......Sainla......Enter the Pachalick of Trebison......Kella Hissar......Afun ......Nixar......Almos..... Tokat, the city of the Plague......Amasia......Wallachian Exile......Nursewan......Dowlut......Osmanjook...... Toksia ...... Karajillar......Boli ......Ismid......Arrive at Constantinople.

NEXT morning I was awoke out of a sound sleep by the smell of a rich cheese near me, and by the noise of two men talking French. One was an intelligent-looking person dressed in the Turkish costume, who informed us he was Doctor Bekey, *premier medecin de cour;* the other was an Armenian merchant from Constantinople, who brought us a present of cheese and biscuits. The Pacha and Siraskier of Azeroom (Siraskier means general; as he is commandant of all the troops in the provinces of Kars, Van, Moosh, Akhiska, and Beiazeed, the pachas of these are also subordinate to him) sent requesting to see us; but my companion said he was indisposed with the fatiguing journey. The Pacha returned for answer, that to-morrow, perhaps, we should be sufficiently recovered to wait on him. As the delay of a day did not exactly suit us, we mounted the splendidly appointed horses which had been sent for us, and entering the court-yard of the palace, were first conducted to the kaia, and then went up stairs to the Pacha. He was a most respectable-looking old man, with a mild and pleasing expression

pression of countenance. He had been formerly Reis Effendi, or minister for foreign affairs, but had been degraded from his office by court intrigue. His name is Alli Pacha. He was very anxious for us to stay with him during the day, and so was his physician. The Pacha almost insisted on our taking a guard with us; but we had had enough of the Delibash, and declined his kind offer. After taking leave, and being provided with a passport, we left this populous city (which contains, I imagine, one hundred thousand souls) in the afternoon, and marched with the Tartar nine saut, or thirty-six miles, to Askalar. It rained all the way; and whether it was owing to the moist atmosphere, or that the old Tartar had been tippling, he slept on his saddle nearly the whole stage. He attempted to smoke, but his chebook fell out of his hand, and his head, surmounted by the high Tartar cap, nodded in a most ridiculous manner. He was constantly calling out to the sooragees, or postillions, '*yawash, yawash*; gently, gently.' At last his horse led him into a ditch, and they both came down together in the mud, which dirtied his red embroidered dress terribly, and this accident kept him awake till we arrived, cold, wet, and hungry, at the munzil, previously crossing the Euphrates by a ford. It was ridiculous to observe the attention shewn to the Tartar by the people of the post-house: they ran out, and lifting him off his horse, carried him into the house, pulled off his boots, and placed him by the fire. They merely cast a glance at us, leaving us to get off as we best could, carelessly asking the Tartar what *giours* (infidels) he had got with him. The lower orders of Turks have a great contempt for Christians of all nations: to Europeans, they are not insolently rude; they merely give a reluctant *khoosh geldee*; 'you are welcome,' and

are

are not at all attentive to their comforts. I have frequently been awoke by a fellow who had lifted the covering off my face, and was scrutinizing my features with a lamp in his hand. This night I was aroused by a rascal throwing wet cloaks upon me to get at his own, which was underneath. He thought, I suppose, that I would tamely submit to this, like a pusillanimous Armenian; but I soon shewed him the contrary, and he took himself off in double quick time.

On the 4th we marched to Karakulukh, sixty-four miles. The Tartar said, at starting, that he intended to go very rapidly now, and was only afraid that we should delay him, which was not at all likely, as I never saw a person in a greater hurry, or more anxious to get over the ground than my companion. We had been prevented from making much progress in Persia by the badness of the chupparee horses. The postmasters in Persia have a paltry allowance from Government, which miserable contract disables them from keeping good horses. Nothing is paid for posting in Persia, only a small present to the postillions: in Turkey, on the contrary, thirty paras per saut are paid for each horse, and the horses are excellent, trotting and galloping the whole stage. There are forty paras in a Turkish piastre; twenty-seven piastres in a ducat, which is nearly ten shillings; so that posting in Turkey is little more than a penny a mile for each horse.

We rode for several miles along the banks of the Euphrates, which winded gracefully through a small valley covered with willows. It rained in torrents the whole day. I, as usual, got the worst horse of the party; they thought, I suppose, that any thing was good enough for the young giour. Much blood have my spurs to answer for.

What

What could be more annoying than labouring with hand and heel at the flanks of a miserable brute that went on three legs, whilst my companions were trotting gaily out of sight, occasionally hallooing to me to come on. If there was a pony in the party, I was sure to get it; if there was a horse which stumbled twenty times during the stage, that fell to my share. It was fortunate that I was of a light build, or the cattle apportioned to me never would have brought me to the end of the stage; but my length of limb was inconvenient, and occasioned me to be terribly splashed. The Tartar, of course, got the best steed; then the servant, from being paymaster; then my companion; and lastly, my unfortunate self.

After riding half the stage we came to a caravanserai, where was a guard to protect travellers in passing that place of ill fame, Sheitan Dura (Devil's valley). The guard mounted, and galloped at a tremendous rate to the valley of dread, which runs up from the river at right angles: it is a deep dell, in the bottom of which, amongst white sand-stone rocks, fringed with brushwood, brawls a mountain torrent. We were slowly descending the side of the glen, when two wild-looking men, armed with long guns, dashed out from under a rock: I clapped my hand to the butt of a pistol, but they ran down before us to guide us in the proper path. Some distance from Sheitan Dura we passed a tract of blueish tuffa, which was rent and torn in every direction by a recent earthquake: huge rocks had slid from their beds, and the shrubs and stones were lying in confused heaps. We passed considerable flocks of sheep of the Cape breed, browsing on verdant hills, covered with trees of the *juniperus communis*, and yews growing in a moist loamy soil.

Great numbers of deer are found in this district, principally the

cervus

cervus elaphus; black bears are frequent in the woods, and the ibex and wild sheep are met with among the hills.

Drenched with rain, we arrived at a very clean post-house, but in which we could not keep ourselves warm the whole night. I was beginning to doubt whether this chilly cleanness was preferable to the close and dirty hovels we had hitherto met with.

The wooded districts through which we passed in the next day's ride appeared like rich carpets. It was the most beautiful season of the year, that preceding the fall of the leaf, when the forests were variegated with autumnal tints of every hue. The dark green firs, junipers, and yews, formed the ground, on which were scattered the diversified tints of wild apple and pear trees, loaded with fruit, and oaks with deeply indented leaves: the latter were the *quercus cirris*, the native of Asia Minor, from the Bosphorus to Syria, and from the shores of the Archipelago to the frontiers of Persia, producing the gall-nuts of commerce, with which the shoots of the young branches were thickly covered. The houses of the villages were all built of logs, the interstices stopped up with mud: the roofs were flat; the minarets were of plank. The country was picturesque in the extreme, and like a well-cultivated garden; to me, so long accustomed to the sterile and forbidding plains of Persia, it appeared delightful. The Turks are to be envied the possession of such a country as this.

We went now at such a rapid rate, that the Tartar was completely knocked up, and we were obliged to leave him. We slept at Sainla, seventy-two miles. My companion was accustomed to chuparee journeys and to travelling Tartar, but this was the first that I had made; and the only cause which I can assign for my enduring the fatigue so well as I did, was the diet which I rigidly adhered to. Since leaving Tabreez I had not touched meat of any kind, nor any liquid besides the pure element and milk, of which last I drank large quantities: in fact, I subsisted entirely on bread and milk. Those few Englishmen who have gone this route have complained bitterly that they were starved; because, I suppose, they could not get a beef-steak or mutton-chop at every stage. In travelling rapidly, when you mount immediately after swallowing a hasty meal, viands that are easily and quickly digested are decidedly the best: butchers' meat ought to be entirely dispensed with.

The country became more beautiful as we advanced. We left now the pachalick of Azeroom, and entered that of Trebison. The sides of the road were lined with apple and pear trees, under which the fruit was thickly scattered, greedily devoured by fine large buffaloes. Red and black barberries were seen at every step. Numerous magpies were the only birds observed.—In Asia Minor there seems to be an unaccountable scarcity of wild animal life: the woods are silent, uncheered by a single feathered songster; even the passing hum of an insect is seldom heard. I cannot explain this: perhaps the severity of the winter is the reason. Unlike this are the jungles of India, which continually resound with the plaintive notes of the wild pigeons and doves, whilst every leaf teems with animation.

We arrived at Kella Hissar, seventy-two miles, a large and flourishing town, seated under a precipitous hill on which is a fort. The town is surrounded with villages, hamlets, and gardens, along the hedge-rows of which are planted poplars, laurels, and walnut-trees. The vine is extensively cultivated here. The people had a very fair and healthy appearance; light hair was very common;

many

many of the children had white curling locks, and all were fresh and rosy-cheeked. There were an infinite number of fountains in and about this delightful town. Hares and partridges abound in the neighbourhood; we saw several parties of sportsmen coursing on foot, a great exertion for Turks.

We rode next day for the first part of the stage along the hilly and dangerous banks of a river, which was much swollen and exceedingly deep. In many places we passed extensive pine forests, and slept at the village of Afun, seventy-two miles, where the people were extremely kind to us.

On the 8th we had a most beautiful ride, passing several rocks, in which were cut small apartments, with a low square door-way. We descended a hill, the upper part covered with beech trees, from the branches of which the wild vines hung in graceful festoons; also different varieties of *convolvulus*, amongst which was the snail-creeper.

In riding down this wooded hill, every tree which is found in England was observed; oaks, elms, alders, planes, ash, &c. The fruit-trees were medlars, apple and pear trees, and that called in Persia the zoghal, with silky heart-shaped leaves, producing a fruit like a long light-coloured cherry, of which an excellent preserve may be made. I collected a quantity of the seeds, and those of the acorn-bearing holly. The ground was carpeted with ferns, crocuses, primroses, and violets. We arrived at Nixar, a large town, the houses of wood three and four stories in height, containing several families; they were covered with tiles, and were almost exact counterparts of those of Ava. This town seemed most unhealthy; the people were wan and sickly in appearance.

After leaving Nixar, we rode through one of the most frightful-

 looking

looking passes I ever saw. It was a deep valley between hills covered with a thick wood, and was so dark that we could only see a few yards before us. We rode along the narrow road, canopied with branches for some miles: a hoarse and swollen brook crossed our path several times. We passed a fire, around which were seated a number of fierce-looking men, who scowled at us as we rode by: it was the most likely haunt for banditti I ever saw. We slept for a few hours at the deserted village of Almos, eighty-eight miles.

On the 9th we entered the hot and sultry region of plague. After a ride of five saut we arrived at the town of Tokat, where the bloated demon of pestilence had established his head-quarters: he had committed dreadful ravages during the last summer, not only here but all the way from hence to Constantinople. I prepared myself for the worst. The site of the town (in which the population is dense) is the sloping side of a red sand-stone hill, at the bottom of which is a clear river: the temperature was very high. We did not enter the town, but breakfasted in an open building near a handsome stone bridge, and sent a man in for the fresh horses. We set off, as usual, at a rapid pace. When passing between garden walls, over which rich clusters of grapes hung, the girth of one of the pack-saddles broke, and the load rolled under the horse. Whilst repairing the damage, a respectable-looking Turk issued with his servants from his garden to assist us: he presented us with several ripe bunches of grapes, observing that for the last three months he had resided constantly in his garden, being afraid to venture into the city, where, out of a population of thirty thousand, a third, or ten thousand, had been swept off within the last two or three months, and that still forty or fifty died *per diem;* but that, *Inshallah,* 'God willing,' the

the *taoon* (pest) would cease at the commencement of winter. Thanking him for his civility, we proceeded on, and had pointed out to us the tents of the exiled Capedun Pacha, who but little distinguished himself against the Greeks. Passing through the post town of Toorka, eight saut from Tokat, we slept at a guard-house, after a ride of sixty-four miles.

The guard-house was a small log-building: the arms of the guard (who reposed on skins outside, around a large fire) were hung against a great tree, opposite to which was a gibbet. This scene was laid in a wooded glen, so that the whole had a very bandit look.

We rode next day to Amasia, a very ancient city,* seated in an amphitheatre of hills, on one of which is a strong fort. On the face of the rock were several excavations, which I suppose were sepulchres. In passing through the town, where we were told there was no plague, I saw several very antique-looking buildings, with buttresses and gothic windows. Over several door-ways were Greek inscriptions, surrounded with beautiful friezes. I regretted exceedingly that I could not spare time to examine the remains of antiquity which are so numerous here.

Sitting in an upper room in the Munzil-khana, making a comfortable meal of the fine bread called ismid (which was twisted, like the strands of a rope, into a large ring), dipping it into *yeuort* (curds) sweetened with *sheera*, or the boiled juice of the grape, and finishing the repast with milk and musk-melons, a demure-looking personage walked in the gallery before us, clad in sad-coloured raiment, looking at us attentively, and seemingly very much inclined to open a conversation.

* The birth-place of Mithridates and Strabo.

versation. At last he took courage, and asking us if we spoke French, he came and sat down by us, and told us that he was an exile of the family of the Prince of Wallachia. He surprised us a good deal by saying that the plague had lately visited Amasia, and that still four or five died daily. His assertion was confirmed when we cast our eyes towards a burial-ground close to the post-house, in which were many recent graves, round which the *iris* was planted.

Leaving Amasia we passed through the large town of Nursewan. Here, also, they denied there was plague, although the first thing we saw was a funeral, and grave-diggers busily employed. We slept at Dowlut, ninety-two miles.

We breakfasted next morning at Osmanjook, a town overlooked by a hill fort. On the face of the rock were many excavations. Across the Kisil-sou, or Golden River, was a very handsome bridge of many arches: the country around seemed to be parched for want of rain, and provisions were dear. The women here wore the black veil, which in Persia is peculiar to the Hajee women, those who have performed the Mecca pilgrimage: with this article of dress, and enveloped in a white sheet, they resemble apparitions. From Osmanjook it was eight saut to Hajee Humza, and thence eight to Toksia; the whole eighty-eight miles.

On the 12th, on leaving Toksia, we were surprised by seeing a European running after us, and calling out in French to us to stop, and speak to an old friend. This was Doctor Fontaney, a French naturalist, sent by the society of the *Jardin des Plantes* to travel in Asia: he had spent some time in Persia, and was now on his way to Constantinople. In stopping to examine some wild yellow jessamines, woodbines, and hop-plants, which grew in the hedges, a

little

little English squirrel ran up a chestnut tree near me; the colour reddish brown with a white belly. We passed large flocks of Cashmere or shawl goats with beautiful white silky fleeces, of which they manufacture shawls, at the village of Oksia, where there was a good deal of plague. Close to this village we crossed the Delidoura river, along the banks of which rice was extensively cultivated.

We were now constantly meeting Tartars, who all said that a third part of Constantinople had been destroyed by fire, on the 1st of September. Passing Karajillan, we slept at Karajillar, seventy-six miles.

We passed next day through a bleak and cold-looking country, and were enveloped in fogs from the Black Sea. On the road-side were many capitals and parts of shafts of Doric and Tuscan pillars, which were placed upright in the ground, and were probably ancient grave-stones. Passing the village of Humamloo, we slept at a caravanserai built of logs, eighty-four miles.

In the morning of the 14th, we arrived at the city of Boli, in which there were whole streets of houses recently built and building. The Pacha here fortunately did not send for us. There were several regiments of the new troops, who were a puny-looking race, dressed in blue with Dutch muskets. The country round this flourishing city was enclosed and divided into fields by wicker and thorn fences. After leaving Boli, we passed a saw-mill driven by water, at which the people seemed busily employed preparing timber for the capital, for which there was a great demand in consequence of the fire: the road was covered for miles with waggons laden with timber. After leaving Boli, we rode for many miles through a beautiful beech wood, along a causeway: green hair-moss hung from the branches in great abundance. The evergreens were the rhododendron,

dron, oleander, laurel, and holly, with myrtles and several varieties of ivy. We slept at Dukja, seventy-two miles.

We proceeded next day to Kunduk, twelve saut: after which we crossed the large river of Sukarea, twelve saut, to Subanja, and from thence six saut, to Ismid, or Nicodeme, seated on the gulf of that name, an inlet of the sea of Marmora. In all we rode thirty saut, or one hundred and twenty miles.

We rode on the 16th along the beautiful and wooded shores of the sea of Marmora, studded with small islands. We passed through many neat sea-ports, near which, in sheltered bays, were lying sharp-built galleys. The copses through which we passed were said to be infested with Janissaries, who had fled from fear of their government. We met many waggons filled with beautiful Turkish ladies, who, escorted by their lords on horseback, were going out on pleasure-parties to the gardens. In the yard of one of the post-houses I observed the marble sarcophagus of a crusader converted into a horse-trough. We passed for miles through the magnificent burial-ground of Scutari, where, amongst high and turbaned tomb-stones with gold-lettered inscriptions, mournful cypresses were thickly planted. The Turks have an idea that Constantinople will ere long fall into the hands of the Franks, and men of family and substance are accordingly carried over and interred in Asia. Except at Ismid we had not previously seen the graceful cypress planted among the tombs: it had a very fine and impressive effect. At last we dismounted at the quay of Scutari, after trotting one hundred and ninety-two miles with only one hour's sleep; for at Ismid some men in the post-house kept thrumming a guitar and singing the whole night.

The

The most magnificent city in the world now rose before us, on the shores of Europe, which I thanked heaven I was again permitted to see. What need have I to describe the splendour of the diversified scene which was now spread out before us? Constantinople is the queen of cities, beyond all doubt. Built on little hills, each crowned with its towering mosque and minarets, with the Sultan's serai, arsenal, and other public buildings, washed by the waters of the Thracian Bosphorus, her site is the finest in the universe.

CHAPTER XIV.

Constantinople......Visit to the British Ambassador......Dragomans......Leave Constantinople.......Camparookchees........Locusts........Enter Bulgaria......Carnabad.......Sheumla......Roóschook......Enter Wallachia......Bucharest......Description of the City and its Inhabitants......Leave Bucharest......The Carpathian Mountains......Rothen Thurn......Quarantine......Hermanstadt......Vienna......Frankfort......Cologne......Brussels......Calais......Paris......Arrival in England.

We were not long in crossing to one of the quays of Pera, a city of itself, inhabited principally by Franks of every nation, but chiefly Italians and French. Great was the astonishment of the people when two sun-burnt men, booted and spurred, armed to the teeth, and arrayed in dark and dust-covered raiment, toiled up the steep and narrow streets, preceded by porters, labouring under leathern bags and Tartar saddles. The cobbler pricked himself with his awl, and the bread of the baker was burnt in his oven, when these two grotesque figures passed on towards the hospitable mansion of the British Consul-General.

Soundly did I sleep that night out of my clothes—a luxury I had not enjoyed since leaving Tabreez. We had performed this journey in a shorter time than it had ever been accomplished by a European. Twenty-three days was the time we took: we could easily have completed it in eighteen or twenty, if we had not been delayed on the other side of Kars by the badness of the horses. The distance is nearly fifteen hundred miles.

Next morning (17th October), after having twice performed our ablutions,

ablutions, to purify ourselves after this harassing journey, we galloped ten miles to the village of Tirepia, on the Bosphorus, to wait on the ambassador, the Right Hon. Stratford Canning. He resided there in a beautiful mansion (as the British palaee in Pera was undergoing repairs) formerly possessed by a Greek prinee, commanding a delightful view of the shores of Asia, the Giant's mountain, and the Black Sea. Mount Olympus was discerned from an eminence above the house. Our ride to Tirepia was over a waste traet eovered with purple heath, the wild fragrance of whieh brought with it a long train of pleasing recolleetions of that dear land, "where blooms the red heather and thistle so green." I ean bear testimony to the truth of these lines:

> " Midst pleasures and palaces though we may roam
> " Be it ever so humble, there's no place like home:
> " A charm from the skies seems to hallow us there,
> " Which, search through the world, is ne'er met with elsewhere.
> " Home! sweet home! there's no place like home!"

We spent five very pleasant days at Constantinople. One day I crossed over and walked about the city, visited the hippodrome, the mosques, serai, &e. In the streets which were lately destroyed by fire they were busy in repairing the damages. The Armenians seemed to have been great sufferers. In the harbour small eutters and schooners were eruising about, to exercise the sailors; and large barracks were ereeting in every direetion for the new troops. There seemed to be a great deal of energy in the government at this time; but they were still constantly deeapitating the disaffected, and levying new taxes: those who grumbled were sent into exile. I saw many shipped for Asia.

Our long stay was owing to our having been requested by the Ambassador to take charge of some important despatches which he was preparing; besides this, our Turkish papers and passports were not ready till the fourth day after our arrival. We engaged a Tartar to accompany us to Bucharest, the capital of Wallachia. We paid him one thousand piastres (£20) for five days: that was merely for escorting us; we bore, besides this, all the expenses of the journey. When the Tartars pay the expenses, the Dragomans oblige you to pay them the large sum of sixteen hundred piastres, which is perfectly absurd. From Azeroom we could have got a Tartar for five hundred.

There are not a set of greater rogues to be met with any where than the Dragomans (interpreters) of Constantinople; they cheat, lie, and intrigue in the most abominable manner. A Dragoman is sent by an ambassador to the Reis Effendi on some business: he transacts it; he then, in the name of the ambassador, asks a place or pension for some friend of his, who has engaged to pay him a large sum if he succeeds. The Reis Effendi, probably, lends a favourable ear to his application, thinking that he is conferring a favour on the ambassador. Frequently they extort money from rich Turks, quietly hinting that "if you don't give me such a sum, "you'll find yourself shortened by the head in a day or two." One mode of raising money amongst them was exhibited a few weeks before our arrival. A British vessel was wrecked at the mouths of the Danube; the captain was the only one saved. He came to Yiasse, the capital of Moldavia, to recover eight thousand piastres, which he had lent to a merchant there: the man denied the debt; the captain applied to a Dragoman, who engaged to recover the money,

money, provided he was allowed half (four thousand). This the captain would not agree to, and he was immediately thrown into prison for endeavouring to raise money on false pretences. The Dragoman proceeded against the debtor, recovered the money, and kept the whole to himself. The allowances of the Dragomans are small, yet they all make large fortunes : the above will shew in what manner.

In the afternoon of the 21st, after bidding adieu to our kind entertainer, the Consul-General (Mr. Cartwright), from whom we had received the greatest attention, we mounted, and rode to Telivree, twelve saut, or forty-eight miles, on the sea of Marmora, passing through a very bare country.

On the next day's march we met large bodies of Camparookchees (bombardiers) going to muster. Our Tartar, Ahmed Aga, a fine stout young fellow of about twenty-seven years of age (he was the best Turk I had yet seen, both as to appearance and affability of manners), told us that he had formerly been a Camparookchee. Some new mortars were to be tried, which it was supposed were not sufficiently strong. None of the men would venture to fire them. At last, Ahmed Aga fearlessly stepped forward and applied the match : the mortar burst into a thousand pieces, knocked him down, dreadfully wounding him in four places. The Sultan was a looker-on at some distance. Seeing the accident, he ordered the sufferer to be brought before him, and, pleased with his gallantry, gave him a pension of one thousand piastres per annum ; and the prime minister taking a fancy to him, made him a Tartar (courier). Some how or other, he took such a liking to me that there was no end to his attentions. I now always got the best and easiest-going horse, even better

better than his own; he never would allow me to mount or dismount but ran up and assisted me as if I had been a delicate female: I was quite ashamed. He constantly brought me little presents of fruit, or any thing that he thought would please me, and provided a warm corner for me to sleep in at night. I never had so much attention shewn me before as what I received from this kind-hearted fellow. I was convinced he was not a Turk, and at last he confessed that he was a German by birth, and had been stolen from his parents when a child. He was fond of a little *rackee* (arrack), which the Turks prepare with aniseed. He said that *chok rackee*, too much of it, was bad; but that a little made him go like the devil: and certainly he was one of the best travellers I ever saw, seemingly requiring hardly any food or rest. It is the broad shawl which Tartars wear round the waist, together with the well-padded saddle, which enables them to hold out in long journeys. I had adopted the shawl from the first, and found incalculable benefit from it.

We travelled through a country in which there was a good deal of plague, and passed a tract covered with locusts: the males were yellowish, and the females a brownish grey. They lay thick on the ground, and were greedily devoured by larks. We slept at Girk Kalissa (forty churches), twenty-eight saut (one hundred and twelve miles).

On the 23d we entered Bulgaria, the peasants of which are Christians, but half the population of the towns is Osmanee. This is a very wild but beautiful part of Europe. Where the country is not covered with oak forests, it is well cultivated. In the oak-woods through which we passed there are vast numbers of wild hogs: of these the Bulgarians make the finest hams in the world. I saw many hundreds

hundreds of these animals: the boars were all black, but the swine were white and mottled. I did not signalize myself by slaughtering any; my horse was so jaded that it could not carry me within shot. I only sabred a black snake, six feet in length, which possessed the poisonous fangs. Bears, wolves, and deer, inhabit likewise these fine forests. I saw a brown bear four feet in height. One of the horses in this day's march was particularly sluggish: the Tartar, in a rage at being delayed, sprung furiously from his saddle, drew his sword, and cut off a great part of the animal's tail, which is a common practice among Tartars, as it prevents the postillions from tying a halter to the horse's tail again. He likewise capsized one of the Soorajees, and gave him a severe beating for providing such an animal.

The towns through which we passed were particularly clean and neat, with large clocks on the minarets. After a march of twenty-two saut (eighty-eight miles), we slept in a Bulgarian cottage. Nothing could exceed the cleanness of the habitation: the walls were wattled, the interstices filled with mud; inside they were neatly plastered. The mother of the family and grandmother were dressed in chemises, white as the driven snow; their petticoats were of a dark stuff: round the head and under the chin was tied a white handkerchief. Two or three white-headed children lay opposite the fire on a rug, and the infant slept on a square board suspended to a beam by four strings. The master of the house was dressed in brown, with a skull-cap edged with black fur on his head. They were most attentive and civil to us: the young mistress of the family pulled off our boots, and placed before us the best fare the house afforded.

We rode on the 24th four saut, to Carnabad, a town of some size: from

from thence sixteen saut to Sheumla, in all eighty miles. Our unfortunate fellow of a servant, a Venetian by birth, whom we had engaged at Pera, now began to exhibit symptoms of insanity, in consequence of the excessive fatigue, to which he was unaccustomed. He said piteously that we had brought him here to kill him; that he should certainly die that night, and wanted a confessor.

We passed next day through a country abounding in game, particularly pheasants; and in the evening came in sight of the dark-rolling Danube. We slept on its banks in the fortified town of Rooschook, to which it was my last ride on horseback for some time. I had been constantly in the saddle since the beginning of June, and from the shores of the Persian Gulf to the banks of the Danube had ridden three thousand four hundred miles. This town was once taken by the Russians, but with great loss; which I am surprised at, as it is completely commanded by heights on the south-eastern face. On an island near this town a Turkish Seraskier and his whole army surrendered to the Russians, who had a superior force on the river. In Rooschook there was a great deal of plague; in fact, it was flying about every where in the dominions of the Grand Seignor. The march this day was eighty miles.

Our servant now went raving mad. He took a strange notion into his head that the Tartar wanted to kill him; nothing could persuade him to the contrary. He came and delivered up his papers and watch to my companion, who would not take charge of them. The only reply he could get was "*vous étes fou:* go to sleep." I took compassion on him, put him to bed, thinking that a sleep would restore him, and took charge of his effects for his brother in Constantinople, as he said this was the last of his days. Next morning he was little better, but

but clung to me in a desperate fright, praying me to defend him against the Tartar, whom he would not approach within twenty yards.

Having crossed this noble stream, half a mile in breadth, in a large single-masted boat with a projecting prow, we entered Wallachia, and mounted (for Bucharest, the capital, distant twelve saut) the most horrible conveyances that were ever contrived for jolting the soul out of the body of a poor sinner. They were low waggons, each containing a single person, who sat in straw two feet from the ground. They run on four wheels, have no springs, and are each drawn by four galloways. The postillion sits on the near wheeler, with the reins of the leaders round his neck. They rattle over the stones at a furious rate. We took six waggons, or *carouches*, so that we set off in great state with our two dozen horses: we were choaked, however, with dust. We changed horses four times. Half way between the post-houses we halted, and the postillions rubbed the eyes and pulled the ears and fore-locks of the horses: they refreshed themselves by drinking the *vin de pays*, which I tasted and found to be like bad Sauterne. The Tartar, after finishing half a jar, made wry faces, discovering it was sour.

We passed through a perfectly flat and highly cultivated country: on the sides of the road were innumerable large wooden crosses. The dress of the male peasants was a long whitish coat, descending to the middle of the thigh: some wore white sheep-skins, the wool inside; some black large-brimmed round hats; others white sheep-skin caps, like a hat without the brim. The women wore white kerchiefs over the head and under the chin, a dark-coloured petticoat trimmed with red or blue, and aprons. I saw several with cloth drab trowsers, which enabled them to ride on horseback like the men.

We crossed a river by a pontoon-bridge, and passing several large monasteries, Bucharest at length rose before us, amongst groves of trees. The appearance of the city, was very beautiful: the houses were white-washed, and there were many churches, each surmounted by a handsome steeple. It was now evident that we were in Furingistan. When we were about to enter the city, one of the wheels of the leading carouche (my companion's) broke in two: a spar was rigged on the axle to prevent the vehicle from capsizing, and in this ridiculous state we drove through the town. The streets were all floored with planks from side to side, and we went jolting and nodding our heads at the people over this uneven surface, in the most ludicrous manner imaginable, led by a waggon hopping on three wheels: our appearance was most absurd. We passed dozens of handsome carriages filled with boyars, or nobles (wearing enormous round grey caps), and well-dressed females: the latter, when we passed, burst into loud peals of laughter.

The streets would only admit of three carriages abreast, and the houses were irregular, with high roofs. Passing a palace, we came to long lines of houses of all sizes, then a church and another palace, and so on.

The Germans, French, and Italians wore foraging caps; the Wallachians round caps without peaks, and long furred robes: and the women seemed very fond of sporting fur of all colours. I need not describe my feelings on seeing so many rosy-cheeked females unveiled; it was what I had been for years unaccustomed to. In fact, I now thought every woman beautiful.

We arrived at two in the afternoon, so that we were exactly five days from Islambool: the distance is four hundred miles. Tartars commonly

commonly take six and seven days to perform this journey. We visited the British Consul, Mr. Blutte, and then went to the German Hotel.

In the evening we went in a drosky to a Turkish bath. We were first taken into a private room, where we undressed; from thence into a small and lofty apartment filled with vapour from three small cisterns, into which, from cocks, hot or cold water was conveyed. After a copious perspiration had broken out, we were rubbed with a hair glove, then shampooed, covered with a lather of soap, and quantities of hot water thrown over us. We were then carefully covered and reconducted into the dressing-room, where we were made to lie down for half an hour, the cloths being changed as we cooled. We smoked nargeels, drank coffee, and took a spoonful of preserve and a draught of water. The last part of the process is much better conducted than in Persia.

Bucharest covers a large extent of ground: it is an open town, and built in the form of a cross; the population is one hundred thousand. The Ospadar, or Prince-Governor of Wallachia, resides here. Formerly the Sublime Porte conferred this office on a Dragoman of the Court, but the present Ospadar is of a noble Wallachian family. The government is very despotic. The Ospadar can order a boyar to be decapitated without trial. This is seldom resorted to. Most commonly they are sent in chains to work in the salt-mines (there are two very large ones in Wallachia*), when they incur the

 displeasure

* These are farmed by the Baron Metane, who has the contract for paving the streets, &c., and is besides a great banker: in short, he is the Rothschild and M'Adam here. We had the pleasure of being introduced to him.

displeasure of the Prince, where they cannot exist beyond a twelvemonth! The Ospadar is assisted by twelve senators, who meet in divan twice a week: the metropolitan commonly presides. There is also present a Turkish officer, a sort of licensed spy, called the Divan Effendi, who watches their proceedings. In divan they discuss projects for raising money, paying off debts, hear and finally decide appeals from inferior tribunals, &c.

The boyars, and Wallachians in general, are weak enough to wish for a change of masters, and the Russians above all others. If the Russians possessed the country, there would be an end to all the emoluments which the boyars at present enjoy. There is a regular series of offices, each of which they can hold for a year; such as Minister for Foreign Affairs, Minister of the Interior, Superintendent of Police, &c. Now under the Russians these would be all filled with their own people: the boyars would dwindle into insignificance. They would not then be enabled, as some of them now are, to keep six carriages and a hundred servants, and to give splendid fêtes; they would then be obliged to take off their caps to every Russian ensign they met.

The calipak, or large cap of grey lamb-skin, which the boyars wear, is a most singular article of dress. The size is restricted to so many Turkish inches in circumference: if it exceed the measure, the wearers are subject to decapitation; yet they are so fond of large calipaks that each boyar has two, one of the authorized dimensions which he wears in the day, another with which they skulk about from house to house at night, and so preposterously large that they cannot come through a door without taking it off and passing it in sideways.

Bucharest

Bucharest is a very dissipated place: every female is of loose habits, from the highest to the lowest; their character is as bad as that of the Venetians. It is pretty evident, even to a stranger, that they are not particularly modest, as the walls of the rooms which I saw were painted with naked virgins (as large as life) bathing; Diana and her nymphs, &c., which were well executed by Italian artists. There is no theatre, but throughout the winter there are constantly balls and parties.

The basis of the language of Wallachia (since it was a Roman province) is Latin, very much corrupted; they have adopted many Turkish words, and a few Greek. The character is the Russian, which is a modification of the Greek. A Latin scholar would find little difficulty in understanding the Wallachians: *bon* is good; *lac*, milk; *rote*, a wheel, &c.

The Turks derive little revenue from Wallachia, though it is a rich country: thirty thousand piastres, and a few sheep for the troops at the capital, is all that is collected by the Porte. The guards in Bucharest are Albanian soldiers, dressed as Turks, and the police consists of sixty Turks.

There is a great deal of ceremony attending every little event at Bucharest. When a new consul arrives, carriages, servants, and guards are sent to escort him to court, where upon being presented he makes a set speech, which is duly answered. After this ceremony he must stay at home for a month, to receive the visits of all the boyars: another month is then spent in returning them. Consuls are here looked upon as ambassadors. Formerly their situation was very comfortable, as they were allowed forage, fire-wood, &c., and had a certain number of serfs attached to them; so that one man engaged

engaged to supply them with game, another with poultry, fish, &c.; but all this, a short time since, was done away with, in consequence of a French Consul refusing to take the Government allowances. The rest all suffered for the foolish pride of this individual.

Provisions are very cheap. The price of a hare is a halfpenny, without the skin; a goose a penny; a turkey three half-pence, &c.; but articles of luxury, as furniture, carriages, wines, &c. are enormously expensive. Their wines are all very bad; Cypress was the best I met with here.

In the afternoon of the 27th, after paying a heavy bill for very indifferent fare, we again mounted those accursed vehicles, the carouches. When I gave my hand to the tender-hearted Tartar at parting, he cried like a child, saying, "In Ingliterra you'll soon "forget Achmed Aga." I purchased his sword, to complete my collection of Oriental arms; but it was with difficulty I could prevail on him to take any thing for it.

We travelled the remainder of that day and the whole of the night through a rich country. Next morning it became more picturesque; little wooded hills rose on each side, with fertile vallies between them, in which appeared white-washed churches, near numerous villages and hamlets. We entered the Carpathian mountains, which are greatly infested with bears and wolves: here the people seemed much afflicted with goitres. Our progress was now slower. At ten, P. M., after crossing a river in a large flat boat, we passed the first Austrian post, and entered the quarantine of Rothen Thurn.

We had only been thirty hours from Bucharest, and till we entered the mountains had gone at the rate of eight and ten miles an hour, without food or rest. The distance must be nearly two hundred

miles.

QUARANTINE.

at Rothen Thurn

miles. Disgusted with the jolting of the vehicle, I had ridden several stages on horseback.

The quarantine station of Rothen Thurn, or the Red Tower (so called from an ancient and ruinous tower which was constructed for the defence of the pass), is situated on the banks of a considerable and rapid river, which winds through a narrow valley in the Carpathian mountains, bounded on each side by wooded hills, very steep, and of four or five hundred feet elevation. The basis of these hills seems to be grey wacke, superimposed on quartzose rock and mica slate; some fine specimens of the latter may be picked up in the bed of the river. The quarantine station consists of a dozen houses, a small chapel, and a hotel. A detachment of Austrian infantry is posted here.

We were placed in a large and clean apartment, in a single-storied house surrounded by a court-yard, inclosed with a wooden wall, in which was a door with a grated window, through which we communicated our wants. There was a French marquis and a king's messenger in quarantine. To the latter I delivered the despatches from the Ambassador at the Sublime Porte. It was ridiculous to witness the forms that were gone through previous to his being allowed to receive them. I was taken into an apartment in the inspecting-house, and was put with the bag into a part of the room which was railed off; here the bag was opened by a man whom the others never approach; the packets had a large needle driven through them in twenty places; afterwards they were put into a cask, under which were placed live embers strewed with sulphur. After having been fumigated for half an hour, they were delivered to the messenger, who left next morning. At the quarantine they open all letters to

or

or from their own subjects. As I went in or out, all the doors were thrown wide open before me, and the people ran back when I passed: the papers were received from me, or handed to me, with a pair of long tongs or pincers. I began to think that I was really infected.

Next morning we were obliged to open and hang up all our clothes, under the superintendence of a medical man; and for half an hour each day we were allowed to walk up and down the banks of the river, under a sentry. We were confined only seven days: on the sixth our clothes and ourselves were fumigated with sulphuric acid.

The Right Hon. Stratford Canning having requested us to wait a day or two longer for despatches, Mr. Willock proceeded to the town of Hermanstadt to purchase a carriage, in order that no time might be lost, and I remained for three days at the hotel until the despatches arrived, which I brought to Hermanstadt.

I spent my time very pleasantly at the gast-haus, or inn. The landlord and his wife were most kind and attentive to me, and the hand-maids, their two daughters, were the prettiest girls I had almost ever seen.

Having reached the quarantine, it is needless to carry the reader further through a circumstantial detail of our progress in countries that have so often been described by journalists and tourists. Let it suffice to state, that we left the town of Hermanstadt on the 7th of November, and travelling in an excellent carriage and four through Transylvania, Hungary, and Austria, by way of Diva, where is an ancient hill-fort; the large and strong town of Temeswar, and Offen, or Buda, the capital of Hungary, on the Danube, we arrived at the imperial city of Vienna in five days, where, having waited on the Ambassador, Sir Henry Wellesley, from whom we received

received despatches, and after staying part of three days and seeing what was worthy of notice, on the 14th November we left, and passing through St. Polten, Lynch, &c., entered the kingdom of Bavaria.

We passed through Passau, Strasburgh, and Ratisbon, with its noble cathedral; Wutzburgh on the Maine, with its beautiful palace, citadel, and bridge; the free-town of Frankfort on the Maine; and at the town of Mantz entered the dominions of the Grand Duke of Hesse: after which we passed through a part of the Prussian dominions, and the very ancient town of Cologne, where the cathedral and churches highly delighted us. At Maas we entered the dominions of the King of the Netherlands, and passing over a part of the ever-memorable field of *Waterloo*, entered Brussels, which, after waiting on the Ambassador, Sir Charles Bagot, and seeing the attractions in this fine city, we left on the 22d, and entering the French territories, passed through the noble fortifications of Lisle, and arrived at Calais on the 23d. We saw Albion's white cliffs exactly two months (to an hour) after leaving Tabreez. My companion sailed for Dover; and having some business in the French capital, I repaired thither, and finally landed in England on the 10th of December 1826.

CONCLUSION.

It may gratify the curiosity of the reader to be acquainted with the amount of expense I incurred in performing this overland journey. The sum I expended, from the time I left Bombay till my arrival at Calais, was £250. Out of this sum I purchased, in Persia, two chargers, kept three servants for four months, and defrayed the hire of three mules for a like period. I also paid my travelling expenses through Asia Minor and Europe. It must be observed, that I paid nothing for my passage from Bombay to Bushire, and that the abundant table of the Envoy occasioned no outlay on my part in the way of living, whilst I had the honour of being attached to his suite.

Three hundred pounds will cover every expense of travelling respectably and comfortably, by either the Turkish or Russian route; in the former, if celerity is attempted, the fatigue is great, attended with risk, from plague and the dangers arising from the Pachalicks being occasionally at war with each other, or in rebellion against the Porte: but all these considerations are amply compensated by the pleasure of traversing the beautiful and classic country of Asia Minor. In the Russian route, comparatively speaking, there is little or no fatigue; the traveller enters a carriage at Teflis, and is carried on without exertion on his part to St. Petersburgh in a month, if in summer; but then, with the exception of the magnificent scenery of the Caucasus, and the two Russian capitals, there is nothing whatever to interest him—the region traversed is monotonous in the extreme. A person of a delicate constitution might easily accomplish the latter route in four or five months; but let no one who does not possess considerable stamina attempt the former: and if expedition is desired, great privation in the article of food must be endured; as well as want of rest, and risk from pestilence and banditti. Probably ere long, if *steam* is extended to the west of India, the Egyptian route will be a beaten tract.

APPENDIX.

No. I.

A CHRONOLOGICAL EPITOME OF THE EVENTS OF THE BURMESE WAR.

No. II.

SUMMARY OF THE CAUSES AND EVENTS OF THE EXISTING WAR BETWEEN RUSSIA AND PERSIA; 1826-27.

No. III.

ITINERARY OF THE JOURNEY THROUGH PERSIA, ASIA MINOR, AND EUROPEAN TURKEY.

APPENDIX, No. I.

A CHRONOLOGICAL EPITOME OF THE EVENTS OF THE BURMESE WAR.

1823.

August. The Rajah Tooroo Wyn demands, in a peremptory letter to the Bengal Government, the removal of the British guard from the island of Shapuree.

Sept. 23. A Burmese force expels the British guard from the island.

Oct. 17. The Bengal Government remonstrates.

Nov. 21. Shapuree re-occupied by the British without opposition.

December. The Burmese invade Cachar.

1824.

January The Burmese invade Jynteea.

—— 17. Major Newton defeats the Burmese on the frontiers of Sylhet. British loss, 34; Burman, 185.

—— 20. Seizure of Mr. Chew, of the H. C.'s schooner *Sophia*, by the Burmese.

Feb. 13. Capt. Bowe defeats the Burmese at Budderpore. British loss, 39; Burman, not known.

—— 21. Lieut. Colonel Bowen attacks Doodpatlee, and is obliged to retreat. British loss, 155; Burman, very severe.

March 5. Proclamation of war by the Governor-General of India.

—— 22. Brigadier MacMorine enters Assam.

April. The Burmese invade the Chittagong district.

May

1824.

May 10. Expedition under Sir Archibald Campbell (which sailed the middle of April) arrived at Rangoon, which was occupied next day.

—— 19. Cheduba reduced by Brigadier General McCreagh. British loss, 44; Burmese, very considerable: the Rajah of Cheduba taken.

—— 17. Capt. Noton and his detachment (consisting of eight companies of regulars, a party of provincials and Mughs, with two guns and a detail of artillery) routed by the Burmese at Ramoo. British loss, 6 officers, and about half the detachment; Burman, not known.

—— Negrais taken by Major Wahab. British loss, 8; Burman, not known.

June 6. The stockades at Kemmendine assaulted and taken by the British army. British loss, 138; Burman, considerable.

July 1. General attack on the British position at Rangoon by the Burmese army, twelve thousand strong, who were defeated without the loss of a single British soldier killed or wounded. Burman loss, 100.

—— 8. General attack of the enemy by the British army, which is successful. British loss, 76; Burman, 800.

Sept. 9. Tavoy surrendered to Lieut. Col. Miles, with one hundred and sixty-seven pieces of ordnance.

October. The Burmese forced to evacuate Cachar.

—— 6. Mergui assaulted and carried by Lieut. Col. Miles: one hundred and forty-three pieces of ordnance captured. British loss, 31; Burman, 500.

—— 7. Lieut. Col. Smith forced to retreat in confusion from the enemy's stockade at Keykloo. British loss, 95; Burman, inconsiderable.

—— 30. Martaban stormed and taken by Lieut. Col. Godwin; one hundred and sixteen pieces of ordnance captured. British loss, 21; Burman, great. The voluntary submission of Tenasserim, and the town and province of Yeah, followed.

Dec.

1824.

Dec. 1. Maha Bundoolah, at the head of sixty thousand men, accompanied by the Princes of Tongho and Sarawuddy, commences an attack on the British post at Kemmendine, which is defended for six days by a small force under Major Yates.

— 5. The left wing of the Burman army defeated.

— 7. The right wing advances against the British, and is defeated. British loss (from 1st to 7th), 224; Burman, 5,000.

— 14. Rangoon fired by emissaries from the Bundoolah's army.

— 15. The Bundoolah rallies his troops and pushes forward a force to Cockain (or Cambah), which is routed, with the loss of its commander. British loss (from 10th to 15th), 206; Burman, most severe.

1825.

Jan. 11. The stockade and pagoda of Syriam stormed by Lieut. Col. Elrington. British loss, 36; Burman, not known.

— 30. Rungpore, the capital of Assam, surrendered to Lieut. Col. Richards. The Burmese troops evacuate the province.

Feb. 3. Attempt on the island of Ramree, by Lieut. Col. Hampton, unsuccessful through the treachery of the guides. British loss, 28; Burman, not known.

— 6. The enemy's works at Tantabain (or Quangalle) stormed and taken by Lieut. Col. Godwin. British loss, 10; Burman, severe.

— 16. The British army advances from Rangoon (a proclamation being previously issued by the Commander of the Forces addressed "to the inhabitants of the Burmese Empire"): the land column, under Sir A. Campbell, marches in the direction of Prome; the marine column, under Brig. Gen. Cotton, towards Panlang and Donabew.

March 3. Basscin occupied by Major Sale; 101 pieces of ordnance captured.

— 6. Brig. Gen. Cotton arrives before Donabew, where the Bundoolah commanded.

1825.

March 7. Unsuccessful attack on Donabew. British loss, 129; Burman, about 500.

—— 8. The Brig. Gen. retires to Youngyoun.

—— 16. Sir A. Campbell reaches U-andeet.

—— 24. Brig. Gen. Morrison, with the south-east division, enters Arracan.

—— 29. The heights near the capital of Arracan stormed and carried without loss by Brig. Gen. Richards.

April 1. The city of Arracan abandoned by the enemy and occupied by the British. Loss from 26th March to 1st April: British, 250; Burman, very great.

—— Sir A. Campbell retrogrades, and joins Brig. Gen. Cotton.

—— 2. Batteries of heavy guns and mortars opened upon Donabew. The Bundoolah killed by a rocket from the British batteries; the place evacuated; large depôts of grain and one hundred and forty pieces of ordnance left by the enemy. Loss, from 25th March to 1st April: British, 75; Burman, not known.

—— 22. The island of Ramree captured by Brig. Gen. McBean, without opposition.

—— 24. Sir A. Campbell reaches Prome, which is evacuated by the Burmese and taken possession of by the British, with one hundred pieces of artillery and stores of grain.

June 1. Rajah Gumbheer Singh, accompanied by Lieut. Pemberton, recovers Munipore, his capital.

Sept. 17. Armistice agreed to at Meeaday for a month (afterwards prolonged till November 2d), preparatory to a treaty of peace.

Oct. 2. Negociations commenced between the British and Burmese chiefs, at Nenbenziek.

—— 20. Sir A. Campbell announces in General Orders that the Burmese army is in full march to attack the British army.

Nov. 15. A British detachment, under Col. McDowall, forced to retreat from Wattygaon, with the loss of its commander. British loss, 219; Burman, not known.

Dec. 1 & 2.

1825.

Dec. 1 & 2. The Burman army under Maha Nemiow defeated at Simbike and Napadee. British loss, 157; Burman, most severe.

— 5. The enemy's right wing on the west bank of the river, dislodged by Brig. Gen. Cotton. British loss, 5; Burman, 300.

— 17. Sir A. Campbell reaches Meeaday, which is evacuated by the enemy.

— 27. He advances with the Madras division to Patanagoh.

— 31. A treaty of peace agreed to: signed January 3d, 1826.

1826.

Jan. 7. Lieut. Col. Conroy, sent with a detachment against Setoung (or Zittoun), killed, and his troops obliged to retreat. Zittoun afterwards carried by the force under Colonel Pepper. British loss (on 7th and 11th), 117; Burman, 500.

— 19. The treaty not being ratified on the 18th, as stipulated, Sir A. Campbell assaults and takes Melloun. British loss, 71; Burman, severe.

— 31. The British army, on its march to Amerapoora, met by a deputation sent from that capital to treat for a suspension of hostilities.

Feb. 9. The Burmese army routed at Pagam Mew. British loss, 18; Burman, not known.

— 14. The Commander of the Forces continues his march towards the capital.

— 24. Treaty of peace signed at Yandaboo, whereby the King of Ava renounces all claims upon Assam, Cachar, and Jynteea; acknowledges Gumbheer Singh as Rajah of Munipore; cedes the whole principality of Arracan, including Ramree, Cheduba and Sandowey, the provinces of Yeah, Tavoy, Mergui, and Tenasserim, with their islands and dependencies; consents to pay a crore of

 rupees

rupees (£1,000,000) and to admit a Resident at his court, with an escort of fifty men. The troops thanked in General Orders, for the courage and perseverance with which they had sustained an arduous conflict of two years' duration; and as a reward of their meritorious services, they bear "Ava" on their colours, and are promised *A Medal.*

The loss of the British in action may be computed at about 3,000. The mortality by sickness was immense, but no returns have appeared of the amount. At Rangoon alone 2,000 Europeans, and at least 5,000 sepoys, were cut off by disease; at Arracan, likewise, great numbers. Many hundreds of invalids met a watery grave before reaching India; from one transport, in a passage of ten days from Rangoon to Madras, three officers and forty men were consigned to the deep.

APPENDIX, No. II.

SUMMARY OF THE CAUSES AND EVENTS OF THE EXISTING WAR BETWEEN RUSSIA AND PERSIA; 1826-27.

THE remote cause of the hostilities between Persia and Russia may be traced to the last treaty of peace concluded between the two powers, and signed at Gulistan in October 1813. The want of precision in marking the exact boundaries by which the respective empires were in future to be discriminated from each other, necessarily led to violations of territory on the part of the rude and ignorant tribes inhabiting the countries on the frontiers, which afforded to a state, like Russia, anxious for an excuse to encroach upon its neighbour, a decent pretext for war.

This was the *natural result* of a treaty so injudiciously framed: but the impatience of the Russian authorities on the frontiers seems to have anticipated this result, and to have hastened the period of collision between the two states by an act of aggression.

The treaty of Gulistan, which was negociated under the mediation of the British Ambassador at the Persian Court (Sir Gore Ouseley), thus defined the limits of the two empires on the Georgian frontier, according to the *status quo ad præsentem:* The boundary line commences from the beginning of the plain of Adinah Bazar, and runs direct through the Sahara, or desert of Mogham, to the west of Yedibolak, on the river Arras or Araxes, and then on the northern bank of that river, until its junction with a river named Capanek, at the back of the hill of Mogree. From the right bank of this river, the boundaries of Karabaugh and Nukshiwan are marked by a line drawn on the summits of the mountains of Pembek and Aligus. The line then continues from the top of the Pembek

Pembek mountains to the angle of the boundary of Shuragil, then over the snowy mountains, and passing through Aked, runs along the limits of Shuragil and between the village of Misteri, until it reaches the river Arpachai.

It is obvious that boundaries thus described, and which are not marked by any natural barriers, or even by towns or fortresses, must be extremely vague and uncertain. Accordingly, there exists between the two empires a district, the sovereign of which is doubtful, and which is inhabited by hordes of Koords and Illyauts, who often plunder both territories indiscriminately, and occasion mutual demands for satisfaction.

The exact and final adjustment of the frontier, which no description on paper could effect with any accuracy, was to be made by commissioners on both sides, who were jointly to survey the country, and settle the new line of demarcation conformably to the terms of the treaty.

Negociations, on this subject, commenced between the Russian and the Persian courts immediately after the peace; and it was hoped by the latter that, through the mediation and good offices of Great Britain, the Autocrat of Russia might be induced to relax a little in the hard terms imposed upon Persia, and to consent to the re-cession of some portions of the territory relinquished by her.

The solicitations of the Persian Ambassador, backed by the recommendations of Lord Cathcart, at the court of St. Petersburgh, had no effect upon the Russian cabinet, which referred the matter to General Yermoloff, the Governor-general of Georgia, who put an end to all the hopes which might have been indulged by the court of Tehran, of recovering a part of its lost possessions.

Some time elapsed before the appointment of Commissioners to settle the line of demarcation, probably owing to an expectation, on the part of Persia, that Russia might relent; but when the appointment took place, and when the commissioners proceeded to the adjustment of the respective frontiers, such a vast difference appeared in the views of each party, that it was plain there was little probability of their coming to an agreement. The Russian Commissioners, Generals Paulonawich and Yermoloff junior, absolutely refused to listen

listen to the representations of those of Persia; they declared what *they* considered as the true boundary line, and positively refused to admit of any deviation from it. The Persian Commissioners, therefore, proceeded no farther than Karabaugh, when they were recalled by the Prince Royal, who had the charge of administering the affairs on the frontier.

The Russian Government, meanwhile, established posts upon a strip of country which extends along the north and north-east shores of Lake Gokcha, and upon a district situated on the borders of Karabaugh, between the Capan and Mogree rivers. The former territory was uninhabited; but it belonged indisputably to Persia. Her title to the other district was less clear and unembarrassed. It is doubtful whether it was in the occupation of either power antecedent to or during the war: the proprietors of the soil, indeed, considered themselves under the protection of Persia; they were the peasants of Abul Futteh Khan, a Persian subject, and probably reoccupied this district as soon as tranquillity was retored.

It is impossible to disover the grounds upon which the Russians could lay claim to the Gokcha territory. When, at a subsequent period, the Prince Royal of Persia remonstrated with General Yermoloff on account of his sending the tribes of Shumsheedeenloo and Kusakh, protected by a detachment of Cossacks, into this district during the summer months, to seek pasture for their flocks, which were withdrawn in winter, (characterizing it as a violation of the Persian territory,) the General acknowledged that it was an infringement of the treaty, but excused the proceeding, on account of the district being uninhabited, alleging that it was equally to the advantage of both empires. What is still more to the point, the Russian declaration of war states that the Emperor did not dispute the right of Persia to the Gokcha territory, and required only that the district of Capan should be given up by Persia, which the document alleges was expressly assigned to Russia by the treaty. The acknowledgment of General Yermoloff was singularly at variance with the statement of General Wilheminoff, the Lieutenant-Governor of Georgia, who at a later period declared, in a letter to the Shah, that Russia had been in possession of the territory

territory in question ever since the peace of Gulistan. It may be here necessary to explain, that though the district of Gokcha is waste and unfertile, yet it commands the pass of Ganja, affording to Persia an easy entrance to Georgia, and to Russia the means of rapidly overrunning the province of Erivan; therefore the one power was as reluctant to give it up, as the other was eager to seize upon it.

With respect to the Capan territory, the Russians assert that the river running in the neighbourhood of Mogree is called *Capanek*, and forms the boundary; and that Persia exceeds her limits, as defined in the treaty, if she occupies the country as far as *Capan*. The Persians, on the other hand, maintain that there is no river called *Capanek*; that the river running in the neighbourhood of Mogrée is called *Mogree Chai;* that the Capan Chai forms the true boundary; and that the country between these two rivers has been in the possession of Persia since the termination of the war.

The statements of the Persian government are fully warranted by a map of Georgia, published by authority of the Russian government in the year 1819. In this official document, the Capan forms the actual boundary of the two empires, and no river named *Capanek* is laid down. The claim of Russia, therefore, which was not set up till some time after the treaty, is destroyed by her own evidence.

Under such circumstances, negociations took place between the Court of Tabreez and the Governor-General of Georgia, which were productive of angry disputes and much irritation on the side of Persia; there being visible in the conduct of Russia a consciousness of superiority, and an eagerness to catch at every pretext for advancing its frontiers towards the Arras.

After some fruitless efforts at an adjustment, a proposal was made to the Prince Royal by M. Mazarovitch, the Russian *Chargé d'Affaires*, for the arrangement of these differences, and which was accepted by his Royal Highness. When this agreement was submitted to General Yermoloff, he refused to ratify it, alleging that the Russian minister had exceeded his instructions.

Soon after, a mission was sent from the Prince Royal to Teflis, and the Persian

sian Envoy, Futteh Ali Khan, returned with a *projet* of arrangement offered by General Yermoloff, which was not, however, satisfactory to the Prince. Futteh Ali Khan was then despatched on a second mission from the Prince Royal. The result of his negociations at Teflis was the settlement of a frontier line, by an agreement between himself on the part of Persia, and Generals Wilheminoff and Mududoff on the part of Russia. By this agreement, the Gokcha district was relinquished to Russia, as an equivalent for the Capan territory, which was thereby acknowledged to belong to Persia. To this agreement, however, Futteh Ali Khan did not affix his seal.

In the month of March 1825, General Yermoloff, having received no formal ratification of this agreement from Prince Abbas Mirza,* and apprehensive, from the notorious uncertainty of Persian politics, that his Royal Highness might be disposed to recede from the agreement of his agent, addressed a letter to Mirza Abul Hussun Khan, the Minister for Foreign Affairs, the object of which was to obtain his Majesty's ratification of the arrangement. The Shah, however, positively refused to ratify it.

General Yermoloff, therefore, in the summer of 1825, despatched M. Mazarovitch upon a mission to Tehran, to endeavour to prevail upon the Shah to confirm the agreement entered into by Futteh Ali Khan. The objections of his Majesty, however, became more confirmed, and he peremptorily refused to sanction the arrangement.

Finding this to be the determination of the Persian Court, the Russian Emperor,

* It would appear that the Prince Royal had consented to the agreement entered into by his agent, Futteh Ali Khan, from a despatch of Prince Menzikoff, dated Sultania, July 5 (17), wherein he says: "This morning I had a conference with the Ministers of the Shah, at which "Alaiar Khan presided, and was the only person who spoke. He renewed strange pretensions, "particularly insisting on the restoration of the coast of Lake Gokcha. I opposed to this the "letter of the Prince Royal to General Yermoloff, whereby he consented to give up this coast "to us in exchange for the tract between the Capan and the Capanekchai. He answered that "the Shah had never given his consent or approbation to such an exchange, and that it was "inadmissible."

Emperor, or rather General Yermoloff, affected to consider the unsealed and unratified treaty of Futteh Ali Khan, the agent of the Prince Royal, as binding upon the Persian Court; and setting it up as the warrant for his proceedings, ordered a Russian force, of sufficient strength to prevent the Persians from immediately dislodging them, to take permanent possession of the Gokcha territory: the troops accordingly posted themselves there in an entrenched camp.

As soon as this unjustifiable act was known at the Persian Court, the Shah sent a confidential agent to Teflis, with a letter of remonstrance addressed to General Yermoloff, stating very fully and explicitly the circumstances under which the treaty of Gulistan had been concluded, and disavowing any power or authority on the part of the frontier Government to contract for the relinquishment of the Gokcha district to Russia. The agent was, moreover, directed to protest against the occupation of that district by the Russian troops, as a violation of the Persian territory, and to suggest that the troops should be immediately withdrawn, whilst a reference upon the subject was made to St. Petersburgh. The agent was also instructed to demand, in case the Russian authorities in Georgia refused to listen to this proposal, that they would distinctly declare it to be their intention to retain possession of the country by force; as such a declaration would enable the Court of Tehran to come to a determination respecting the ulterior measures proper to be adopted in such an emergency.

The reply which was returned to this letter imported that General Yermoloff was not authorized without permission of the Emperor to relinquish possession of the Gokcha territory, or any other which up to that period (*i. e.* January 1826) was in the actual possession of Russia: it was, however, proposed that Gokcha should be evacuated by the Russian troops, provided Persia consented to withdraw her troops from the Capan territory, which she had occupied in alleged contravention of the treaty of Gulistan.

The Russian declaration of war, with reference to these transactions, which are but loosely adverted to in it, states that the Court of St. Petersburgh, during the whole of the negociations, had used the utmost endeavours to avoid all

all acts which could give to Persia any just ground of complaint or *suspicion.* How far this profession can be reconciled with the eagerness with which every plea for encroachment was signed by Russia, and especially with the arrogant tone assumed by the Georgian authorities, in all their communications with the Persian Government on the frontier, it is extremely difficult to perceive.

At this critical period a new turn was given to affairs by the death of the Emperor Alexander, and by the appointment of Prince Menzikoff, by the reigning Emperor, on a special mission to the Court of Tehran, ostensibly to announce the succession of the Emperor Nicholas, but authorized (in the language of the Russian declaration) " to conclude an agreement respecting the " *only* point which delayed the demarcation of the frontiers, to renew the " proposal for an exchange of territory, or, *in order to consult still more the* " *interest of Persia, and to place the views of Russia in their true light,* to add to " the territory already occupied by the Persians a part of the district of " (Talish) Talychyne."

Before the result of this mission is stated, it will be proper, at the expense of a slight digression, to describe shortly the relations subsisting between the Court of the Prince Royal of Persia and that of Russia.

It had been a great object of the Emperor Alexander's crafty policy to secure the Heir Apparent to the Persian throne in his interests, in order to facilitate his designs of pushing the Russian frontier to the Arras. With this view he consented to a stipulation in the treaty of Gulistan, which, though it merely bound Russia to recognize as the lawful heir to the throne of Persia that son of the Shah whom his Majesty should appoint as his successor, was in effect (as secretly understood) a guarantee that Prince Abbas Mirza should be supported by Russia to the prejudice of his elder brother; and upon his nomination by the Shah as Heir Apparent, he was so recognized by the Court of St. Petersburgh. By the death of that brother, Abbas Mirza's right to the succession became indisputable.

Previous to this event, however, Abbas Mirza felt so much his dependency upon the Russian Emperor, that the latter acquired such an influence at the Court of Tabreez as was viewed by the Shah's Ministers with considerable jealousy and alarm. The intrigues carried on at that Court, under the able management of the Russian Minister, M. Amburger, were of the most deep and dangerous character; and the Prince, who secretly entertained a dislike to Russia and a regard for the British, was prevailed upon, partly by his hopes and fears, and partly by misrepresentations, to look passively upon the encroaching system of Russia, and to listen to projects which were hostile to the interests of Great Britain in the East.

The death of Alexander, the diminished dependence of Abbas Mirza upon the Russian Court, the growing suspicions engendered by the conduct of that Court,* and perhaps more than all, the skilful and unremitted exertions of Major Hart and Dr. Cormick at the Court of Tabreez, who possess much of the Prince's confidence, brought about a decided change in the sentiments and policy of his Royal Highness.

Accordingly, when the mission of Prince Menzikoff was announced to the Court of Tabreez, the Prince Royal, in reporting it to the Shah, desired that he might be authorized to oppose the Russian Ambassador's advance to Tehran, unless he previously consented to the evacuation of Gokcha.

The Shah appeared at first to be disposed to listen to his son's proposition, more especially as he wished to avoid the embarrassment of being obliged to receive the Envoy at his Court and to refuse him an audience, as he had determined to do, in the event of a refusal to evacuate Gokcha, the possession of which by Russia the Shah considered as endangering the safety of the province of Erivan, which is, (as formerly stated), a barrier against the encroachments of the Russians; the Surdar of which province, in the last war, successfully withstood the attacks of their troops.

The Shah was, however, persuaded by his Ministers, who were supported by our *Chargé d'Affaires*, not to refuse the Russian Envoy admission to his Court, which might be a rejection of favourable overtures from the new Emperor.

Some

* It has been said that opprobrious terms were actually applied to the Prince Royal in letters to his Ministers.

Some reports likewise prevailed at Tehran that a civil war was likely to occur in Russia, through disputes regarding the succession to the crown.

Whilst Prince Menzikoff was still in Georgia, a detachment of Russian troops advanced to Åberan, on the frontier of Erivan, and which has always been regarded as Persian territory. This simultaneous march of a Russian force into Persia, and an appointment of a special mission to the Court of Tehran, were incongruities inexplicable by the Ministers of the Shah, and led them naturally to believe that the mission was a mere blind, and that submission to former insults had emboldened Russia to commit further aggressions. The troops were, however, soon afterwards withdrawn.

Upon the arrival of Prince Menzikoff on the Persian frontier, he was received with great respect, and experienced a friendly reception from Prince Abbas Mirza at Tabreez. He proceeded from thence to the royal camp at Sultania, where he was treated with distinction; and although he did not experience at his audience those marks of favour with which the British Envoy was honoured, this circumstance was partly attributable to a failure in etiquette, as is remarked in page 208. Prince Menzikoff states that the letter from the Emperor was not taken from his hands by the Shah, conformably to the ceremonial regulated before-hand; but when he offered it, his Majesty signified by a sign that he should lay it on a cushion.*

Negociations were immediately opened by the Persion Ministers, namely, the Asuf-ud-Dowlah, Alaiar Khan, who is of the Kujur family, and son-in-law of the Shah; Mirza Abul Hussun Khan, and Mirza Abdul Wahab. Upon the Ministers' inquiring the powers of the Russian Envoy, he declared that he had no authority to recede from the engagements entered into by the Georgian authorities, in concert with Futteh Ali Khan; that he had nothing to offer beyond this, and could not consent to the evacuation of Gokcha until the Persians retired from the territory bordering on Capan.

In the mean time, the aggressions and the insolence of the Russian authorities in Georgia, and more particularly their interference with the religious tenets and

---

* The principal present to the Shah was a cut-glass bed.

and prejudice of their Mahomedan subjects, had excited the resentment of the warlike tribes on the Georgian frontier, who offered to co-operate with the Persians in a war with Russia. The Mooshtaed, or head of the Persian church, was applied to, in order that he might use his endeavours for the same end. All the Moollahs took up the cause, and loudly called upon the Shah in the name of Allee to avenge the insults offered to their religion, on pain of being loaded with the curses of the faithful. The petitions of the discontented and injured Georgian Chiefs; the representations of his Prime Minister, by whom the petitions were recommended; the denunciations of the Moollahs; and the urgent solicitations of the Prince Royal, who now became as eager for war with Russia as he had formerly been subservient to her policy, did not induce the Shah to precipitate his subjects into a contest with so powerful an empire as Russia.

In this resolution his Majesty was supported by some of his ministers. He declared, indeed, that if Russia positively refused to relinquish Gokcha, he would declare war; because he felt that the safety of Erivan depended upon the preservation of that apparently insignificant district.

The Persian Ministers, assembled at the tent of the Premier, made a further effort to extort from Prince Menzikoff some concession, however trifling, which might save the honour of the Shah, and preserve him from the appearance of retracting the declaration made to his subjects. The only proposal which Prince Menzikoff offered, was to suspend the negociations till he could receive fresh instructions from St. Petersburgh, and in the mean time to visit the points on the frontier which were in dispute. The Persian Government consented, proposing only that the Gokcha district should be abandoned by the Russians, with the understanding that the Persians should not occupy it till the result of the reference to the Russian Court was known. To this proposition, however, Prince Menzikoff could not be prevailed upon to consent.

The ferment in Persia now increased; the Moollahs called upon the Shah to redeem his pledge; the tribes on the frontiers were already in arms; and the enthusiasm inspired into all ranks throughout Persia, gave the expected contest the aspect of a religious war, and made it impossible for the Persian Ministers to disappoint the wishes of the people.

The

The reflections of the Persian Government upon the conduct adopted by the Russian Court, impelled it to believe that the latter was bent upon war, otherwise so easy an expedient to prevent that evil as the temporary evacuation of the Gokcha territory, which Russia had always the power to reoccupy, would not have been declined by the Envoy. The delay occasioned by a reference to St. Petersburgh would at all events have retarded hostilities for a year, since before the return of an answer to the reference, the approach of winter would have forced the Persian troops to retire to their own country.

The Shah felt keenly the disappointment of his hopes, when he found that the special mission, which he expected would evince the desire of the Emperor Nicholas to maintain amicable relations with him, was sent merely to demand the ratification of Futteh Ali Khan's agreement with General Yermoloff, which had already been formally refused by his Majesty. Sensible that he was committed to the nation, urged by the importunity of the Border chiefs and the ecclesiastics of Persia, and conscious that, should he submit to the humiliation of concession, under existing circumstances, he could have no security against future encroachment, the Shah determined, at length, upon resistance, though with a full sense of the danger.

It was, nevertheless, still intimated to Prince Menzikoff, that the negociations which were broken off might be resumed at some town on the frontier: and Mr. Willock was requested by the Shah to communicate with the Russian Envoy (unofficially), with a view of interposing his good offices to prevent a rupture between the two states. This interposition, however, had no effect in procuring a pledge for the evacuation of Gokcha, the Envoy declaring he had no control over General Yermoloff. Prince Menzikoff therefore left the royal camp at Sultania on the 26th of July. The Shah proceeded from Sultania to Ardebeel, thence to Achar, and war was formally commenced on the part of Persia.

About this period the Russian subjects in Dagistan, Shervan, and Shekee were in arms. In Talish the people rose and cut off the detachments dispersed throughout the country; they then took Askeran, and in concert with a Persian army laid siege to Lankeran on the Caspian, which had been taken by the

Russians

Russians in the last war. It was now garrisoned by a weak battalion of regulars, who, alarmed probably by the massacre of the troops in Askeran, withdrew in the night to the island of Sari, leaving in the fort six pieces of cannon, military stores, and provisions in abundance.

The exasperation of the inhabitants of the Georgian provinces had risen to such a height, that the Russians were cut off by them whenever they were met with and could be overpowered. The insurgents bitterly complained of the tyranny and barbarity of the Governor-General, Yermoloff, and his subordinate officers, who paid no regard to the religious prejudices of the Mahomedans, violated the women, and were guilty of great enormities. General Yermoloff is reported to have amputated the right hands of a whole tribe, because a Russian detachment in the Caucasus was fired at; and a Russian soldier having been murdered near a village, the inhabitants of which refused to surrender the perpetrator of the deed, men, women, and children, horses, dogs, and every living creature within the walls, were exterminated by the General's order.

The conduct of the other party was nearly as barbarous, as the following occurrence will prove:—The Russian commandant at Karakalissa, threatened by the Surdar of Erivan, sent for a reinforcement to Ganja, which was garrisoned by a battalion one thousand strong. The officer in command at Ganja conceived that, if the people were sworn to fidelity on the Koran, they would remain true to the Russian cause. The people took the oath, having been told by their Moollah that there would be no sin in taking it, and none in breaking it. Seven hundred of the garrison then marched for Karakalissa, leaving three hundred behind in Ganja. The Moollah, having secretly distributed a quantity of spirits amongst the soldiers, invited the officers to an entertainment, in the midst of which they were murdered, together with their intoxicated men. The Moollah then set out, with about four hundred horse, after the detachment on its march to Karakalissa; he overtook them on a halt: proceeding to the commanding officer's tent, he told him that he came with news of the disaffection of the people of Ganja, and requested him to return. Whilst the Moollah held the officer in conversation his horsemen mixed with the unsuspecting Russians,

Russians, and, at a signal, attacked and cut them up; two hundred only escaped.

When the Russian Envoy, Prince Menzikoff, reached Tabreez, on his return to Teflis, he was treated with much disrespect. His couriers had been stopped, and one or two murdered, between Tabreez and Sultania, and their despatches detained. He wished to procure the attendance of the English serjeants at Tabreez, on his journey to the frontiers, as he had no European escort except a serjeant's guard of Lancers. But the British officer in command of the troops was obliged to refuse his request, as they formed part of Abbas Mirza's army. On his arrival at Erivan, August 16th, the Envoy was arrested by the Surdar of that province, and detained there for twenty-five days, experiencing many affronts. Prince Menzikoff communicated this outrage upon the law of nations to the British Envoy (Colonel Macdonald), who instantly made such strong remonstrances upon the subject to the Shah's Ministers, that a Royal firman was despatched to the Surdar of Erivan for the immediate release of the Prince and his suite. In order to obviate any difficulty or impediment which might be created by the Surdar, Major Monteith was sent to Erivan with another firman, to effectuate their liberation if it had not already take place, and to accompany the Russian Envoy across the frontier, to Teflis, or any other Russian station. The Prince, however, had been released, and had reached Teflis, when the Major arrived at the Surdar's camp. It appears that the cause of this detention of the Russian Envoy was owing to a rumour that General Yermoloff had been removed from his office of Governor-General, and that Prince Menzikoff was appointed his successor: the Persian Court therefore thought, that if the Envoy was detained, the troops in Georgia would be left without a head.

The army under the orders of the Prince Royal which took the field against the Russians amounted in number (including irregulars) to forty-five or fifty thousand men. The *Surbaz* (resolute), or disciplined battalions, were twelve thousand strong; there were also a few companies of foot artillery, and several hundreds of Russian deserters. The Shah's military force, except ten or twelve thousand disciplined *Janbaz* (contemners of life), is but an untrained rabble, who plunder their own countrymen more frequently than their enemy, and, under pretence of collecting contributions for the prosecution of the war, rob the villagers, as well as travellers, of their valuables. The Russian force on the southern side of the Caucasus consisted of thirty-two thousand infantry, twelve hundred dragoons, six thousand Cossacks, and two battalions of artillery; but they were mostly dispersed in detachments throughout Georgia.

Previous to the two armies coming into actual contact several affairs had taken place, in which both parties had been, at different points, successful.

The Surdar of Erivan, who had distinguished himself during the previous war, was not idle. A Russian force, seven thousand strong, with twelve battering guns, under the direction of the chief engineer, had been collected at Karakalissa, evidently with a view of reducing Erivan. The Surdar had, however, taken Goomree, slaughtering the male inhabitants (who were Armenians), whose heads he sent into camp. He recovered Gokcha, Balikloo and Aberan from the Russians, and had taken about five hundred prisoners; Karakalissa was evacuated on his approach, the Russian force which occupied it retiring upon Looree, a stronger position, after the reinforcement from Ganja had been cut off by the Moollah of that place, as already mentioned. The Surdar and his troops are represented by the Persian accounts to have had a narrow escape upon entering Karakalissa: the Russian commandant had dug a mine, intending to blow up the Surdar's army as they entered the town; but it exploded too soon and did no harm.

The Prince Royal directed his march towards Sheesha, in Karabaugh, at the end of July. This is a rich and beautiful country; the vallies are covered with forests of the finest timber, from whence it derives its name of "The Black Garden." Wild oats wave luxuriantly over the plains for miles together, far, indeed, as the eye can reach; whilst the landscape is improved and the soil fertilized by the clear streams of numerous rivers which meander through the vallies, where herds of deer abound.

Sheesha is a considerable town; its inhabitants are partly Tartars and partly Armenians.

Armenians. It is built on a lofty precipitous rock, and the houses, upwards of two thousand in number, appear to hang in a very perilous situation. . The Russians had sustained some loss in this quarter: the garrison of Sheesha having sent a detachment to attack a Persian force which had collected in the neighbourhood, the inhabitants of Karabaugh had cut them off.

The Persian army, under the Prince Royal, having advanced to the Arras, crossed the river, and pitched near a noble bridge called Khoda Afereen, where he made prisoners a detachment of Cossacks sent to reconnoitre. From these he learned that the Russian troops, ignorant of the war, were dispersed throughout Karabaugh; and that a battalion of infantry twelve hundred strong, with four field-pieces, quartered near Gourous, could be cut off. On the 26th July he marched, and hearing that the Russian battalion was retreating towards Sheesha, the Prince sent forward his son, Ismael Mirza, with the Karabaugh cavalry, and the Ghoolam Tafunchees, to harass their rear and impede their march, whereby he was enabled to come up with them. He attacked the Russians in a pass called Kunjerik: four hundred Russians were killed and wounded; the rest laid down their arms; one lieutenant-colonel, eight other officers, and four guns, fell into the hands of the Persians. These were some of the officers seen at Ardebeel; their statement of the causes of their defeat may be seen in page 190.

The Prince, encouraged by this success, and urged by Mhatee Khoulee Khan and Abul Futteh Khan, the exiled chiefs of Karabaugh,* proceeded to Sheesha, in Karabaugh (the inhabitants of which country had paid him 10,000 ducats), took the town, and invested the hill fort, containing a garrison two thousand strong, but unfurnished with provisions. The abominable misconduct of the Russian functionaries may be conceived from the behaviour of the Governor of Karabaugh. He sold last year all the grain in the magazine of Sheesha, there having

2 o 2 been

* There were also in camp the discontented chiefs of Sherwan, Shekee, Talish, the chiefs of the Lesgees, and the son of the Waly.

been a scarcity in the adjoining provinces, and pocketed the proceeds of the sale. The garrison, upon evacuating the town and shutting themselves up in the fort, found it unprovided with grain. Their former supply was contained in two magazines outside the fort, which the Persians seized the first day. The commandant in consequence was forced to agree to surrender the fort in eight days, if not sooner relieved.

About this time the Shah deputed a messenger to Constantinople, to communicate the intelligence of the success that had attended his arms, and for the purpose of exciting the Porte to declare war with Russia.

Whilst the Prince Royal lay before Sheesha, he despatched his eldest son, Mahomed Mirza (governor of Hamadan), accompanied by Ameer Khan, maternal uncle of the Prince Royal, and a body of ten thousand men, with six field pieces, on the road to Teflis. They encountered a Russian force of six thousand infantry and three thousand cavalry, under General Mududoff,* who had previously sent a detachment of six hundred men to surprise a Persian post; but this body falling in with Mahomed Mirza's army, sustained a loss of two hundred men. A battle took place between the two armies on the 2d September, near Shamkhar, five fursungs from Teflis, when the Persians were defeated. They lost a considerable number of men, and also Ameer Khan, whose head was laid at the feet of the Russian general. Notwithstanding the provocations given to the Russians, by the heads of their slain being sent to the royal camp and built into pyramids, Mududoff ordered the head and body of Ameer Khan to be decently interred.

The Russians, after this success, advanced to Elizabethpol, or Ganja, from which they drove the Persians with great loss. The Persians had previously slaughtered the unwarlike Armenians, and swept off a colony of German Moravians settled near the town, whom they sold as slaves to the Koords, for three and four tomauns each. On this being communicated to his Persian Majesty,

* Who is an Armenian by birth. He was educated by a Russian priest, and entering the army, *Russianized* himself by adding *off* to his Arabic name of *Mudud* (assistance).

Majesty, he asked if any of the German women were handsome: on being answered in the negative; "then let the Koords keep them," said he.

The Prince Royal, upon receiving the news of these disasters, hastily raised the siege of Sheesha, and marched towards Teflis to revenge the death of his uncle and the disgrace of his son. The Armenians of Karabaugh continued hovering on his flanks and rear, and cutting off stragglers during his advance. A considerable portion of his army was engaged in foraging and marauding excursions; but, as he advanced by slow marches, he collected forty thousand men, half Nizam or disciplined troops (for he had been joined by Alaiar Khan, the prime minister of Persia, with a considerable force); the remainder cavalry and irregulars, with twenty field-pieces.

On the 25th September, the Prince Royal found himself opposite to the Russian army, commanded by General Paskevitch, which was strongly posted about five miles from Elizabethpol, waiting his approach. The Prince resolved to attack them, and divided his army into three bodies, with the cavalry in the intervals and on the flanks. After a cannonade had been kept up for some time on both sides, the Prince, finding that the heavy metal of the Russians (they had brought battering guns of large calibre into the field) was doing great execution amongst his troops, ordered a general charge upon the Russians, who were drawn up in hollow squares. When the Persian troops approached the enemy, the latter quickly formed line, and met the advance of the Persians, whose first line, being broken, fell back upon the second, and threw it into disorder. The reserve, seeing the fate of the other troops, fled towards the camp without firing a shot. Several standards and four field-pieces fell into the hands of the Russians; the other guns, under the direction of Serjeant Dawson, were saved. The gallant artilleryman retreated in so masterly a manner, that he kept the Russian light infantry completely at bay. The loss sustained by the Persians amounted to two thousand; the Russians lost five hundred killed and wounded.

The Prince, perceiving the fate of his army, fled with a few horsemen, and

and did not halt till he was fifty fursungs on the Persian side of the Arras. His troops made for the camp to collect their effects; a general scramble ensued, and the cash-chest of the Prince was plundered by his own soldiers. All order and discipline being at an end amongst the wreck of the army, each soldier betook himself to his home.

When the news of this total overthrow was communicated to the Shah, he was of course extremely dejected: he at length broke out into invectives against the Prince Royal, for his rash sacrifice of so fine an army in a single day; but subsequently relenting, he invited his son to the royal camp. Abbas Mirza replied to the invitation, by acknowledging that he was ashamed to appear in the presence of his father and brothers. After some delay he ventured to visit his royal father, and his approach was announced, unexpectedly, to the camp. Major G. Willock was deputed by the British Envoy to meet and console him. The spirits of the Prince seemed to be quite sunk; he confessed that he had acted with great imprudence in attempting to contend against a well-appointed and disciplined army in the open field; and declared that had he acted differently, agreeably to the advice he had received, he might easily have driven his enemies out of Georgia. In passing the lines of the Janbaz infantry, loud expressions of dissatisfaction, and even hootings, were heard, which were extremely galling to the feelings of the unfortunate Prince. The Shah received him graciously, and endeavoured to cheer the drooping spirits of his favourite son, whilst the governors of the different provinces were despatched immediately to re-assemble their respective troops.

The Surdar of Erivan having also sustained a check in his advance, and having intercepted a correspondence between the Armenians of Yeuch Kalissa and those in Georgia, which proved that they were disaffected towards him, he fell back and occupied the Three Churches, sending the priests into Erivan.

General Mududoff making a demonstration of his intention to march upon Erivan, the Shah broke up his camp, and marched to Tabreez. A tremendous storm of wind and rain burst upon the plain of Achar just as his Majesty was about to leave the ground. He refused to sleep in Tabreez, but remained for some days outside the city, in a garden-house belonging to the Prince Royal. The Shah finally encamped about twenty miles from Tabreez, in the direction of Murand. In the early part of October he returned to Tehran.

General Mududoff finally took up a position opposite to Áslandoos (where the Persians had sustained a defeat during the last war), and made incursions, at the head of five thousand men, into the Persian territories, in the direction of Erivan. Retaliating upon the unhappy people the disorders and cruelties committed by the troops of Persia in Georgia, he laid waste the country, burnt the villages, and massacred the inhabitants.

The Prince Royal having collected another army, took post upon the Arras. His troops hovered about the frontier, and occasionally penetrated into Georgia on marauding expeditions. Nothing, however, of any moment occurred on either side, and towards the close of October, it appears, his Royal Highness retreated towards Ardebeel, having closed the campaign until the spring.

It was generally believed in Persia that the Russians would attempt no enterprize of any moment till next season, although they had transported, by the co-operation of the Georgians, a heavy battering train from Teflis, destined probably for the siege of Erivan, and great preparations were making at St. Petersburgh to supply the arsenals with shells and rockets for the prosecution of the war.

The interposition of the British Government, it may be rationally expected, will be the means of preventing another campaign.

If the Russian Cabinet, however, has really instigated the measures of the local Government of Georgia, and is determined, in spite of the mediation of a friendly power, to profit by the present opportunity of accomplishing the schemes of aggrandizement which it has cherished from the time of Peter the Great, success is not so easy of attainment as may at first be supposed. Persia, though not provided with artificial bulwarks of defence, is strong by nature; and if the greater part of her army is undisciplined, and ill calculated to cope with the Russians in pitched battles, and according to the system of European warfare,

fare, yet the bulk of her population consists of warlike tribes, who, if a proper impulse were given to them, would furnish a more effectual defence to Persia than if the country were studded with fortresses. Nor is such an impulse wanting in the present contest, which has arisen from a belief that the Russians have insulted the Moslem religion. The war is regarded by the Persians as a holy war: they are persuaded by their Moollahs that their religion has been invaded; and no motive is so well calculated to excite all the energies of a Mahomedan population as a belief that their faith is menaced by an infidel power.

Should the Russians, therefore, continue the war, and march their heavy dragoons and infantry into Persia, the Persians need only remove the provisions, forage, &c. from their line of march, and harass the invaders with their numerous and superior cavalry, in order to impede effectually the enemy's advance across barren plains.

If Persia had a chief like Nadir Shah, the event would be easily calculated. But a great obstacle to the exertions of the Persians, and a drawback to their success, is the excessive parsimony of the Shah, who, though possessed of immense wealth, is unconquerably averse to opening his treasury. For this very reason he has no army of reserve; although he could assemble without difficulty (if he would pay them) ten thousand robust troopers, mounted on strong and active horses, from Khorasan and Kerman, and a like number from Ispahan, Kermanshah, Hamadan, from the Bucktiaris, and the wandering tribes of Louristan; besides at least three thousand from the towns and Illiauts of Fars.

The successes of the Persians at the commencement of the present war shew that there is less inequality than might be expected between the respective forces; and the result of the last war, in which, after ten or twelve years' exertion, Russia was unable to push her boundaries to the Araxes, affords a strong proof of the same fact. In the present war the Russians labour under greater disadvantages than during the last; they have to convey their munitions of war over an immense tract of country, in which they must leave strong posts,

not

not merely to keep up the communication with their magazines, but to overawe their disaffected subjects in Georgia.

Upon the whole, it may be concluded that, although Persia may be compelled to submit to some further sacrifices, if the war continues, the conquest of that empire by the Russians is perfectly chimerical, and the invasion of India by them a mere bugbear.

That the interests of Britain are deeply concerned in the present contest cannot be doubted. If Russia shall force the Shah to make peace, the extinction of British influence at Tehran will doubtless be stipulated for, as well as the dismissal of the British officers in the service of the Prince Royal, and perhaps the substitution of Russian subjects,—a proposal for disciplining the Persian army by Russian officers was made by General Yermoloff immediately after the peace of Gulistan. In the mean time, the continuance of hostilities imposes upon the British Government the obligation of deciding whether the contest was or was not caused by the aggression of Russia, since, in the former case, we are bound by treaty with Persia to renew the subsidy of two hundred thousand tomauns. If we decide that the *casus fœderis* has not taken place, we lose our ascendancy at the court of Tehran; and if we adopt a contrary policy, and subsidize Persia against Russia, it seems impossible for us to maintain that neutral system of measures, in respect to Persian politics, which has been the result of a sort of understanding between our court and that of St. Petersburgh; and it will perhaps be difficult for us to avoid embroiling ourselves in a dispute with the latter.

The embarrassments of our situation are very obvious; but they might easily have been foreseen at the period when the treaty of subsidy was concluded; it may therefore be assumed they were, (as they ought to have been,) provided against.

APPENDIX, No. III.

ITINERARY OF THE JOURNEY THROUGH PERSIA, ASIA MINOR, AND EUROPEAN TURKEY.

Names of Stages.	Places passed.	Distance travelled per Diem in Miles.
BUSHIRE TO		
Chakota	Chakaduck	24
Borazgoon		16
Dalkee	Kootul Moolah	12
Konartukht	Kootul Kumeredge	16
Kumeredge		14
Devist	Shapoor	12
Kazeroon	Kootul Dokhtur	12
Perizun	Kootul Perizun	20
Dustiajun		15
Khonahzunnion		12
Shiraz		28
Zergoon		16
Bund Emir		16
Persepolis		14
Futeabad	Istakar	12
Mayen		24
Imaum Zada Ismael	Kootul	12
Oojan		16
Aspas		12
Kiosk-i-Zurd		20
Deygurdoo		28
Yezdikhurst		30
Muksoodbeggee		24
Ghomesha		12
Mayar		16
Ispahanek		24
Ispahan		8

Names of Stages.	Places passed.	Distance travelled per Diem in Miles.
ISPAHAN TO		
Nujufabad	....	20
Teiran	....	15
Askeran	....	20
Domina	Konsar	20
Wo Nishan	Imaum Zadah,—Gilpaegah	28
Komin	Leihan..............................	28
Hoormabad	....	22
Amarut	....	10
Khooshbajan................	Kazeroon	20
Khoondab	....	20
Kurdahoor	....	16
Barwund	....	16
Hamadan	....	14
Shevereen	....	4
Moran	....	16
Kaboot' Rahung	....	12
Gao Souar..................	....	20
Tousley	....	16
Hissar	Hyder Pyghumber..................	26
Bool Mulledge	Sultania	20
Zunjan	Koorkundee	20
Zohra	....	12
Armaganah	....	12
Achkund	The Mines	28
Mamoon	Kootul..............................	18
Herees	....	25
Kureem	....	25
Ardebeel	....	20
Talib Kishlak	....	12
Furukabad..................	....	24
Ahmedbegloo	....	24
Mizan	....	10
Royal Camp near Achar ...	....	20

Names of Stages.	Places passed.	Distance travelled per Diem in Miles.
ACHAR TO		
Tabreez	Sophian	64
Murand	Gurgur, River Arras..............	40
Nukshiwan	....	64
Shuheroor	....	40
Erivan	Yeuçh Kalissa, Mount Ararat ...	56
Kuremarchee	....	32
Nukshiwan	Hajee Bairamloo	56
Kars	....	48
Ben Ahmud	....	12
Misingird	Hussun Kella........................	52
Azeroom	River Euphrates	72
Askalar	Sheitan Dura	36
Karakulukh	....	64
Sainla..........................	....	72
Kella Hissar	....	72
Afun	Nixar	72
Almos..........................	Tokat, Toorka	88
Guard House	Amasia, Nursewan	64
Dowlut	Osmanjook, Hajee Humza	92
Toksia	Oksia, Karajillan	88
Karajillar	Humamloo	76
Caravanserai	Boli	84
Dukja	Kunduk, Subanja	72
Ismid	....	120
Constantinople	....	72
Telivree	....	48
Girk Kalissa	....	112
Bulgarian Cottage	Carnabad	88
Sheumla........................	....	80
Rooschook.....................	....	80
Bucharest	....	50
QuarantineatRothenThurn	....	200

VIGNETTES

ORIGINALLY INTENDED AS HEAD-PIECES TO THE CHAPTERS.

1.

3.

2.

6.

4.

5.

7.

8.

9.

12.

10.

11.

15.

14.

13.

16.

17.

18.

21.

19.

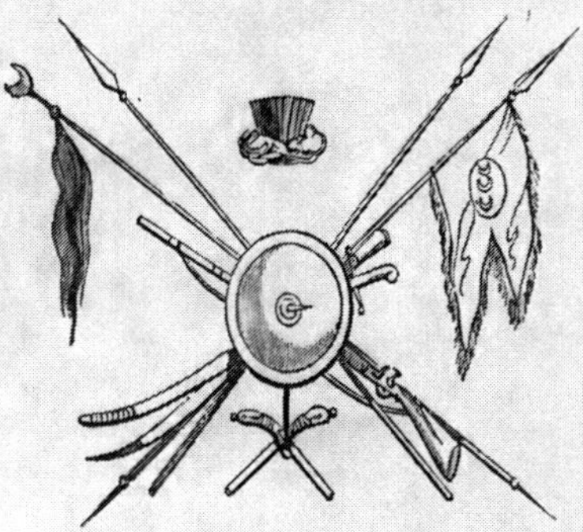

22.

20.

ERRATA.

Page. Line.
20...26, *for* orce *read* force.
43... 4, *for* Tavai *read* Tavoy.
48...28, *after* Martaban *insert* in the former voyage.
55...20, *for* salloon *read* saloon.
62...26, *for* sides *read* side.
80... 6, *for* of *read* at.
20, *for* 182,000 *read* 108,000.
81... 8, *for* in a succeeding chapter *read* in the Appendix.
82...22, *for* Curreem *read* Cassim.
96...14, *for* Muschuks *read* Mussbuks.

Page. Line.
96...28, *for* sex *read* six.
99... 6, *for* mafruches *read* mafrushes.
116...24, *for* After having *read* We.
135... 2, *for* Kiosk-ki-zurd *read* Kiosk-l-zurd.
15, *after* Lalla Rookh *insert* though we did not find them applicable.
147...12, *omit* under Nadir Shah.
154... 9, *for* new residence *read* new edifice.
177... 7, for *rosa uniflora* read *rosa berberifolia*.
208... 4, for *reshha pur* read *bur reshha*.
239...26, *omit* after leaving Boli.
